Selected Correspondence of Bernard Shaw

Bernard Shaw and Nancy Astor

Selected Correspondence of Bernard Shaw

Bernard Shaw and Nancy Astor

Edited by J.P. Wearing

UNIVERSITY OF TORONTO PRESS
Toronto Buffalo London

Published by University of Toronto Press Incorporated
Toronto Buffalo London
Printed in Canada
ISBN 0-8020-3752-6

   Printed on acid-free paper

Library and Archives Canada Cataloguing in Publication

Shaw, Bernard, 1856–1950.
  Bernard Shaw and Nancy Astor / edited by J.P. Wearing.

  (Selected correspondence of Bernard Shaw)
  Includes index.
  ISBN 0-8020-3752-6

  1. Shaw, Bernard, 1856–1950 – Correspondence.   2. Astor, Nancy
Witcher Langhorne Astor, Viscountess, 1879–1964 – Correspondence.
3. Dramatists, Irish – 20th century – Correspondence.   4. Women
legislators – Great Britain – Correspondence.   I. Astor, Nancy
Witcher Langhorne Astor, Viscountess, 1879–1964.   II. Wearing, J.P.
III. Title.   IV. Series.

  PR5366.A43 2005   822'.912   C2004-905525-9

The General Editor and the University of Toronto Press express appreciation for the support of the late John Wardrop, whose generosity
helped make this series possible. We also thank the Academy of the
Shaw Festival for its support.

University of Toronto Press acknowledges the financial assistance to its
publishing program of the Canada Council for the Arts and the Ontario
Arts Council.

University of Toronto Press acknowledges the financial support for its
publishing activities of the Government of Canada through the Book
Publishing Industry Development Program (BPIDP).

Contents

General Editor's Note

This volume is the sixth in the series entitled *Selected Correspondence of Bernard Shaw*. The first two volumes – *Bernard Shaw and H.G. Wells*, edited by J. Percy Smith, and *Theatrics*, edited by Dan H. Laurence – appeared in 1995. The third – *Bernard Shaw and Gabriel Pascal*, edited by Bernard Dukore – was published in 1996, and the fourth and fifth volumes – *Bernard Shaw and Barry Jackson*, edited by L.W. Conolly, and *Bernard Shaw and the Webbs*, edited by Alex C. Michalos and Deborah C. Poff – appeared in 2002.

The volumes in this series are of two kinds. Percy Smith's inaugural volume represents an example of the first kind: correspondence between Shaw and another individual of distinction in his or her own right. Bernard Dukore's and my own editions are further examples of this kind, as is the present volume, J.P. Wearing's *Bernard Shaw and Nancy Astor*. *Bernard Shaw and the Webbs* is a minor variation on this model in that it deals with Shaw's relationship with *two* distinguished individuals.

This approach replicates other editions of Shaw correspondence published prior to this series: Christopher St John's *Ellen Terry and Bernard Shaw: A Correspondence* (1931), or Alan Dent's *Bernard Shaw and Mrs. Patrick Campbell: Their Correspondence* (1952), among others. The advantage of this approach, of course, is that it gives the reader two (or more) voices rather than one, with all the stimulation that can arise from complementary or adversarial views on issues, events, or people. Such an approach also allows for insights into the nature of close personal and professional relationships, with all the emotional and intellectual drama that usually accompanied such Shavian associations. While matching the epistolary Shaw in full flow is a tough challenge, people like Wells, Pascal, Jackson, the Webbs, and Nancy Astor – hardened professionals all – were not easily intimidated by Shaw's sharp wit, searing logic, or intellectual aggression. Thus the sparks sometimes fly, from which light as well as heat is generated.

This attempt to capture Shaw's *dialogue* with friends and colleagues differs, of course, from collections solely of Shaw's letters to individuals, be they single individuals as in C.B. Purdom's *Bernard Shaw's Letters to Granville Barker* (1957) or Samuel Weiss's *Bernard Shaw's Letters to Siegfried Trebitsch* (1986), or hundreds of individuals as in Dan H. Laurence's monumental edition, *Bernard Shaw: Collected Letters* (4 volumes, 1965–88). And both of these approaches differ again from the second kind of volume in this series, Shaw's letters to a variety of individuals *on a particular subject.* Thus, Dan Laurence's *Theatrics* provides the opportunity to explore Shaw's ideas on theatre and theatricality. Similar volumes on Shaw and publishers and Shaw and musicians are in preparation.

And so through a variety of approaches the magnificent edifice of Shaw's correspondence is gradually constructed, drawing, in this series, largely on previously unpublished letters and, in many instances, opening up new insights into Shaw's life and achievements, as well as the life and achievements of his correspondents. Over half of the letters in this volume, for example, are here published for the first time, shedding much new light on one of the most celebrated and unlikely friendships of the twentieth century. On the face of it, as Professor Wearing points out in his Introduction, the wealthy American-born Tory politician (the first woman to take a seat in the British House of Commons) and the Irish socialist reformer had little in common, but their differences as well as some unexpected common interests held them together (sometimes more closely than Shaw appreciated) for the eventful last twenty-five years of Shaw's life. Politics, of course, feature prominently in the correspondence, as do many of the major political figures of the period, but so do more mundane concerns over health, finances, travel, domesticity – 'seeming trifles,' as Professor Wearing puts it, that 'flesh out Shaw's and Nancy's public personae and render them as ordinary beings coping with the quotidian travails of life.'

Introduction

'Not bloody likely.' Liza Doolittle's now legendary ejaculation in *Pygmalion* (1914) might well have applied to the improbable prospect of a close friendship between an ardent Fabian socialist who espoused communism and a wealthy Conservative Member of Parliament with a mercurial temperament. However, that is precisely what occurred between Bernard Shaw and Nancy Lady Astor in the final two and a half decades of Shaw's life. In fact, Shaw and Nancy shared a surprising number of characteristics, and the wonder is why the two did not meet and become friends earlier in their lives.

Certainly the delay was not attributable to Nancy. A great collector of people of her day (her friends and occasional foes included Hilaire Belloc, T.E. Lawrence, Winston Churchill, Lloyd George, Neville Chamberlain, and H.H. and Margot Asquith, to mention but a few), Nancy had made overtures to Shaw long before they met. In a letter dated 8 July 1926 to their mutual friend, Edith 'D.D.' Lyttelton, Shaw wrote:

> I am *not* well; but I play for sympathy in vain, as everyone congratulates me on my recovery. I have work to finish: that is the only interest I have in lagging superfluous. Man delights me not, nor woman neither.
>
> The inimitable Nancy has laid many snares for me, but never the right one. She thinks I want to meet people: I dont. But Charlotte sometimes does, if they are the sort of people that interest her; and she takes her lion with her. He lets himself be taken to lunches (never to dinners) and dutifully jumps through his hoops for her hostesses; but he does not go alone; and if he were to say 'I wont come unless I may bring my wife' his wife wouldnt come on those terms, naturally.

> So you must tell Lady A. that I am not available for next Thursday, and
> convey to her that the approach must be made from the other side.[1]

At this stage in his life (he was nearly seventy), Shaw's primary interest
lay in whatever work he might yet produce (although virtually all his
significant work was behind him). However, there is no reason to doubt
Shaw's assertion that it was Charlotte Shaw who wanted to meet people.
Charlotte was a snob who, as Beatrice Webb observed in November 1927,
possessed an 'inveterate love of all that accompanies wealth and social
prestige and [a] dislike of "little people."'[2] Nancy Astor's social standing
and astonishing wealth rendered her precisely the right class of person
in Charlotte's eyes and so Shaw yielded eventually to Nancy's importuni-
ties. Exactly when Shaw and Nancy first met is undocumented; however,
as Letter 1 reveals, a relationship had developed by 1926 or 1927, and
Charlotte was a less than reticent partner. Once established, the friendship endured through Charlotte's death in 1943 and ceased only with
Shaw's death in 1950.

Superficial appearances to the contrary, Shaw and Nancy Astor shared
common experiences and characteristics.[3] Born in erstwhile British possessions, both, by the time of their friendship, were expatriates who,
nevertheless, were attached strongly to their roots. Shaw was born in
Dublin on 26 July 1856 to a Protestant family that boasted landed-gentry
forebears but that lived in indifferent, though hardly poverty-stricken,
circumstances. His father, George Carr Shaw, was devoted more to
alcohol than familial duties, while his mother, Lucinda, found musical
and other solace with Vandeleur Lee, a Svengali-like singing teacher and
musician. Nancy Astor was born (also in less than affluent circumstances) in Danville, Virginia, on 17 May 1879; she was christened Nannie
Witcher, after her mother, and it is uncertain when she adopted the
name Nancy.[4] Interestingly, her mother, Nannie Witcher Keene, claimed
distant Irish ancestry, while her father, Chiswell Dabney Langhorne, was
born in Lynchburg, Virginia. Chiswell (always called 'Chillie,' pronounced
'Shillie') was fond of his southern tipples; however, unlike Shaw's father,
Chillie did not abrogate his familial responsibilities, and gradually he
raised both the financial and social standing of his family. Neither Shaw
nor Nancy forgot their families, and, once financially stable, assumed
responsibility for the welfare of numerous relatives.

That stability took time to attain, more so for Shaw than for Nancy Langhorne. Shaw struggled in London (whence in 1876 he had followed his mother, who had followed Vandeleur Lee there four years earlier), first as an aspiring novelist, and then with increasing success as an art critic, music critic, drama critic, and ultimately as a dramatist. However, only the close of the nineteenth century brought Shaw any significant financial security. It was confirmed by marriage in 1898, after several bouts of philandering, to the comfortably well-to-do Charlotte Payne-Townshend. Shaw called Charlotte 'my Irish millionairess' who, he said, and perhaps only half-jokingly, could provide him with 'so many hundreds a month for nothing.'[5] Their marriage was unconventional because Charlotte 'had succeeded in obtaining a marital arrangement that entirely excluded sex (they had agreed initially even to maintain their separate domiciles in London), and she was free to indulge what she later described as a "managing, domineering strain" inherited from her mother.'[6]

On the other side of the Atlantic, Nancy Langhorne's early adult years were sometimes unsatisfactory. In New York, at Miss Brown's Academy for Young Ladies, she was regarded as an inferior by her fellow young ladies: Virginia was deemed a backwoods state, contrary to Nancy's own elevated opinion of her home and herself. In 1897 (just one year before Shaw's marriage) Nancy married Robert Gould Shaw, scion of a distinguished family. It proved a marriage of incompatibles. Nancy was not a submissive, compliant Southern belle; indeed, her character was exceptionally paradoxical: 'For she was at once overbearing and modest, censorious yet kind, fierce and direct yet sympathetic, tactless at the same time as sensitive, didactic and even minatory yet remarkably intuitive and willing to learn.'[7] For his part, Robert Shaw was simply an alcoholic ne'er-do-well. The marriage seems to have induced an aversion to sex in Nancy, although in 1898 she did give birth to a son, Robert, who was always her favourite child. A series of separations ensued and (despite Nancy's strong religious beliefs to the contrary) divorce followed in 1903. After that experience, Nancy became more matrimonially circumspect: '[S]he was icily virtuous ... as her puritanism did not only mean that she went to church regularly and only drank tea and barley water, but that she did not scruple to threaten with exposure and ridicule anyone who even hinted at dishonourable transgression of the very lightest kind.'[8] Further promising (though ultimately failed) courtships followed, and Nancy, stunning beauty that she was, also had any number of suitors during her first visit to England in 1905. While she was crossing the Atlantic for a second visit in December 1905, Nancy was spotted on board ship by the phenomenally wealthy Waldorf Astor (born in New York City on Nancy's revised birth date, 19 May 1879). He was the son of William Waldorf Astor, who had moved permanently to Britain in 1890 and who later became a British subject and a peer. Nancy and Waldorf were mutually attracted and their relationship developed swiftly: they were engaged in March 1906 and married on 3 May 1906. Nancy thereby achieved the sort of secure financial and social position that is usually confined to fairy tales. Nancy's 'palaces' included one of England's huge country houses, Cliveden (a wedding present from Waldorf's father), which sits impressively high above the River Thames in Buckinghamshire, and a sumptuous town house at 4 St James's Square, London (other properties in Kent, Plymouth, and Scotland were to follow at later dates).

So, in the first decade of the twentieth century, these two emigrants found themselves in England – married, stable, disinclined to sex (for varying reasons), and, to boot, confirmed teetotallers because of earlier detrimental experiences.

Both marriages endured. Shaw became the most famous dramatist of his day and a pundit on innumerable topics. Charlotte enjoyed luxurious travel and insisted on taking an often reluctant Shaw with her; travel was also supposed to provide Shaw with a break from work (although, as the correspondence reveals, this stratagem failed). Charlotte's attempts to spare Shaw from the strains of overworking could even lead her to express forthright disapproval of Nancy herself (Letter 44). Charlotte also tolerated, in varying degrees, Shaw's continued philandering, with, for example, Mrs Patrick Campbell and Molly Tompkins (the latter December–May romance was flourishing when Shaw's friendship with Nancy began). Ultimately, however, the Shaws' marriage was contented and is captured perhaps in Pra and Prola's discussion of their marriage in Act 2 of *The Simpleton of the Unexpected Isles* (1935):

> PROLA: We have now grown together until we are each of us a part of the other. I no longer think of you as a separate possibility.

PRA: I know. I am part of the furniture of your house. I am a matter of course. But was I always that? Was I that in the childhood of our marriage?

PROLA: You are still young enough and manlike enough to ask mischievous questions.

PRA: ... Did you ever really care for me? I know I began as a passion and have ended as a habit, like all husbands; but outside that routine there is a life of the intellect that is quite independent of it. What have I been to you in that life? A help or a hindrance?

PROLA: Pra: I always knew from the very beginning that you were an extraordinarily clever fool.

PRA: Good. That is exactly what I am.

Shaw revealed his deep concern and care for Charlotte during her declining years when she suffered painfully from osteitis deformans or Paget's disease. (Coincidentally, the latter was correctly diagnosed for the first time while the Shaws were staying at Cliveden in 1942; Letter 103). Indeed, many of the letters here provide a touching chronicle of a partnership withstanding the physical ravages that sometimes accompany old age.

Nancy and Waldorf Astor generally worked well together. Nancy was instrumental in promoting Waldorf's career as a politician and canvassed for him when he stood for the Plymouth (Sutton division) seat in the House of Commons in the January 1910 general election. However, Waldorf had to wait until the second 1910 election (held in December) to be elected. Their roles were reversed when, elevated to the peerage by his father's death in 1919, Waldorf reluctantly gave up his seat (after he had sought unsuccessfully to renounce his title). Nancy ran in his stead and so in 1919 became the first woman to take her seat in the House of Commons, although she was not the first woman to be elected (Letter 228). Nancy was an effective campaigner, as was evident in the vigorous climax of her 1919 adoption speech: 'If you want an M.P. who will be a repetition of the 600 other M.P.s don't vote for me. If you want a lawyer or if you want a pacifist don't elect me. If you can't get a fighting man, take a fighting woman. If you want a Bolshevist or a follower of Mr Asquith, don't elect me. If you want a party hack don't elect me. Surely we have outgrown party ties. I have. The war has taught us that there is a greater thing than parties, and that is the State.'[9] Her ready wit deflected interruptions at the hustings effortlessly: 'A countryman in her constituency thought to floor her with "Missus, how many toes have a pig got?" I'm sure Nancy wouldn't know, but what he got was: "Take off your boot, man, and count them for yourself."'[10] Waldorf supported Nancy unobtrusively and unwaveringly; he did her research and drafted her speeches. Unfortunately, Nancy invariably wandered from her text: unlike Shaw, her mind was not orderly and her thoughts would drift until her argument became obscure. Writer and National Labour MP Harold Nicolson recalled: 'She has one of those minds that work from association to association, and therefore spreads sideways with extreme rapidity. Further and further did she diverge from the point [of her speech] ... I was annoyed by this, as I knew that I was to be called [upon to speak] after her. It was like playing squash with a dish of scrambled eggs.'[11] In the 1940s it became clear that Nancy was losing her parliamentary grip, and Waldorf and the family, prompted by love rather than other motives, pressured Nancy to resign her seat. The result was a permanent rift in their relationship; despite Waldorf's entreaties, Nancy remained decidedly cool, if not icy, until Waldorf's death in 1952. Nancy and Waldorf's relationship had been strained earlier by Nancy's platonic friendship with Philip Kerr (later 11th Marquess of Lothian), whom she converted to Christian Science from Roman Catholicism. One of Nancy's biographers, Maurice Collis, has recorded how Nancy's son, Bill Astor, 'described some of the private stresses and troubles which existed in the background of the brilliant Cliveden period of the twenties and thirties. Nancy, though sexually frigid, had a great need for men friends. Her affection for Philip Kerr, Lord Lothian, was very deep, and Waldorf was jealous of the friendship. She had also a very deep fondness for Bernard Shaw.'[12]

That fondness was established quickly once Nancy and Shaw did meet finally, although their firm friendship did not render Shaw averse to expressing his opinion of the Astors. In a 12 December 1941 letter to Upton Sinclair Shaw reported:

> I spent three weeks with the Astors at Cliveden last August. I had not been there for eleven years! Waldorf, though like myself he is an absentee landlord, is by temperament a Communist who offended his father by introducing a Bill in the House of Lords to enable people like himself to get rid of

their peerages. Nancy is a unique and amusing phenomenon. It would take
me a whole chapter to describe her. Her hospitality is utterly indiscriminate
as far as class and party is concerned; only you must be 'good' or you shant
darken her doors. She wont give you a strong drink, as she is a bigoted
teetotaller. She is a Christian Scientist, and, though she is as fiercely Protestant as if she was a Belfast lady instead of a Virginian aborigine, she eschews
the Church of England. A Speaker of the House of Commons told me that
she was more trouble than ten Maxtons and Gallachers (both Left extremes). Her philosophy begins and ends with her being a good sort; and
her being a Conservative means no more than that she lies where she was
dropped, as the scope of her mind is not Marxian. I refused all her invitations until I happened to meet her in person at a London party. In ten
minutes we were as thick as thieves; and that is what will happen to you if you
come to England and make her acquaintance.[13]

For her part, Nancy maintained she was attracted by Shaw's cerebral
qualities (a sharp contrast with her own delight in wealth and its trap-
pings): 'I absolutely agree about G.B.S. being entirely mental and spiri-
tual; that is why I liked him and that is why I think he had such a good
brain: it wasn't clogged up with material things.'[14] Nancy's friendship
with Shaw satisfied another, darker aspect of her psychology: 'Nancy's
ambition was not just to meet people but, wherever possible, to enslave
those about her.'[15] Put more simply, Nancy was aggressively bossy and
wanted her own way in even the smallest of matters. However, as her
long-serving maid Rosina Harrison proved, the best course of action with
Nancy was to counterattack, and Nancy admired people who stood up to
her.[16] Shaw was definitely not enslavable, but he was forced frequently to
fend off either Nancy Astor's invitations to stay with her or her offers to
visit him. Nancy's judgment above on Shaw's attitude to material wealth
is only partially true. Letters 93, 100, and 110 reveal that, as he grew older
and considerably wealthier, Shaw became more vexed by the heavy
taxation he suffered, even in times of national crisis, such as the Second
World War. Moreover, it is worth noting that the Shaws' house in Ayot St
Lawrence was more than tolerably spacious, that over the years Shaw
possessed several expensive cars (which invariably he drove erratically,
even to the extent of causing Charlotte injury [Letter 39]), and that,
even in wartime, the Shaws employed several servants. However, there

was a Spartan aspect to Shaw – his vegetarianism, teetotalism, Jaeger clothing, and love of exercise. While Nancy was surrounded by and enjoyed opulent luxury, she took a daily cold bath and, even in old age, could boast of her athletic prowess in golf, tennis, skating, and skiing. To boot, she could and did turn cartwheels!

Other similarities between Shaw and Nancy Astor were more obvious. Both were quick-witted personalities and entertainers who relished attention: a Christmas at Cliveden provided just one of many such opportunities (Letter 2). Both were outspoken, Nancy more so than Shaw, and their frankness paid scant consideration for other people's sensibilities. In the political arena, as the first woman to sit in the hitherto all-male preserve of Parliament, Nancy inevitably had to give as good as she received. When she challenged Winston Churchill to explain why he ignored her in Parliament, 'he replied that he found a woman's intrusion into the House of Commons as embarrassing as if she had burst upon him in his bathroom when he had nothing to defend himself with but a sponge. "Nonsense, Winston," she retorted. "You're not good-looking enough to have fears of this sort."'[17] Despite such wit, Nancy often spoke before she thought; she maintained that she did not know her opinion on a particular subject until she had spoken about it. Nevertheless, she was consistent in her commitment to certain social issues and, although a Conservative, she was an advocate for vulnerable members of society. Her parliamentary preoccupations, which Waldorf shared, included

> [n]ursery schools, votes for women at twenty-one, the subsidized provision of children's footwear, improved treatment of juvenile offenders and women in prison, the protection of married women (who lost their citizenship if they married a foreigner), equal guardianship for mothers and fathers, the abolition of the death penalty for expectant mothers (she was also against any death penalty), and slum clearance. She believed in state health care and town planning, advocating a massive housing program 'as important as building battleships in 1914'; she also advocated raising the school-leaving age. She supported the Trade Boards, to protect workers from exploitation and employers from being undercut; she supported the international eight-hour day. She tried to bring in a bill preventing prostitutes from being convicted on the evidence of a single policeman.[18]

That was an agenda Shaw the socialist could endorse and, throughout her
political career, he provided Nancy with both general and specific political
advice and support, as many letters in the correspondence illustrate.

Religion was one significant area where their views diverged. After an
early life of orthodox Christianity, Nancy became a committed Christian
Scientist in 1914; without fail thereafter, she read the daily lessons in
Science and Health with Key to the Scriptures by religion's founder, Mrs Mary
Baker Eddy. However, given Nancy's woolly intellectual abilities, her
belief was probably founded on instinctual faith. Indeed, an essential
tenet of Christian Science, the ability of the mind to overcome physical
ailments, requires a blind, unwavering faith. For Nancy it worked: once
she converted to Christian Science, she never experienced illnesses
much beyond the common cold. However, her faith had nearly disastrous consequences when her daughter, Wissie, was injured while horse
riding and, initially, Nancy refused to allow her conventional medical
attention (Letter 14). Her convert Philip Kerr almost certainly died as a
result of his Christian Science beliefs because he did not seek conventional medical attention, which could have remedied his uremia. Nancy
Astor's Christianity also failed to amend her other shortcomings. Henry
Channon, Conservative MP and author of delightfully indiscreet diaries,
described Nancy as 'warm-hearted, a whirlwind and a wit ... but an
unconscious snob and a hypocrite. Her Christian Science wraps her in a
veil of sham and she believes, as they all do, only what she wants to.'[19]
More seriously, Nancy's family members were affected. In 1933 her son,
David Astor, after suffering a breakdown, 'told Waldorf that he could no
longer get on with Nancy, for whom he had lost his respect. He went
further, accusing his mother of hypocrisy; that what was dressed up in
great acts of unselfishness was always driven by personal motive.'[20] Interestingly, as Letters 14 and 44 suggest, Charlotte Shaw was attracted to
some aspects of Christian Science, and she attended some services with
Nancy. However, Charlotte consulted traditional doctors about, for example, her own debilitating Paget's disease.

Shaw teased Nancy about her Christian Science, although without any
apparent intent of changing her opinion (Letter 5). In the theatrical
arena, however, both Christian Science and orthodox medicine were fair
game for Shaw's satirical attacks. Act 1 of *Too True to be Good* (1932)
contains this exchange:

THE DOCTOR: I am a faith healer. You dont suppose I believe the bottles cure
people? But the patient's faith in the bottle does.

THE MONSTER: Youre a humbug: thats what you are.

THE DOCTOR Faith is humbug. But it works.

THE MONSTER: Then why do you call it science?

THE DOCTOR: Because people believe in science. The Christian Scientists
call their fudge science for the same reason.

THE MONSTER: The Christian Scientists let their patients cure themselves.
Why dont you?

THE DOCTOR: I do. But I help them. You see, it's easier to believe in bottles
and inoculations than in oneself and in that mysterious power that gives us
our life and that none of us knows anything about. Lots of people believe in
the bottles and wouldnt know what you were talking about if you suggested
the real thing. And the bottles do the trick. My patients get well as often as
not. That is, unless their number's up. Then we all have to go.

Whatever Shaw's complex philosophy, religion, or beliefs – and he
certainly was far more widely read, logical, analytical, and philosophical
than Nancy – they were fundamentally intellectual, while Nancy's were
instinctual.

While Shaw and Nancy were famous individuals before they met, their
friendship was spotlighted and rendered notorious by their visit (accompanied by Waldorf, Kerr, and others) to Russia in 1931. This was an
improbable venture – wealthy capitalists accompanying an avowed communist into Stalin's heartland. Perhaps it was 'merely Shavian "impish-
ness" that persuaded [Shaw] to ask the Astors to travel to Russia with
him. His sense of fun, nothing more, suggested that it would be well
worthwhile to see what the Astors made of the Soviet Union, or what the
Soviet Union made of the Astors – or both.'[21] Curiously Shaw, for all his
acknowledged communist sympathies, was apparently not particularly
observant during the tour (although he enjoyed the adulation lavished
upon him).[22] Shaw could be excused for falling asleep during some
horse races laid on to celebrate his seventy-fifth birthday, but 'David
Astor found it difficult to understand how Shaw could apparently show
so little signs of being aware of what was all around him that was different
from his home background. Neither a visit to Leningrad, generally
admitted to be the most beautiful of Russian cities, nor the beautiful and

varied landscapes through which they were taken on the long railway journey from Moscow to Leningrad and back seemed to have any appeal to Shaw.'[23] On the other hand, Waldorf Astor took a very keen interest in the agricultural aspects of the Russian economy.[24] The highlight of their visit was a two-and-a-half-hour interview with Stalin by whom, typically, Nancy was not in the least cowed: 'The honours of the occasion were won by Lady Astor who, having no veneration for dictators nor any awe of eminent persons, frightened the wits out of the interpreters ... by asking that cunning Caucasian [Stalin] why he had slaughtered so many Russians. The interpreters were loth to translate it, nor did they do so, until Stalin, observing their fearful embarrassment, demanded to be told what Lady Astor had said.'[25] Instead of shipping his guests off to Siberia, Stalin treated Nancy's remarks with genial indifference. Quite the opposite response faced the travellers on their return to England.

The furore was fomented by a newspaper article written by Winston Churchill (Letter 32), who directed his withering sarcasm at the visit as a whole:

> Ah! But we must not forget that the object of the visit was educational and investigatory. How important for our public figures to probe for themselves the truth about Russia: to find out by personal test how the Five Year Plan was working. How necessary to know whether Communism is really better than Capitalism, and how the broad masses of the Russian people fare in 'life, liberty and the pursuit of happiness' under the new regime. Who can grudge a few days devoted to these arduous tasks? To the aged Jester, with his frosty smile and safely-invested capital, it was a brilliant opportunity of dropping a series of disconcerting bricks upon the corns of his ardent hosts. And to Lady Astor whose husband, according to the newspapers, had the week before been awarded three millions sterling returned taxation by the American courts, all these communal fraternizings and sororizings must have been a pageant of delight.[26]

Churchill then depicted aspects of the real Russia the Shaw/Astor party had ignored: 'a vast, dumb people dwelling under the discipline of a conscripted army in war-time; a people suffering in years of peace the rigors and privations of the worst campaigns; a people ruled by terror, fanaticisms, and the Secret Police ... Here we have a system whose social achievements crowd five or six persons in a single room; whose wages hardly compare in purchasing power with the British dole; where life is unsafe; where liberty is unknown; where grace and culture are dying; and where armaments and preparations for war are rife.'[27] Shaw responded gallantly to the personal attacks that Churchill levelled against Nancy Astor (untrue and irrelevant accusations that she dabbled in betting on horse races); however, Churchill's charge of the group's realpolitik myopia cannot be gainsaid.[28]

The 1930s saw Shaw and Nancy embroiled in other controversial politics. Shaw's predilection for the superman (or at least someone with 'the *personality* to change the world'[29] found him voicing his approval of Oswald Mosley, Mussolini, Hitler, and Stalin. These men were his lions, in both the present correspondence and, among many examples, the preface to the Nancy Astor–inspired *The Millionairess* (1936), where Shaw extolled Mussolini's rise to power in post–First World War Italy: 'Here was clearly a big opportunity for a man psychologist enough to grasp the situation and bold enough to act on it. Such a man was Mussolini ... Mussolini refused to be turned aside from his work like a parliamentary man to discuss "incidents." ... [H]e was delighting his own people by the spectacle of a great Italian bullying the world, and getting away with it triumphantly.'[30] Shaw offered an equally unpopular appraisal of Hitler at the beginning of the Second World War: '[W]e made all the mischief, we and the French, when we were drunk with victory at Versailles; and if that mischief had not been there for him to undo Adolf Hitler would have now been a struggling artist of no political account. He actually owes his eminence to us; so let us cease railing at our own creation and recognise the ability with which he has undone our wicked work, and the debt the German nation owes him for it.'[31]

Nancy achieved nationwide notoriety in 1937 when the countless weekend gatherings of politicians and other notables at Cliveden were dubbed the 'Cliveden Set' and condemned as exerting undue influence on British policy, particularly with regard to Hitler and Germany. Nancy's own categorical denial of such an organized 'set' appeared in a letter to the *Daily Herald* on 5 May 1938: 'There is no group which week-ends at Cliveden in the interest of Fascism or anything else. For years my husband and I have entertained men of all political creeds (including Bolsheviks) of all nationalities, of all religious faiths, of all social inter-

ests. As regards the imaginary Cliveden set, some who are said to belong
to it have never been to Cliveden, others not for years.'[32] While Nancy
and many of those Cliveden guests were anti-fascist, she supported Prime
Minister Neville Chamberlain's policy of appeasement with Hitler. In
this policy Nancy was encouraged by Philip Kerr's remarkable assessment of Hitler after his meeting with the dictator for two and a half
hours in 1935: 'Hitler is a prophet – not a politician or an intriguer.
Quite straight, full of queer ideas, but quite honestly wanting no war.'[33]
Interestingly, Kerr had been a member of Lloyd George's personal staff
at the 1919 Paris Peace Conference and had opposed the impossible
reparations imposed on Germany that led ultimately to Hitler's rise.
However, Kerr *was* responsible for drafting the article in the peace treaty
by which Germany accepted guilt for the war.[34] Shaw responded to the
scathing newspaper attacks on Nancy and Cliveden by pointing out that
the gatherings at Cliveden were so eclectic that a concerted conspiracy
there would be impossible (Letter 66).

When the likelihood of war became more inevitable, Nancy abandoned her earlier appeasement stance. She began in July 1939 by encouraging Chamberlain to bring Churchill into his cabinet as a warning
to Hitler. Henry Channon noted: 'The Astors surprisingly enough, take
a strong pro-Churchill line. Lady Astor, frightened by anonymous letters
and gossip about the so-called "Cliveden Set" has thrown over her principles and is urging Chamberlain against his better judgement, to take
the plunge.'[35] Less than a year later, on 8 May 1940, Nancy Astor was one
of forty government MPs to vote with the Labour opposition on a
motion that resulted eventually in Chamberlain's fall and in Churchill
becoming prime minister. The ever-observant Channon remarked: 'Lady
Astor rushed about [in the House of Commons], intriguing and enjoying the fray and the smell of blood: she has joined hands with the
insurgents, probably because she must always be in the limelight, and
also because I think she is seriously rattled by the "Cliveden Set" allega-
tions which were made against her before the war, and now wants to live
down.'[36]

Certainly more admirable was Nancy Astor's brave conduct as Lady
Mayoress of Plymouth (Waldorf had been elected Lord Mayor in 1939)
during the devastating German air raids on the city. She stayed frequently in her house there even after it suffered damage, visited people

in bomb shelters, helped put out fires, and participated in the nightly dancing on Plymouth Hoe that helped boost the populace's morale. Noel Coward recounted in his diary a morning spent with Nancy in July 1941: 'A strange experience. Lady A. very breezy, noisy and *au fond* incredibly kind. Banging people on the back and making jokes. The people themselves stoic, sometimes resentful of her, but generally affectionately tolerant. The whole city a pitiful sight. Houses that have held sailor families since the time of Drake spread across the road in rubble and twisted wood.'[37] And, as in the First World War, the Astors handed over most of Cliveden for a Canadian hospital, where Nancy often provided deliberately brusque bedside comfort in order to challenge wounded soldiers to stop feeling sorry for themselves and to get better: 'The ward woke up at once on her appearance, everybody galvanized to attention, jokes answering her back. She carried a basket and marched through like a fishwife on the Barbican.'[38] Occasionally she even cajoled Shaw into sending a book for one of the solders (Letter 85). Meanwhile, the Shaws retreated from the London blitz to the relative safety of Ayot, although that was not without its occasional hazard (Letters 151–2). Their flat at Whitehall Court suffered bomb damage in both 1941 and 1944, as did a bust of Nancy Astor on the latter occasion (Letter 162).

The 1940s marked a progressive decline in both Shaw's and Nancy's fortunes. Shaw's case is unsurprising because he was already in his mid-eighties, although he had a decade to live. However, the world's press still beat a path to his door, his longevity affording a cachet to his opinions on current events. Shaw remained productive: in addition to newspaper articles and letters, his works included *Everybody's Political What's What?* (published 1944), *Buoyant Billions* (completed 1947), *Far-fetched Fables* (written 1948), *Shakes versus Shav* (written 1949) and *Sixteen Self Sketches* (published 1949). However, only diehard Shavians would argue strongly for much of his 1940s work. For her part, Nancy was drifting into a parliamentary eclipse from which she never recovered. Her personality was the root cause: 'As she grew older her outrageous outbursts became less and less tolerable and she became even more petulant when thwarted than formerly.'[39] Violet Markham (a public servant and liberal activist) reported to the eminent civil servant Thomas Jones (a close friend of both Waldorf and David Astor) that she believed Nancy's private behaviour bordered on lunacy. Markham had witnessed some of Nancy's violent, uncontrolled outbursts against several of her *bêtes noires* – Catholics, the Pope, Communists, Russians.[40] Her public performance was little better. In August 1942 Nancy gave a speech at a rally in Stockport in which she belittled Russia as a former German ally and the Russians for doing no more than defending themselves. However, the truth of the matter was that the Russians (defending the 4000-mile-long eastern front) were then in the midst of the Battle of Stalingrad, which resulted in over one million Russian dead and proved to be a turning point in the war in the east. People were shocked. Clementine Churchill observed: 'Nancy Astor has made an ungracious & clumsy (I was about to write "ass of herself" – But I will not compare her to the animal which bore Christ in triumph) speech which has repelled everybody.'[41] Two years later, Nancy was berating English troops: 'Lady Astor did not have a good press in my family. My father had served in North Africa and Italy with the Eighth Army, which Nancy had asserted in the House of Commons in 1944 was "dodging D-Day." They returned singing to the tune of "Lili Marlene": We're the D-Day Dodgers, out in Italy, / Always on the vino, always on the spree. / Eighth Army scroungers and their tanks, / We live in Rome among the Yanks. / ... Dear Lady Astor, you think you're mighty hot, / Standing on a platform talking tommy rot. / You're England's sweetheart and her pride: / We think your mouth's too bleeding wide.'[42] That same year, Violet Markham confirmed Nancy was continuing to engage in her screaming rows, citing one with her son, Bill, in which she demanded that some evacuees be returned immediately from Cliveden to London.[43] In addition, Nancy maintained her hostility to her sons' marriages by refusing to attend Jakie Astor's wedding in 1944 (Letter 176). Her uncontrolled, wilful behaviour is captured most poignantly in the midst of Waldorf's plea for a reconciliation: 'You are naturally combative and have developed a habit of increasing your combat, of getting involved in unnecessary or wrong combats but always insisting on augmenting the assault even when the consequences will be damaging – Now I don't like to see my Prima Donna getting the gilt knocked off her ginger bread nor do I want to look for & get into losing battles just for the sake of battling!'[44] So it was apparent to Nancy's family that she could not continue as an MP.[45] Further, many people realized that, despite what Churchill had achieved during the Second World War, a Labour government was a decided probability after the war and that Nancy would suffer the humiliation of losing her Plymouth seat after twenty-five years. (In the event, a Labour candidate did take the seat; a slight consolation for Nancy might have been that the victor was a woman. See Letter 181.) Despite her reluctance (and truculence) over this matter, Nancy decided to retire from Parliament, with Shaw as ever providing sideline advice, though firmly refusing to intrude between husband and wife (see Letters 178, 180–1, and 184).

Nancy's retirement came just two years after Charlotte Shaw's death after her long and painful illness. Nancy convinced herself Charlotte had 'bequeathed' Shaw to her to look after. In a sense, Nancy's new task was little more than a continuation of her solicitousness for both the Shaws as they grew older, more feeble, and, she believed, more alone.[46] Also, in the years leading up to her retirement (and after Philip Kerr's death), Nancy viewed Shaw as her one solid true friend, quite unlike her own traitorous husband and family. Indeed, with Charlotte dead and a rift established with Waldorf Astor, Nancy saw Shaw almost as a substitute husband.

Shaw did not want the overwhelming, domineering attention Nancy lavished upon him as a widower. However, he could not prevent all Nancy's visits to him. In about 1946, Nancy brought the budding dramatist William Douglas Home with her to see Shaw:

> Lady Astor turned the handle of the shed door, pulled it open, and I saw within a figure seated at a table working on a manuscript.
>
> 'Come out of there, you old fool,' Lady Astor said. 'You've written enough nonsense in your life! The figure raised its head and, with its head, a long white beard – or was it faintly yellow?
>
> 'Go away,' it said. 'I'm working. Go away, and I'll give you some tea when I've finished.'
>
> ...
>
> 'You're a lonely old man' I recall her saying, 'since poor Charlotte died. You ought to come and live in London. I'll look after you!'
>
> 'I don't like London, Nancy,' he replied.
>
> 'Then I'll come and live down here,' she told him.
>
> 'Nothing,' he said, 'would move me to London quicker than that.'[47]

In fact, Shaw enjoyed his newly found isolation and freedom, and he still had servants enough to tend to his daily needs. Moreover, he had had enough of the 'pursuing woman' he had attracted in his early years and showed no signs of or capacity for octogenarian philandering. But, as the correspondence reveals, matters were not entirely straightforward because Nancy enlisted Shaw's secretary, Blanche Patch, as a compliant ally and informant to keep her apprised of Shaw's domestic circumstances. Doubtless this action was well-intentioned; it also reflected Nancy's innate jealous bossiness. Nancy's alliance with Blanche Patch also allowed both women to vent their mutual dislike of F.E. Loewenstein (Shaw's self-appointed bibliographer and founder of the Shaw Society)[48] and of Clare and Stephen Winsten, Shaw's neighbours at Ayot.

Shaw's final accident and illness in September and October 1950 found Nancy as attentive as ever. On 15 October 1950 she wrote an account of her several visits to Shaw's bedside that included a colourful Shavian tale: 'He told me his night nurse was a scream; was fifty and dressed like a young lady of fifteen. She told him she had nursed Adelina Patti's last husband – a foreigner who took a large house in Wales. He gave a grand gala party with all the best of the neighbourhood there, when, in the midst of a dance, he rushed into the ballroom screaming "Stop the music." The music stopped and he said, "Please all go home. I have found my wife upstairs in bed with a man." He rushed out and the guests began to depart, when he came rushing back and said, "Stop, don't go. The gentleman has apologised."'[49] On 31 October, despite his weak condition, Nancy insisted on seeing Shaw: '"He is very, very tired," Lady Astor told the pressmen as she emerged an hour later; his final words to her, she reported, were "Oh, Nancy. I want to sleep, sleep."'[50] Shaw died on 2 November 1950, the occasion for Nancy to adopt the role of grieving widow. She was prominent among the three dozen or so relatives and friends at Shaw's cremation at Golders Green in London on 5 November,[51] and she contributed a short, if inconsequential obituary for the *Observer* (5 November 1950). However, Nancy was not present when the ashes of Shaw and Charlotte were mingled together and spread in the grounds of Shaw's Corner on 23 November. Later she *was* active on the abortive Shaw Memorial Committee (she served as a vice-president), the swift demise of which was a telling reflection upon Shaw's diminished standing shortly after his death. Waldorf Astor's death in 1952 touched Nancy but a little and her own final years, despite her family's ongoing support, lacked fulfilment. One direct connection with Shaw remained. Appropriately, it was in the form of a lengthy and comforting correspondence (over 300 letters have survived in the Astor Archive) between Nancy and Shaw's cousin, Judy Musters. Their correspondence continued until Nancy's death on 2 May 1964. While Shaw was an ever-recurrent topic of their letters, Nancy's final deathbed thoughts proved to be of her husband: her last word was 'Waldorf.'[52]

The correspondence in this edition captures amply the multifaceted aspects of Shaw's relationship with Nancy Astor, which blossomed swiftly and endured for a quarter of a century. Many letters discuss significant topics – the politics of the era (sharpened by Shaw's and Nancy's opposing viewpoints), major political and theatrical figures, Shaw's plays and other works, Nancy's campaigns in and outside of the House of Commons, the Second World War. Other topics are more humble in nature and embrace the incidental but nevertheless interesting aspects of their lives. There is their mutual fondness (together with Charlotte's devotion to Nancy), concerns over health, financial matters, family and domestic problems, travel plans – indeed, the minutiae of life that affect public and private figures alike. Here those seeming trifles flesh out Shaw's and Nancy's public personae and render them as ordinary beings coping with the quotidian travails of life. Indeed, many letters reveal the more personal side of Shaw's life, particularly as he struggled with Charlotte's declining health and painful illnesses, which in turn led to his more solitary final years. Paradoxically, as one might expect, Shaw declared he enjoyed his newly found solitude, while Nancy did her best to impose her own domineering care on him (thereby avoiding the reality of her own deteriorating marriage brought on her own shortcomings). Ultimately, the Shavian and Astorian canvas encompasses much more than is contained in these letters, but this edition affords a vivid close-up from a unique vantage point.

Notes

1 The letter is in the Archives, Churchill College, University of Cambridge (CHAN 5/19).

2 Norman and Jeanne Mackenzie, eds, *The Diary of Beatrice Webb Vol. 4 (1924–1943): The Wheel of Life* (Cambridge, MA: Belknap Press, 1985), 133. See also Blanche Patch's comments in Letters 114, 132.

3 Both Shaw and Astor are the subjects of numerous biographies. I am indebted particularly to the following works for my own account here and in the notes to the edition.

On Shaw: St John Ervine, *Bernard Shaw: His Life, Work and Friends* (London: Constable, 1956); Archibald Henderson, *George Bernard Shaw: Man of the Century* (New York: Appleton, Century, Crofts, 1956); Michael Holroyd, *Bernard Shaw: Volume 3, 1918–1950, The Lure of Fantasy* (New York: Random House, 1991); Dan H. Laurence, ed., *Bernard Shaw: Collected Letters 1926–1950* (London: Max Reinhardt, 1988); Blanche Patch, *Thirty Years with G.B.S.* (London: Victor Gollancz, 1951); Hesketh Pearson, *G.B.S.: A Full Length Portrait* (New York: Harper and Brothers, 1942)

On Nancy Astor: Michael Astor, *Tribal Feeling* (London: John Murray, 1963); Maurice Collis, *Nancy Astor: An Informal Biography* (New York: E.P. Dutton, 1960); James Fox, *Five Sisters: The Langhornes of Virginia* (New York: Simon and Schuster, 2000); John Grigg, *Nancy Astor: A Lady Unashamed* (Boston: Little Brown, 1980); Lucy Kavaler, *The Astors: A Family Chronicle of Pomp and Power* (New York: Dodd Mead, 1966); Anthony Masters, *Nancy Astor: A Biography* (New York: McGraw-Hill, 1981); Christopher Sykes, *Nancy: The Life of Lady Astor* (New York: Harper and Row, 1972); Derek Wilson, *The Astors 1763–1992: Landscape with Millionaires* (New York: St Martin's, 1993).

4 Grigg, *Nancy Astor*, 15. Most sources give Nancy Astor's birth date as 19 May 1879, which coincides conveniently with that of her second husband, Waldorf Astor. However, Grigg's date is based on an examination of local records, and there appears no reason to dispute it.

5 Dan H. Laurence, *Bernard Shaw: Collected Letters 1874–1897* (London: Max Reinhardt, 1965), 693. In 1897 Shaw's annual income amounted to just over £1000. After their marriage 'Charlotte's solicitors drew up a settlement that guaranteed the income from two trust funds ... to Shaw himself ... Between themselves they agreed to share basic expenses, but to keep their unequal incomes mainly apart' (Michael Holroyd, *Bernard Shaw: Volume 1, 1856–1898, The Search for Love* [London: Chatto and Windus, 1988], 462–3).

6 Dan H. Laurence, *Bernard Shaw: Collected Letters 1898–1910* (London: Max Reinhardt, 1972), 4–5.

7 A.L. Rowse, *Memories of Men and Women* (Lanham, MD: University Press of America, 1983), 25.

8 Sykes, *Nancy*, 69.

9 Ibid., 191.

10 Rowse, *Memories*, 29.

11 Harold Nicolson, *The War Years 1939–1945: Volume II of Diaries and Letters*, ed. Nigel Nicolson (New York: Atheneum, 1967), 285.

12 Louise Collis, ed., *Maurice Collis: Diaries 1949–1969* (London: Heinemann, 1976), 98.

13 Typescript copy in the Astor Archive, University of Reading (ms 1416), of an original in the Lilly Library, Indiana University. James Maxton (1885–1946) was a member of the Labour Party and sometime chairman of the Independent Labour Party; William Gallacher (1881–1965) was a communist MP and a founder of the British Communist Party. Thomas Jones provides an informative vignette of the Astors and Cliveden in *A Diary with Letters 1931–1950* (London: Oxford University Press, 1954), xxxiv–xl.

14 Letter to Judy Musters, 28 May 1951 (Reading). For her part, Judy Musters declared: 'Had I been writing about you, I think I should have stressed what you and GBS had in common: you were both fundamentally serious and frothily gay' (Letter to Nancy Astor, 22 November 1953 [Reading]).

15 Fox, *Five Sisters*, 299.

16 See Rosina Harrison, *Rose: My Life in Service* (New York: Viking Press, 1975).

17 Pamela Brookes, *Women at Westminster: An Account of Women in the British Parliament 1918–1966* (London: Peter Davies, 1967), 22.

18 Fox, *Five Sisters*, 290. Brian Harrison gives a persuasive account of Nancy Astor's 'firm and consistent feminism and her career's major impact on inter-war attitudes to women' in 'Publicist and Communicator: Nancy Astor,' in *Prudent Revolutionaries: Portraits of British Feminists between the Wars* (Oxford: Clarendon, 1987), 73–97.

19 Sir Henry Channon, *Chips: The Diaries of Sir Henry Channon*, ed. Robert Rhodes James (London: Weidenfeld and Nicolson, 1967), 27.

20 Fox, *Five Sisters*, 396.

21 T.F. Evans, 'Myopia or Utopia? Shaw in Russia,' *SHAW: The Annual of Shaw Studies* 5 (1985): 129.

22 The Russians were eager to see Shaw and he was lauded as having 'one of the most untrammeled minds of the civilized world' (A[natoly] Lunacharsky, 'Bernard Shaw, Our Guest,' *Moscow News*, 23 July 1931). See also Anna Louise Strong, 'Bernard Shaw Comes to Moscow,' ibid.

23 Evans, 'Myopia or Utopia?' 134. Shaw's account of his trip given to the

Independent Labour Party Summer School is notable for generalities rather
than specifics (see 'Mr. G.B. Shaw on Russia,' *Manchester Guardian*, 6 August
1931). By comparison, Philip Lothian's speech to the Liberal Summer School
was detailed ('Things That Astonished Lord Lothian in Russia,' *News Chronicle*, 6 August 1931). However, while on the trip, Shaw did send Charlotte
seven letters recounting events (Lawrence, ed., *Collected Letters 1926–1950*,
243–56).

24 Waldorf kept a diary of the trip (Reading). His 6 August 1931 letter to J.J.
Mallon (Reading) captures additional aspects of the trip: 'G.B.S.'s presence
with our party caused every door to be opened to us, even Stalin's ... We
made a solemn vow not to disclose to anybody outside what was discussed
with Stalin, but I don't mind telling you privately that Nancy with her usual
dash and courage put the most searching questions to him on the most
inflammatory points ... [S]he created her own news value. At first all the
crowds concentrated on G.B.S. ... [but] gradually they began to follow her
and feature her and question her to an equal extent.'

25 Ervine, *Berhard Shaw*, 518; and see Letter 74.

26 Winston S. Churchill, *Great Contemporaries* (New York: G.P. Putnam, 1937),
42–3. Churchill's attack first appeared as '"Personalities": No. 4. Lady Astor
and G. Bernard Shaw,' *Sunday Pictorial*, 16 August 1931, which was incorporated into his chapter on Shaw in *Great Contemporaries*.

27 Ibid., 43.

28 'G. Bernard Shaw Replies to "Personalities" Article,' *Sunday Pictorial*, 23 Au-
gust 1931. Waldorf Astor also defended Nancy in the course of an interview,
'Lord Astor Relates His Impressions of Red Russia,' *Western Independent*, 9
August 1931. In 1932 Shaw protested that he had seen the real Russia and
not 'an elaborate show staged for my special benefit' ('Not Hypnotised by
Stalin,' in Dan H. Laurence and James Rambeau, eds, *Agitations: Letters to the
Press 1875–1950* [New York: Ungar, 1985], 286–9). However, in a series of
four articles for the *Morning Post* (5–8 June 1933) entitled 'Russia Revealed,'
Malcolm Muggeridge (related to Beatrice and Sidney Webb by marriage)
reported 'what is hid from tourists' such as Shaw. Muggeridge 'went to
Russia a convinced and enthusiastic Communist. He came away entirely
disillusioned about the Soviet regime.'

29 Holroyd, *Bernard Shaw*, 3:113.

30 *Plays Extravagant* (London: Penguin, 1981), 228–30.

31 'Uncommon Sense about the War,' *New Statesman and Nation*, 7 October

1939, 484. Shaw echoed similar sentiments in a 1940 BBC radio talk (L.W. Conolly, ed., *Bernard Shaw and Barry Jackson* [Toronto: University of Toronto Press, 2002], 109–10).

32 Quoted from Thomas Jones, 'The Cliveden Set' (typescript), National Library of Wales, Thomas Jones Collection, Class Q, vol. 2, f. 108. Waldorf Astor repudiated the 'fiction' in his letter, 'The "Cliveden Set,"' *The Times*, 5 May 1938. For a thorough, even-handed discussion of the Set, see Norman Rose, *The Cliveden Set: Portrait of an Exclusive Fraternity* (London: Jonathan Cape, 2000).

33 1 February 1935 letter to Nancy Astor (Reading), quoted in Sykes, *Nancy*, 385. See also Channon, *Chips*, 180: 'But the Astors want peace with Germany, due, I think to Lothian's influence on Lady Astor.'

34 Sykes, *Nancy*, 184–5.

35 Channon, *Chips*, 204.

36 Ibid., 246.

37 Graham Payn and Sheridan Morley, eds, *The Noël Coward Diaries* (Boston and Toronto: Little, Brown, 1982), 7–8.

38 Rowse, *Memories*, 31.

39 E.L. Ellis, *T.J.: A Life of Dr Thomas Jones, C.H.* (Cardiff: University of Wales Press, 1992), 463.

40 23 October 1942 letter to Thomas Jones, National Library of Wales, Thomas Jones Collection, Class T, vol. 2, f. 119.

41 4 August 1942 letter to Winston Churchill in Mary Soames, ed., *Speaking for Themselves: The Personal Letters of Winston and Clementine Churchill* (London: Doubleday, 1998), 466. See also Ellis, *T.J.*, 463.

42 Stephen Sedley, 'In Judges' Lodgings,' *London Review of Books*, 11 November 1999.

43 8 August 1944 letter to Thomas Jones, National Library of Wales, Thomas Jones Collection, Class T, vol. 3, f. 32.

44 7 May 1947 letter from Waldorf to Nancy Astor (Reading).

45 By 1945 Nancy's public speeches were invariably embarrassing. During one such 'came another tug from Waldorf, so strong that Nancy sat down suddenly with an expression of pained surprise. I suppose her rambling is amusing, but it rather saddens me, as I like her, and I wish that she would not make quite such an idiot of herself in public' (Nicolson, *The War Years*, 451).

46 Nancy Astor claimed 'in fact Judy [Musters] and I were his [Shaw's] only

intimate friends after Charlotte died' (2 August 1951 letter from Nancy
Astor to John Mason Brown, Houghton Library, Harvard College Library,
Harvard University).

47 William Douglas Home, *Mr Home Pronounced Hume: An Autobiography*
(Newton Abbot: Readers Union, 1980), 69.

48 The degree of Nancy Astor's anti-Semitism is debatable; however, there is
anecdotal evidence to illustrate her enmity. For example, in 1938, Alan
Graham, a Conservative MP on Parliament's Foreign Affairs Committee
'came up to Nancy and said, "I do not think you behaved very well." She
turned upon him and said, "Only a Jew like you would *dare* to be rude to
me." He replied, "I should much like to smack your face." I think she is a
little mad' (Harold Nicolson, *Diaries and Letters 1930–1939*, ed. Nigel
Nicolson [New York: Atheneum, 1966], 327).

49 Nancy Astor's account exists in holographic and typescript form (Reading).

50 Laurence, ed., *Collected Letters 1926–1950*, 883.

51 Ibid., 885–6.

52 Sykes, *Nancy*, 524.

Editor's Note

This edition contains 229 pieces of correspondence (mostly letters): 150 are from Bernard Shaw to Nancy Astor; 34 from Nancy Astor to Shaw; with the remainder from Shaw to Waldorf Astor, Nancy Astor to Charlotte Shaw, Charlotte to Nancy, Nancy to Blanche Patch, and Blanche to Nancy. Of those letters, 135 are published here for the first time, 26 have been published previously in their entirety, and 37 as substantial extracts. Very brief extracts (often no more than a few words or a phrase) of a further 31 have been published only in Michael Holroyd's *Bernard Shaw: Volume 3, 1918–1950, The Lure of Fantasy* (1991). Numerous extracts from Shaw's and Nancy Astor's letters with other correspondents will be found in the headnotes and endnotes to the correspondence. The vast majority of the 229 letters published here are located in the Astor Archive at the University of Reading Library. Eight are located in the British Library and six in the Bernard F. Burgunder Collection, Division of Rare and Manuscript Collections, Carl A. Koch Library at Cornell University. The source for previously published letters and extracts is given at the start of a letter. Some slight incidental material (indicated by ellipses) has been omitted only from a handful of letters by Charlotte Shaw and Blanche Patch.

Nancy Astor preserved her correspondence with Shaw systematically, whereas Shaw appears to have destroyed most of Nancy Astor's letters to him, which accounts for the imbalance in their correspondence. Indeed, if Nancy Astor had not retained carbon copies of her own letters, only five or six to Shaw would have survived; however, she was not as prolific a correspondent as was Shaw, and she also appears to have preferred to telephone rather than to write. Unfortunately, those carbon copies usually lack the holographic additions Nancy Astor scrawled frequently once a letter had been typed. The remaining correspondence with Waldorf Astor, Charlotte Shaw, and Blanche Patch has been included because it acts as a form of surrogate correspondence. For example, Charlotte Shaw's writing to Nancy Astor from one of her world cruises with her husband is similar, in content at least, to what Shaw himself might have written. All such correspondence is interesting intrinsically, relates directly to the two chief figures, and thereby fleshes out the overall picture that emerges from the correspondence.

Shaw's letters present few difficulties in transcription. Generally his holographic letters are straightforward to read, even when his hand became somewhat shaky with old age. His correspondence typed by either himself or his secretary (usually Blanche Patch) contains only slight typographical vagaries. Almost without exception Shaw's letters are dated carefully and accurately. Nancy Astor's correspondence is an entirely different matter and caused consternation in many of its recipients. Ramsay MacDonald complained jokingly that Nancy Astor's handwriting was worse than a tame spider kept as a secretary by a certain Lady X, while Nancy's husband, Waldorf, often professed defeat when trying to decipher a note from her. A similar fate has befallen the present editor on a number of occasions, and holograph letters included here are littered with editorial conjectures. Possibly Nancy Astor wrote poorly in order to disguise her weak spelling, or to cover up some other inadequacy; her handwriting is, nevertheless, frustratingly drawn out and almost evokes, chirographically, her Virginian drawl. Her carbon copy letters are an easier proposition, although a few are badly smudged, and rarely do they indicate from which of several possible addresses they were dispatched. Nancy Astor could also be as careless with dates as she was with her handwriting.

I have endeavoured to tamper as little as possible with the letters themselves, and have done so only where confusion might otherwise have ensued. Shaw's well-known idiosyncratic spelling and punctuation have been retained, as have his sometimes fanciful salutations to Nancy Astor ('Asthore'). I have corrected silently any obvious typographical errors or omissions as well as a few consistently misspelled proper names ('Mosely' for Mosley, 'Atlee' for Attlee); the editorial '[*sic*]' appears as infrequently as possible. Nancy Astor's correspondence, as indicated above, has required a more obtrusive editorial hand, as will be obvious from the conjectures placed in square brackets.

The correspondence in this edition shares features in common with other volumes in this series. It is printed chronologically in a standard format (particularly for addresses and dates). The recipient of each letter is identified in boldface type at the head of each letter. Headnotes to letters provide contextual background information and narrative links. Endnotes to letters endeavour to identify people, places, and events (whether historical, political, literary, or theatrical) as well as allusions and other references. (However, figures such as Plato or Shakespeare are not so annotated.) The subject of each annotation is indicated in boldface type. A very few subjects have proved impossible to elucidate, and are so indicated. A forward slash '/' has been used to denote line breaks in poetical extracts and paragraph breaks in prose passages. Souces cited by author's name in the head- and endnotes are given in full in the Reference section.

Acknowledgments

Leonard Conolly, a long-standing friend and colleague since our post-graduate days together at the University of Wales, first suggested this volume to me, and he has provided unfailing support and encouragement during its various phases. He and Michel Pharand (University of Ottawa) read an early draft of the edition and both spared me from errors and omissions, for which I am most grateful. Much of my work here rides unashamedly on the back of the magnificent scholarship in the volumes of Shaw's correspondence edited by Dan H. Laurence, who also answered my enquiries and opened up his files of Shaviana for me. I am privileged to be in the same company. The companion volumes in the University of Toronto Press series of Shaw's correspondence have also proved a rich resource. I have made extensive use of Tony Gibbs's *Bernard Shaw Chronology*; he also provided me with valuable information.

My research in the Astor Archive at the University of Reading was rendered possible and more than pleasant by Michael Bott and Verity Andrews; my every request was fulfilled with courtesy, kindness, and good humour. I am also grateful to the staffs of the British Library, the

National Library of Wales, the University of Florida Library, and the Florida State University Library. Bay County Public Library (Panama City, Florida) provided me with what must have appeared to be an endless stream of books on interlibrary loan. Without the unfailing assistance of its staff, my research would have taken considerably longer to complete.

Jill McConkey at the University of Toronto Press has been a most supportive editor. John St James has been an admirably perceptive copy-editor, while Barbara Porter has guided the edition through the various stages of production with genial efficiency. I also received useful suggestions from the two reviewers of the edition who were solicited by the Press.

The following people answered my enquiries with invariable promptness and courtesy, and provided valuable assistance without which I could not have completed this edition: Angelina Altobellis (Harry Ransom Humanities Research Center, University of Texas); Linda Amichad (University of Guelph Library); Donna Baker (University of North Carolina Library); Heather Barrett (Ed Victor Ltd); Denison J. Beach (Houghton Library, Harvard University); Judith Brimmer (Churchill Archives Centre, Churchill College, Cambridge); Mark Brown (Brown University Library); Diana Burnham (New York Public Library); Margaret Cook (College of William and Mary); Carolyn Davis (Syracuse University Library); Ann Ferguson (Cornell University Library); Annette Fern (Harvard Theatre Collection); Isaac Gewirtz (Berg Collection, New York Public Library); Christopher Glover (Beinecke Library, Yale University); Michael Holroyd; Penelope and Edward Jackson; Sarah Lewis (Adam Matthew Publications); Rachel Lloyd (Churchill Archives Centre, Churchill College, Cambridge); Hannah Lowery (University of Bristol Library); Anne Morgan (Archivist, Plymouth and West Devon Records Office); Jim Moske (New York Public Library); Sharon Perry (California State University at Fullerton Library); Margot Peters; Katharina Petersen (Churchill College); Carl Peterson (Colgate University Library); Katherine Reagan (Cornell University Library); Michael Richardson (University of Bristol Library); Bella Shand (Granta Books); Iris Synder (University of Delaware Library); Martin Thornton (University of Leeds); Paul Williamson (Curator, Shaw's Corner).

Shaw's letters in this edition are published by permission of the

Society of Authors, acting for the Estate of Bernard Shaw. Letters from the Astor Archive are published by kind permission of the Nancy Astor Archive at the University of Reading. Charlotte Shaw's letters are published by kind permission of the trustees of the will of Mrs Bernard Shaw. Letters from the Dr Thomas Jones Collection are published by permission of the National Library of Wales. Other letters and materials are published by courtesy and permission of the British Library; the Churchill Archives Centre, Churchill College, Cambridge, UK; the Division of Rare and Manuscript Collections, Cornell University Library; and the Houghton Library, Harvard University.

The exceptional and extended hospitality of my good friend Darion Hutchinson allowed me to conduct crucial research for two weeks in the University of Florida Library. I am most grateful. Jerry Worthy has supported my work with patience and fortitude, and this edition would not have been possible without his support.

Abbreviations

Type of Correspondence

ACCS	Autograph 'compliments' (or pro forma response) card signed
ALCS	Autograph letter-card signed
ALS	Autograph letter signed
APCS	Autograph postcard (with photograph on one side) signed
(c)	Carbon copy
(e)	extract
TEL	Telegram
TLS	Typed letter signed
TLT	Typed letter, typed signature
TLU	Typed letter unsigned

Sources of the correspondence

Note: Full publication information for printed sources can be found in the References.

BL	British Library (followed by additional manuscript and folio numbers)
Cornell	Cornell University (Bernard F. Burgunder Collection, Division of Rare and Manuscript Collections, Carl A. Kroch Library)

Dunbar	J. Dunbar, *Mrs. G.B.S.*
Ervine	St J. Ervine, *Bernard Shaw*
Fox	J. Fox, *Five Sisters*
Grigg	J. Grigg, *Nancy Astor*
Halperin	J. Halperin, *Eminent Georgians*
Henderson	A. Henderson, *George Bernard Shaw*
Holroyd	M. Holroyd, *Bernard Shaw*, vol. 3
Kavaler	L. Kavaler, *The Astors*
Lash	J.P. Lash, *Eleanor and Franklin*
Letters	D.H. Laurence, ed., *Bernard Shaw: Letters 1926–1950*
Masters	A. Masters, *Nancy Astor*
Patch	B. Patch, *Thirty Years with G.B.S.*
Pearson	H. Pearson, *G.B.S.*
Reading	University of Reading Library, Astor Archives, ms 1416
Rose	N. Rose, *The Cliveden Set*
Sykes	C. Sykes, *Nancy*
Tompkins	P. Tompkins, ed., *To a Young Actress*
Wilson	D. Wilson, *The Astors*

Letters

1 / To Nancy Astor   Ayot St Lawrence, Welwyn, Herts.
                                                    11th December 1927

[ALS: Reading, Holroyd (e), Sykes (e)]

Charlotte's hint of reluctance to accept Nancy Astor's invitation is perhaps somewhat disingenuous: the Shaws' proposed Christmas visit to Cliveden, the Astors' famous country seat on the banks of the River Thames in Buckinghamshire, was known already to their close friend, social reformer, and writer Beatrice Webb (1858–1943), who noted censoriously in her diary on 5 December 1927: '[Shaw] and Charlotte are spending Xmas with the Astors! They were recently at the Philip Sassoons. Alas! poor Shaw, you have succumbed to Charlotte!' (Mackenzie, Diary, 136). Sir Philip Sassoon (1888–1939), a millionaire-socialite and cousin of the war poet Siegfried Sassoon (1886–1967), was the Under-secretary of State for Air 1924–9.

Dear Lady Astor

We've been thinking furiously about what you said.

We have come to the conclusion that you asked us for Xmas in that delightful and friendly way in a fit of enthusiastic benevolence, & desire to be kind to two old crocks & brighten up their holiday for them.

Now – on thinking it over – are you not appalled at the step you have taken?

If not, & you can really face it, we might – I say we *might* – go to you on Friday or Sat. before Xmas Day (Sunday) & leave you on the Monday or Tuesday following.

What do you say?

If you can't face it now, in cold blood (but your blood is never cold!) one of the servants might have small-pox – or – that sort of thing!

                                                    Yours really appreciatively
                                                    C.F. Shaw

Tell your Sec. to write or telephone to address *above*. We go to London again on Thursday.

2 / To Nancy Astor   Ayot St Lawrence, Welwyn, Herts.
                                                    10th January 1928

[ALS: Reading, Holroyd, Masters, Sykes]

On 23 December 1927 the Shaws began their first Christmas visit to Cliveden, where there were thirty or so other guests, including Thomas 'T.J.' Jones (1870–1955), a well-known civil servant and academic, who described Christmas Day in detail (Jones, Whitehall, 125–7). Cliveden was decorated lavishly, looking more like 'Harrods or Selfridges' amidst piles of presents, one of which was a real pony (T.J.'s own modest gift to Shaw was a sixpenny 'collection of Nursery Rhymes'). After various activities during the day, the 'whole household, family, guests and domestics' were entertained by the famous diseuse, Ruth Draper (1884–1956), noted for her powers of mimicry and her ability to conjure unseen characters during her monologues. Christmas dinner followed, and 'from 9.15 to 11.30 ... we had a characteristic Astorian evening of dance and song all jumbled up in a rollicking way.' With the exception of the Joneses and Shaws, guests donned fancy dress, including Nancy Astor dressed as 'an extraordinary figure – a racing tout in ill-fitting coat, vest, trousers (black and white check squares), face of a low-caste Jew, glasses slung along her side, small bowler hat. The carpet was rolled up in the Library, the records turned on, and she did all sorts of turns with uproarious results, talking the race course jargon all the time.' Shaw's own impressions of the event are conveyed in Laurence, Letters 80–4, where he remarks on the 'over-crowded splendor' of Cliveden, the 'orgy of presents' (his own was a mouth organ), and the amount of talking he did. He also noted: 'I "peacock" here (Charlotte's expression) amid week end crowds of visitors.' Heavy snow, which had fallen on Christmas Eve, prevented the Shaws from returning to Ayot until 9 January 1928. Shaw added a holographic P.S. to Charlotte's letter.

Here we are, dear friend, safe & sound & we both agree that all that has occurred during the last 3 weeks is a wonderful & impossible dream, & that now we are awake again to the buffets & storms of life. But the lovely flower is alive & well to witness that we lie!

My love to——David.

ever

C.F. Shaw

All the same, I dont believe it ever happened. I ask you, is it likely? G.B.S.

David Astor (1912–2001), recipient of the real pony, was the Astors' second son. He served in the marines in the Second World War, and from 1948 to 1975 was editor of *The Observer*, whose fortunes he revived. Nancy, whose relations with David from the mid-1930s onwards were 'glacial,' 'intensely disliked the leftist slant of the paper, and described it in 1950 as "written by Germans for blacks"' ('David Astor' [obituary], *Daily Telegraph*, 8 December 2001).

3 / To Nancy Astor   4 Whitehall Court SW1
27th January 1928

[ALS: Reading, Sykes]

Having snared Shaw once, Nancy Astor was eager to cement the new relationship with a further invitation (broached apparently in a letter to Charlotte), which Shaw parried, as he was to do with many more invitations when other business pressed for his attention.

My dear N——I mean Lady Astor

Charlotte is in bed with a temperature. Nothing serious; but I have to answer her letters.

Just at this moment, and until I get my book finally out I must have deadly quiet week ends; for every Saturday finds me abominably tired; and to ask me to spend a Sunday with a volcano is not reasonable.

Put it off until you get a copy of the book from me.

Then, if you are still of the same mind, ——————!

ever
G.B.S.

Shaw's **book** was his successful *The Intelligent Woman's Guide to Socialism and Capitalism,* which he had begun in 1924; it was published on 1 June 1928.

4 / To Nancy Astor   Oakwood Park Hotel, Conway
25th April 1928

[ALS: Reading]

The Shaws spent 31 March–28 April 1928 touring Wales by car (Gibbs, 269), which did not prevent Nancy Astor from issuing further invitations to them. Although the arrangements mentioned here fell through, the Shaws subsequently spent 26 May–4 June at Rest Harrow, the Astors' fifteen-bedroomed house in Sandwich, Kent. While there Shaw found time to again write flirtatiously (as he had done from Cliveden at Christmas) to erstwhile American actress Molly Tompkins (1898–1960): 'Oh Molly, Molly, Molly, Molly, I must not think about you' (Tompkins, 127). Nancy was far from commanding all his attention.

Nancy Asthore

I arranged to come up by train on Friday, arriving just in time to dine with you, and then to return on Saturday afternoon by the G.W.R. to Shrewsbury, which is within 12 miles of Charlotte's sister's house, to which Charlotte would meanwhile have taken the car. This advanced Charlotte's departure by a day. When your telegram came to say that the Friday dinner was impossible we hurled off telegrams in all directions to revert to our original plan of leaving here together by car on Saturday and not molesting them at Whitehall Court until the end of next week.

When your later telegram arrived proposing two dinners for Friday, to the ruin of your digestion and my disappointment at your having to run away between the soup and the fish, leaving me to pose as a Gibson girl for the rest of the evening, I really didnt dare ask Charlotte to engage in another fusillade of telegrams (a third) with a strong likelihood of fresh infidelities on your part as fresh temptations turned up.

We shall not reach Ayot St Lawrence, which is within an hour and a half of London by car, until Tuesday evening, the day of Dana's departure.

Will you tell him that I am sorry I have missed him, and that we both hope for better luck during his next visit.

Our affectionate regards to Waldorf and the progeny.

Your devoted paramount
G.B.S.

The **G.W.R.** was the Great Western Railway. **Charlotte's sister**, who lived at Edstatson in Shropshire, was Mrs Hugh Cholmondeley (née Mary Stewart Payne-Townshend, 1859?–1929). She had married Hugh Cecil Cholmondeley (1852–1941) in 1885. The **Gibson girl**, the American icon of feminine beauty in the twenty years or so before the First World War, was created in 1890 by the pen-and-ink illustrator Charles **Dana** Gibson (1867–1944). In 1895 he married Nancy Astor's sister, Irene Langhorne (1873–1956), Virginian Southern belle and embodiment of the Gibson girl, whose beauty (and remarkably thin waist) surpassed even her sister's. Nancy's husband, **Waldorf** (1879–1952), was M.P. for Plymouth (Sutton) 1910–19, a newspaper proprietor, and an expert on agriculture.

5 / To Nancy Astor   Ayot St Lawrence, Welwyn, Herts.

29th January 1929

[ALCS: Reading, Masters (e), Sykes (e)]

The Shaw/Astor friendship was clearly progressing. Beatrice Webb noted in a letter to her husband, Sidney (1859–1947), in mid-June 1928: '[Shaw] is evidently very touched by Nancy's personal devotion and Charlotte and Waldorf [seem] to be devoted to her! But he told me that he went among these people because Charlotte enjoyed it so' (Mackenzie, Letters, 300). On 5 July 1928 Nancy hosted a reception for Shaw at her glittering London home, 4 St James's Square, where guests invited to meet Shaw included the American tennis player Helen Wills (1905–98), whom Shaw described as 'a siren!' (Conolly, 34). Also present was A.E. Johnson, an English professor from Syracuse University, who noted Nancy's familiarity with Shaw: '[S]o far from treating Shaw as an idol, [she] jollied him as if he were a bright spoiled boy.' Nancy also declared: '"The trouble with you, G.B., is that you think you're clever: you're not clever, you're only good! Isn't he, Mrs. Shaw?"' (Johnson, 20). At the occasion Shaw also addressed a group of workers from Toynbee Hall, London, led by the Warden, sociologist J.J. Mallon (1875–1961). Nancy told her friend and dramatist Dame Edith 'D.D.' Lyttelton (1865–1948): '[I]t really was most amusing. [Shaw] was in fine form, but Charlotte says that he easily tires' (9 July 1928 letter [Reading]). Later that summer (20 July–2 September) the Shaws vacationed at Cap d'Antibes, France, whose heat and nude sunbathing impressed Charlotte; however, she told Nancy, she preferred the quieter ambiance of Rest Harrow (letters to Nancy Astor, 10 and 22 August 1928 [Reading]). That holiday was followed immediately by another of two weeks in Geneva. For her part, Nancy spent most of the autumn of 1929 in the United States with her husband. The two couples were reunited at a second Christmas house party at Cliveden during which Shaw completed The Apple Cart.

My Charlotte, I regret to say, is in bed with a swamping headful of sin and error and self, known to the mob as a bad cold. So she cannot come up to town this week.

I, on the other hand, must come up to relieve the strain on our small household.

I therefore propose to present myself with you at 1–15 on Thursday as arranged.

I chuckled over the shocking effect of Wissie's example in the House the other day.

The Apple Cart is at the printer's.

G.B.S.

Shaw's description of Charlotte's **bad cold** glances humorously at Nancy Astor's Christian Science belief that illness, like sin and death, is an illusion that can be cured by exercising the power of the mind by prayer. **Wissie** was the nickname of the Astors' only daughter,

8

Phyllis (1909–75), later Countess of Ancaster. Her **example** in the House of Commons is unknown. Shaw began *The Apple Cart* on 5 November 1928 and finished a somewhat rough version on 29 December at Cliveden. He then read the play to the Cliveden house guests, which, Charlotte reported to theatre director and founder of the Birmingham Repertory Theatre Sir Barry Jackson (1879–1961), 'was an entire & overwhelming success – kept them in fits of laughter, & a little frightened at the same time' (Conolly, 37; this volume includes a thorough account of *The Apple Cart* and other Shaw plays produced by Jackson, particularly in connection with the Malvern Festival, Worcestershire).

6 / To Nancy Astor   Ayot St Lawrence, Welwyn, Herts.

11th February 1929

[ALS: Reading, Holroyd (e), Kavaler (e), Masters, Sykes]

Shaw read the now finished version of The Apple Cart *to a gathering of society notables at the Astors' London house on 23 March 1929 at 6.30 pm. Not mentioned among the prospective guests in this letter is T.E. Lawrence ('of Arabia,' 1888–1935), a close friend of both the Shaws and Nancy Astor, who was also invited and did attend. The date of Shaw's reading of the play to 'the Webbs and the Fabian lot' is unknown, but probably took place on or before 25 March. On that date Beatrice Webb noted in her diary: '[The Apple Cart] is a savage burlesque of a Labour government ... [T]he Cabinet is made up of Labour men and two Labour women (caricatures of Susan Lawrence and Ellen Wilkinson, GBS told us) ... [I]t is very good fun – GBS at his cleverest and naughtiest, reflecting the outlook of the Astor set. The love scene [the 'interlude' between King Magnus and Orinthia] ... is an obvious reminiscence of Mrs Pat Campbell and her overtures and GBS's refusal to comply; a very brutal portrait, a tit-for-tat, his belated retort for her publication of his love letters [in* My Life and Some Letters *(1922)] some fifteen years ago' (Mackenzie,* Diary, *160–1).*

Loveliest Nan

As to that list – what about Balfour? what about T.J.? (an authority on Cabinet procedure who needs cheering up)? what about Elliot (for dinner and the last act: he heard the first)? what about Mosley & his Cynthia? (to represent the Labor Party)? Griggs has suffered it all before: need we plague him again? Ward, dear lad, is only one of many journalists; but why not Geoffrey Dawson: wouldnt you like to see him wriggling on my skewer?

Are you on visiting terms with Ellen Wilkinson? Dare she – if you asked her? I should rather like to know how my lampoon would strike her – whether she would detect portraits which dont exist. However, unless she would amuse *you*, disregard this suggestion, as I can easily get at her when I read for the Webbs and the Fabian lot.

I shall have to read the play professionally and privately to Sir Barry Jackson and the producer this week (it has come back from the printer); so there is no *need* to have him, though he might like to come and look at you under cover of the play.

I can't think of anyone else for the moment; but I presume you dont want a mob.

I hope you have not been devoured by wolves, though you would be if I were a wolf. Here it is blastingly, blightingly, blitheringly cold: 8 degrees of frost in the sun out of the wind at midday, and 1000° below zero *in* the wind.

Probably Charlotte, who is up and about the house, is writing.

> In haste: the post goes at 4.30 in this village
> Your
> G.B.S.

PS   Waldorf is bringing in a bill to get Lady Rhondda into the House of Lords to cheer him in your absence. What about *her*?

Arthur James **Balfour**, 1st Earl Balfour (1848–1930) was Conservative/Unionist Prime Minister (1902–5) and had been one of Nancy Astor's sponsors when she was introduced into Parliament in 1919. Balfour was unable to attend (Sykes, 316). **T.J.** was Thomas Jones (see Letter 2). **Elliot** was probably Walter Elliot (1888–1958), Conservative MP for Lanark (1918–23) and Glasgow Kelvingrove (1924–45). Later he held various ministerial appointments including Secretary of State for Scotland (1936) and Minister of Health (1938–40). **Mosley** was Sir Oswald Mosley (1896–1980), an MP for various parties (1918–31) and founder of the British Union of Fascists in 1932. He married Lady **Cynthia** Curzon (1898–1933), a Labour MP (1929–31); dramatically, Nancy Astor declared that Mosley 'practically murdered his first wife, who was one of my dearest friends' (Krause, 155). **Griggs** was in all likelihood Sir Edward Grigg, later 1st Baron Altrincham (1879–1955), journalist, politician, and colonial administrator. His son, John Grigg (1924–2001), wrote the biography *Nancy Astor: A Lady Unashamed* (1980). **Ward** is probably Robert Barrington-Ward (1891–1948), who succeeded **Geoffrey Dawson** (né Robinson, 1874–1944) as editor of *The Times* (1941–8). Dawson served twice as editor of *The Times* (1912–19, 1922–41). 'Red **Ellen**' **Wilkinson** (1891–1947) was a Fabian, suffragist, and Labour MP for Middlesborough East in 1924. She became Minister of Education in the 1945 Labour Government. Jackson's **producer** (director) at the Birmingham Repertory Theatre was the actor H.K. Ayliff (1872–1949). **Lady Rhondda** of Llanwern (Margaret Haig Thomas, 1883–1958) was a feminist and editor of

10

Time and Tide, in which she published a series of her own articles, 'Shaw's Women,' 7 March–4 April 1930. On 27 January 1927 Shaw had chaired a BBC broadcast debate between Lady Rhondda and G.K. Chesterton (1874–1936), entitled 'The Menace of the Leisured Woman' (*Radio Times*, 21 January 1927).

7 / To Nancy Astor

4 Whitehall Court SW1
14th March 1929

[ALCS: Reading]

Shaw suffered an attack of influenza 21 February–6 March 1929 (Gibbs, 273). That, and delays with the printers, threatened the proposed St James's Square reading of The Apple Cart; *however, it did take place as scheduled.*

I have set to work on the proof of The Apple Cart, and have messed it up so frightfully that it will be unreadable until I get a clean revise from the printer. The corrections will not be complete for some days to come – not sooner than the middle of next week – and then the proof has to go to Edinburgh and stay there until the printer's part of the work is done. That puts the 23rd out of the question, I am afraid.

The flu left me with a throat like sandpaper; and I have been cautiously singing Handel & Bach down here to restore it for your sake. It still breaks like a budding boy's. This would add greatly to the effect of the King's speech, but not to the comfort of the reader –

ever & ever
G.B.S.

Shaw's **printer** in Edinburgh was R. & R. Clark Ltd. Shaw is probably refering to King Magnus's long **speech** towards the end of Act 1 in which he analyses his position within the constitutional framework and on which Amanda, the Postmistress General, compliments him: 'You did speak that piece beautifully, sir.'

8 / To Nancy Astor

4 Whitehall Court SW1
15th March 1929

[ALS: Reading]

Charlotte Shaw in her 19 March 1929 letter to Nancy Astor (Reading) confirmed Shaw was suffering from a serious cough and was singing in order to strengthen his voice.

I am posting the first three sheets of the play [*The Apple Cart*] to Edinburgh tonight, and shall get the remaining two off on Sunday, with an urgent requisition for delivery of the revise to me on Saturday morning at latest. I have no doubt that they will be able to put the job through for me; but at worst I can read the sheets I read from at Cliveden, as I have a spare copy of them. Charlotte became violently abusive when I suggested a possible postponement, and woke me up to the enormity of it from your point of view. So let it be the 23rd (unless *you* want to escape) and pray for my poor rasping throat. If I break down, you must finish [the] reading.

G.B.S.

9 / To Nancy Astor   4 Whitehall Court SW1
                                              13th April 1929

[ALS: Reading, Holroyd (e), Letters, Masters (e), Sykes (e)]

Charlotte's sister, Mary Cholmondeley (see Letter 4), died on 5 April 1929 and the Shaws travelled to Edstaston, Shropshire, for her funeral on 8 April. Although Mary had disapproved of Shaw when he first married Charlotte, she grew to like him. Shaw dedicated The Intelligent Woman's Guide to Socialism and Capitalism *to her, although he managed to misspell her name in the first edition (Laurence, Shaw 1: 172–3). The day after this letter, the Shaws embarked on a trip to Trieste, Brioni, Dubrovnik, Split, and Venice, returning to London on 13 June. A highlight of the trip was a lengthy holiday on Brioni with the American heavyweight boxer Gene Tunney (1898–1978), and his wife Polly (Dunbar, 277–8, and see Letter 64). Charlotte told Nancy that Tunney was 'so handsome & gentle & babyish that it refreshes one to look at him' (Holroyd, 210).*

Dear blessedest Nancy

Charlotte is all right. I went down with her to the funeral at the lovely little old village church of Edstaston on a lovely day with a mountain of lovely flowers. I contributed enough comic relief to wipe the black off without going so far as to turn the afternoon tea into a wake. Still, I think we all enjoyed ourselves. The Intelligent Woman had lived her life well out, and exhausted her health so much through her struggle with asthma that it would really have been terrible if she had recovered and had to die all over again. Those who cared felt that all was well. Those who didnt had a pleasant outing, and were relieved to find that long faces were not expected.

If Charlotte ever has more distress than I can pull her through I will send for you. She is very fond of you. So am I. I dont know why.

What the devil was Marion Phillips doing in Plymouth? Sunderland is her shop; and when she goes out raiding she might at least raid a man's constituency. The worst of Plymouth is that it lives by selling drink to sailors, though it has to keep sober itself to do so effectually and profitably.

I have just registered our luggage. All day yesterday I could think of nothing but

As there seems to be plenty of room in the box
I may as well take some additional socks.

Packing is a distracting task; but when it is done it is done. If you have a valet or a maid to do it you are never done with them, and might as well stay at home. That is Charlotte's philosophy of travelling.

Brioni Hotel, Brioni, Istria, Italy is our next address. It was recommended to us as a desert island. We learn now that it is one of the most overcrowded 'resorts' on earth. I wonder how long we will be able to stand it.

ever & ever

G.B.S.

Marion Phillips (1881–1932) was Labour MP for Sunderland (1929–31). Nancy Astor served as Conservative MP for the Sutton division of Plymouth (1919–45), taking over the seat from her husband Waldorf when he was elevated to the peerage by his father's death. She was the first woman to take her seat in the House of Commons (though not the first woman to be elected; see Letter 228). The Astors maintained a home in Plymouth (3 Elliott Terrace, The Hoe) that Waldorf had acquired in 1909 after he had been adopted as a Conservative parliamentary candidate in 1908. Drink and its evils were among Nancy Astor's perennial concerns; her maiden speech in the House of Commons on 24 February 1920 was on the 'horrors of drink' (Brookes, 22–4), and in 1923 her private member's bill to prevent people under eighteen from buying intoxicants was successful. Nancy herself was a confirmed teetotaller, whose first disastrous marriage to the alcoholic Robert Gould Shaw (1871–1930) had ended in divorce in 1903. Shaw provided Nancy with further advice on 'the drink question' in the next letter. The doggerel couplet, As there seems, is unidentified and is possibly Shaw's own.

10 / To Nancy Astor   Grand Hotel Imperial, Dubrovnik, Yugoslavia
18th May 1929

[ALS: Reading, Holroyd (e), Letters, Masters (e), Sykes (e)]

After the Shaws left for Italy, Parliament was dissolved and a general election called for 30 May 1929. The main issues of the election were unemployment and the anti-unions Trade Disputes and Trade Union Act (1927) enacted after the General Strike of 1926. Nancy Astor again defended her Plymouth seat against Labour and Liberal contenders. At the top of his letter Shaw wrote 'Next Week – Hotel Danieli. Venice.'

Dearest Nancy

You will see by the enclosed that I also have had a turn at what I presume to be your main occupation at present. Heaven forgive us both. I gather from an article by Ramsay Macdonald that the election has fallen flat so far; but this can hardly last: the excitement will rise as the candidates strip nakeder and nakeder (nuder, the Americans call it) until they have shed the last rag of scruple and dont care what they say or do to get in. All the better for you; for when the Trade has stooped to its last infamy in reviling you, you need only fold your arms like a Christian martyr and leave chivalrous indignation to do its work. All the same, it is an error to suppose that mud is pleasant when it does not stick, and that lies do not matter as they are not true. On the contrary you get finished without the satisfaction of having deserved it, or the benefit of expiation.

Besides, you are in a difficult situation: a violently Radical Conservative, a recklessly unladylike Lady, a Prohibitionist member of The Trade party, and all sorts of contradictory things, including (on the authority of the late Speaker) the most turbulent member of the Party of Order. The only tune to which you can win in a seafaring constituency is Jack's Delight Is His Lovely Nan. In that sign you will probably conquer in spite of all the sober and virtuous publicans and brothel keepers who minister to the paid-off mariners of our historic port. Knowing that you are on the side of the angels they will give you a vote to set against their profits in the books of the recording angel, believing that you are too jonnick to cut any ice in parliament on your own account. Therefore be extreme on the Drink Question; for if you compromise they will be afraid you might really hurt them, whereas if you go all out for a Dry England they will laugh at pretty Nancy's way and feel sure that you might as well try to dry England with blotting paper as with Prohibition. On the social question, just read chapters of my book at random and give them chunks of it: they will neither know nor care whether it is Socialism or Conservatism if you dont tell them. Give them what you like, and they'll probably like it too; and leave it to the others to 'give em muck' (peche Melba). Tell them you are making enemies all the time because you can't suffer fools gladly and are up against 600 of them every working night of your life, and that under God your refuge is Plymouth, and if Plymouth turns you down it will shut the gates of mercy on mankind. In short, dear Nancy, let yourself rip, and wear all your pearls: prudence is not your game; and if you ride hard enough for a fall you won't get it. And if you want a poster –

> BERNARD SHAW
> SAYS
> 'Lady Astor's Defeat Would Be a NATIONAL
> CALAMITY'

ever & ever
G.B.S.

Shaw **enclosed** an undated cutting from the *East End Star*, 'George Bernard Shaw on the Slums.' James **Ramsay MacDonald** (1866–1937) was elected MP in 1906 and became the first Labour Prime Minister from January to November 1924. He again became Prime Minister after the 1929 general election when Labour gained 287 seats, the Conservatives 260, the Liberals 59, and 'others' 8. During May MacDonald had written several **articles** for *Forward* (Glasgow). The **late Speaker** was the Rt. Hon. E.A. Fitzroy (1869–1943). **Jack's Delight** is a traditional folk tune. The phrases 'Jack's delight, his (un)lovely Nan,' 'Dark Jack's delight, his WHITE unlovely Nan,' and 'Jack's delight was the least unlovely Nan, both morally and physically' all occur in chapter five of *The Uncommercial Traveller* (1860) by Charles Dickens (1812–70). **Jonnick** (or jannock) is an English dialect word meaning honest, fair, straightforward. The **book** was *The Intelligent Woman's Guide to Socialism and Capitalism.*

11 / To Nancy Astor   Hotel Danieli, Venezia, Italy
4th June 1929

[APCS: Reading, Sykes (e)]

On the reverse of the postcard Shaw is seen posing on the deck of a ship, the F. Morosini, Venezia. In the general election, Nancy Astor received only 211 more votes than William Westwood's 16,414 (Labour), while the Liberal T.H. Aggett posted 5430 (Craig, 216). It was her smallest majority during her twenty-five years in the House of Commons. Thomas Jones visited her on 31 May: 'At Cliveden I found Nancy in bed resting from her labours at Plymouth where she had just escaped defeat at the hands of a Labour man from Glasgow whom she suspected of being in the pay of the liquor trade. She was obviously hurt by Ll. G. [David Lloyd George, 1863–1945] coming down to Plymouth to hold one of his big meetings' (Jones, Whitehall, 193). After his return to England, Shaw helped Nancy receive guests when she entertained Rhodes scholars at a garden party given at Cliveden on 9 July 1929 (Gibbs, 274).

The swing of the pendulum and the Unholy Alliance nearly got you; but a miss is as good as a mile. My secretary wired 'Astor yes' the moment the figures were out, which rejoiced us.

On the 11th we start from this hotel in the forenoon and are due in London on the 12th in the late afternoon. Then, piles of work.

G. Bernard Shaw

Shaw's **secretary**, Blanche (Eliza) Patch (1879–1966), worked for Shaw from 1920 until he died. She published her memoir (written with Robert Williamson) *Thirty Years with G.B.S.* in 1951. During Shaw's declining years she became an ally, if not a friend, of Nancy Astor.

12 / To Nancy Astor　　　　　Ayot St Lawrence, Welwyn, Herts.
23rd September 1929

[APCS: Reading, Holroyd (e)]

Shaw spent part of the summer in preparations for the first Malvern Festival before arriving in Malvern on 6 August and remaining there until 12 September. After a dress rehearsal on 18 August, The Apple Cart *opened the festival on 19 August. Later there were performances of* Back to Methuselah, Heartbreak House, *and* Caesar and Cleopatra *(see also Conolly, 44–9). In a letter (26 August 1929, Reading) Charlotte reported to Nancy Astor that Shaw was the attention of huge crowds of people who worshipped him, although she herself found much to complain about in arranging their affairs and in keeping undesirables at bay. On the reverse of the postcard is a portrait of a grim-looking Shaw.*

I am a week after my holiday: just look at me!

The performance was the worst up till then: quarter of an hour too long, and all strained with first night panic.

It is all harrow and no rest for me now: I am at the revolting job of getting together a Collected Edition.

G.B.S.

All harrow and no rest is Shaw's groan-inducing pun on the name (Rest Harrow) of the Astors' home in Sandwich. The **Collected Edition** of Shaw's works was published initially in thirty volumes, 26 July 1930–24 February 1932, with additional volumes appearing in 1934 and 1938 (see Laurence, *Shaw*, 1: 183–94).

13 / To Nancy Astor   4 Whitehall Court SW1
                                           20th November 1929

[ALS: Reading, Holroyd (e)]

Shaw spent an extended weekend (12–15 October) with the Astors in Plymouth. Nancy enlisted him as guest speaker for the opening on 15 October of Astor Hall, a residential student hostel for the University College of the Southwest (now the University of Exeter). Considering the occasion (the hostel was Waldorf Astor's gift), Shaw gave a singularly unamusing and embarrassing speech: he rambled, was self-contradictory, and declared that 'English university education is destroying civilisation' (Collis, 143–4). 'In proposing a vote of thanks ... Nancy said that there were few people who could speak as he did' (Sykes, 307), a suitably diplomatic, if not ironic, phrase for an inappropriate speech. There is no tangible connection between that event and Shaw's invitation to Nancy to hear him speak in London, though perhaps at some level he was trying to make amends.

Dearest Nancy

The enclosed is the only one left undisposed-of: Charlotte's. The front row of chairs on the platform is kept in the family until the chairman & council appear with the lecturer. I shall stand at the chairman's right at the table; and if you take the second chair on that side of him you will be next [to] me.

The meeting is in no sense a party meeting: it is the last of a series of six public lectures open to everyone without distinction of color, creed, age, or sex. The word platform has no more meaning than orchestra at a concert. The papers may say 'Lady Astor attended Mr Bernard Shaw's lecture last night at Kingsway Hall; and her attachment to him as she sat by his side on the platform was very obvious'; but they will not say that you have joined the Labor Party.

I dined in the House tonight in a bevy of Labor ladies, the host being Kenworthy, and hoped – in vain – to meet you in the passages or lobby. K. wanted to take me into the gallery; but I would not break my record & came home to send you the ticket.

ever

G.B.S.

The **enclosed** was a ticket to a lecture Shaw gave at the Kingsway Hall, London, on 21 November 1929; in his engagement diary for that date he noted: 'Kingsway Hall. Myself on Random Speculations.' The other **lectures** were given by G.D.H. Cole (1889–1959), Fabian and successively a Fellow, Reader, and Chichele Professor of Social and Political Theory at Oxford University; H.J. Locke (unidentified); S.K. Ratcliffe (1868–1958), journalist and lecturer; C. Delisle Burns (1879–1942), civil servant and university lecturer; and Mrs (Mary Agnes) Hamilton (d. 1966), Labour MP, civil servant, and biographer. Joseph M. **Kenworthy** (1886–1953), Labour MP, was later 10th Baron Strabolgi.

14 / To Nancy Astor   4 Whitehall Court SW1
                                                         6th February 1930

[ALCS: Reading]

During the previous two months Nancy Astor had been preoccupied with the spinal injuries her daughter Phyllis ('Wissie') had sustained as the result of a horse-riding accident on 18 December 1929. Initially, in accordance with her Christian Science beliefs, Nancy refused to allow Phyllis to be treated by conventional doctors, although she eventually relented. Charlotte Shaw wrote her two sympathetic letters (31 December 1929, 12 January 1930 [Reading]) and offered her help which apparently included some form of telepathic healing power: 'The thoughts seem to go to her so much more willingly – to her own home – where I can picture her' (Sykes, 311–15). Moreover, it seems Charlotte did attend Christian Science services with Nancy (see Letter 44). The Shaws visited Cliveden 1–5 February 1930.

They have started a chain letter in Holland now: the same one. They are sending them to poor and ignorant women who write with difficulty and can afford neither stamps nor stationery, but believe, poor things, that something deadly will happen to them unless they write three letters. You should bring a private bill before the House if you have luck in the ballot.

Davidson worked at me for 2 hours today. He is very keen on your seeing the result before he tackles you. That is his way of interesting you. Highly intelligent man, Jo. I have to give him another sitting tomorrow; and Charlotte is to come at 1 to see the bust and lunch. He begged me to bring you; but as you are in the country nothing could be settled. If you are in London tomorrow you might consider it. He is at the Savoy Hotel, Room 315. The bust looks 90, and convinces me that I do too.

G.B.S.

The specific nature of the **chain letter** is unknown. Shaw sat for the American sculptor Jo **Davidson** (1883–1952) on 6–8 February 1930 (see next letter).

15 / To Nancy Astor 4 Whitehall Court SW1
7th February 1930

[ALCS: Reading, Letters]

Shaw claims he pointed out 'a wrong dimension [in Davidson's bust of him] ... which the callipers verified, [which] obliged him to make a change at the last moment which he had not time to incorporate completely. Still, he turned out a lively presentation of me as a jolly old wisecracker' (Pearson, 274).

Charlotte demanded the entire reconstruction of the bust the moment she saw it. Her criticisms were shattering; but Jo rose to the occasion and did what she wanted with a turn of the hand, leaving her contemptuously dissatisfied because my neck was too thick and the bust looked like flesh and not like flame.

It is a remarkable bit of work all the same; but tomorrow is its last day in London as it has to go off to the moulders & casters.

Post just going.

G.B.S.

16 / To Nancy Astor 4 Whitehall Court SW1
28th February 1930

[ALCS: Reading]

With his note Shaw enclosed one of his printed postcards which reads: 'Mr Bernard Shaw, who is not and never has been a professional lecturer, is now obliged to restrict his appearances as a public speaker to special and exceptional occasions, mostly of a political kind. He therefore begs secretaries of societies to strike his name from their lists of available speakers. Mr Shaw does not open exhibitions or bazaars, take the chair, speak at public dinners, give his name as vice-president or patron, nor do any ceremonial public work; and he begs his correspondents to excuse him accordingly.' To which he added: 'And he NEVER begs for money that should be taken by force from everybody by the Government for the children of the community as in Holy Russia.' Lady Alexandra 'Baba' Metcalfe (1904–95), Cynthia Mosley's sister, regarded Nancy 'as a surrogate mother' (Fox, 326), and doubtless Nancy had encouraged her to approach Shaw.

Sign the enclosed and post it to the Lady Alexandra Metcalfe.

I will not have my affections hired out in this fashion; for to my mind of all mankind I love but you alone, not Alexandra or another.

G.B.S.

17 / To Nancy Astor The Palace Hotel, Buxton, Derbyshire
1st May 1930

[ALS: Reading]

The Shaws began what was supposed to be only a week-long holiday at Buxton on 22 April, although Charlotte was disappointed with Buxton: she thought it 'a dull little town, but some of the country round is fine, with splendid hills and valleys with rivers' (Chappelow, 64). Then, on 26 April, Charlotte contracted scarlatina (not tonsilitis, as Shaw mentions here), and she was forced to remain in Buxton until 28 May in order to recuperate.

My dear Nancy

I have just come down here from London, and have only a few minutes before the post goes out.

I have found Charlotte horridly ill. She has been in bed since I left on Sunday, with a rash, a sore throat, sore eyes, fever, misery, and all sorts of discomforts. The young Irish doctor says Tonsilitis, and declares that it is the usual thing, and will go away as suddenly as it came. She is evidently recovering; but she can't read with her sore eyes, and is very wretched. Her temperature was normal this morning, and is only 99 now (nothing for her); so I have great hopes of her being able to get up tomorrow.

But fancy her left alone in this hotel whilst I was rehearsing in London!

You must fill up your rooms without considering us; for I cannot bother to make decisions until she is stronger. The grasshopper is a heavy burthen just at present, though the doctor talks of her travelling on Monday.

Forgive this bothersome bad news; but she will worry if I dont write to you.

Fortunately the people here are nice, and have been kind.

ever
G.B.S.

Shaw had been **rehearsing** *Jitta's Atonement,* which was performed at the Arts Theatre 30 April–4 May 1930 with Violet Vanbrugh (1867–1942) as Jitta. **The grasshopper is a heavy burthen** echoes Ecclesiastes 12:5.

18 / To Nancy Astor The Palace Hotel, Buxton, Derbyshire
5th May 1930

[ALS: Reading, Dunbar (e), Letters]

It is clear from this and the next two pieces of correspondence that Nancy Astor had immediately volunteered to visit Charlotte and to have her recuperate at Cliveden. Although Shaw resisted both suggestions, Nancy did visit Charlotte in Buxton (see Laurence, Letters 21–2).

My dear Nancy

Charlotte has been washed.

I should have liked to talk to you on the telephone; but it is so situated that I cannot be sure that Charlotte will not hear what I say; and I am deceiving her (as we all are here) about her illness: she thinks she has tonsilitis, which is not alarming, whereas she really has scarlatina.

One of the tricks of scarlatina is to start on your glands when it has finished with your throat, in which event your restored normal temperature suddenly shoots up again. That is what happened to Charlotte yesterday. When I sent you my telegram she was normal and almost well. Before you read it her temperature had risen to 102° and she was in despair. She said to me very earnestly 'Have I got mumps?' 'No,' I replied with conviction: 'you havnt got mumps.' This morning I did what I wanted to do on Thursday when I returned from London. I engaged a nurse. When I first suggested it Charlotte wouldnt hear of it. 'I couldnt bear it' she said. 'She would be trained to be cheerful and to keep up my spirits. She would WARBLE at me all the time.' And so she was left to me and to the unskilled and overdriven chambermaids. But after six days without washing she welcomed the nurse, who is an excellent young woman. She does not warble; but when I took the doctor for a drive and the patient became anxious for my safe return, she cheered her up with a faithful account of all the most frightful recent motor smashes in Buxton.

So Charlotte is still in bed in a fairly high fever; and the doctor says she will have two days of it, or rather the remainder of two days, one and a half having already elapsed. She is improving visibly; and the mump is yielding instead of gaining. But our departure cannot take place before the end of this week or the beginning of next. Meanwhile she is now being properly nursed and is comparatively comfortable.

The doctor declares that the case is not infectious, though a child of five might perhaps catch it. But scarlatina is scarlatina; and you must not let it into Cliveden until the last scrap of rash has peeled and been forgotten for, say, three weeks. When Charlotte *knows*, she will not let you take the slightest risk. She loves you. I am myself far from indifferent. I will send you bulletins the moment there is any news.

Goodnight & blessings.
G.B.S.

19 / To Nancy Astor   Buxton
                                                          12th May 1930

[TEL: Reading]

FRIDAY NIGHTS LETTER HAS ONLY JUST ARRIVED. DO NOT COME TODAY. DOCTOR SAYS NO MADLY EXCITING VISITS YET AND IS EVIDENTLY RIGHT. SHE HAS WRITTEN TO YOU THIS MORNING. I MUST COME UP ON WEDNESDAY AFTERNOON FOR A FEW DAYS. WILL YOU LUNCH WITH ME ON THURSDAY AT WHITEHALL? AM WRITING FULL PARTICULARS. BERNARD SHAW.

20 / To Nancy Astor   The Palace Hotel, Buxton, Derbyshire
12th May 1930

[ALS: Reading, Holroyd (e), Letters]

Dearest Nancy

Charlotte is reposing and peeling and eating voraciously and getting along beautifully; but though she would dearly like to see you for a moment I dare not let you loose on her. You have not the least notion of her genius for worrying, and her conviction that nothing will be done unless she gives exact instructions just as she did in her youth to her Irish servants, and as you did to your negroes. She would feel obliged to order rooms for you, to order meals for you, to explain carefully to you how to eat them, to buy your railway ticket and see that you were washed and disinfected; and she would never believe that I was doing all this properly or that you were quite comfortable and happy without her immediate supervision. In short, you would give her an hour's happiness at the cost of a mountain of imaginary anxieties which might throw her back seriously. Her sense of responsibility is appalling. At Cliveden she is happy because running the house is not her job and she must not interfere; but here–!

The novelty of being able to read and write a little, and sleep and eat a great deal, and the blessed relief of being out of pain, is enough for her for the present. I am going up to town for a day or two mainly because she is beginning to worry about keeping me here. If I leave her she will feel that she may take her time about returning home. We must get back to Ayot: our unexpected absence has created a state of arrears in her work and mine which puts Cliveden, I fear, quite out of the question. It certainly does for me; and she wont go without me.

Now as to Thursday. Before all this happened I had invited to lunch a certain Miss Mabel Shaw (no relation), a woman with a craze for self torture, who broke off her engagement with a clergyman (he died of it) to bury herself in the wilds of Africa and lead negro children to Christ. She has a very graphic pen; and some of her letters were shewn to me. She has come home on missionary-furlough, and is to lunch with me at 4 Whitehall Court on Thursday next at 1.30. I am afraid it will be a tête à tête unless you come to protect me, with Phil or anyone else you like, or no one. It is of course mostly an excuse for seeing you. I come up by the afternoon train on Wednesday.

Charlotte is actually out of bed and installed in a chair; but after 5 minutes of my energetic conversation she had to send me away. Dont bother about bedjackets: I have been sending for them to Ayot & Whitehall and think she must have enough. She is in a state about all your work and says you mustnt be let add to it by doing things for her.

My notion of enjoying Parsifal is to have a box and sit across the back of it with my calves up on a second chair out of sight of the stage.

ever & ever

G.B.S.

Shaw's association (Laurence, *Letters*, 55–6, 88–90, 281) with **Mabel Shaw** (1889–1973), a missionary in Northern Rhodesia (Zambia), was the inspiration for Shaw's *The Adventures of the Black Girl in Her Search for God* (1932). Shaw lunched with Mabel Shaw and Nancy Astor on 15 May. **Phil** was Philip Kerr (1882–1940), who became 11th Marquess of Lothian in 1930. An intimate friend (and arguably a surrogate though non-sexual husband) of Nancy Astor, he was a fellow Christian Scientist, statesman, and in 1939–40 British Ambassador to Washington, where he died from uremic poisoning (treatable by conventional medicine, which Kerr refused). **Parsifal** (1882) by Richard Wagner (1813–83) was performed at Covent Garden on 16 May.

21 / To Nancy Astor   4 Whitehall Court SW1
                                        15th May 1930

[ALCS: Reading]

Since Nancy Astor had to attend a function in Nottingham, she was able to coordinate a visit on 21 May 1930 to Buxton to visit Charlotte. The arrangements Shaw outlined here were modified somewhat, since he escorted Nancy to her function (Collis, 145).

There is only one good train from Buxton to London with a through carriage and restaurant car with afternoon tea service. It starts at 2.25 and reaches Paddington at 6.15. I propose to send the car on Wednesday morning to wherever you may be staying in Nottingham, and fetch you to Buxton, where you will have time to see Charlotte, lunch with me, and get away by the train as above. If that will suit you let me have the Nottingham address or hotel.

You made the lunch today delightful. Thanks and blessings.

G.B.S.

22 / To Nancy Astor The Palace Hotel, Buxton, Derbyshire
19th May 1930

[ALS: Reading]

After his lunch with Nancy Astor and Mabel Shaw (Laurence, Letters 20–1), Shaw returned to Buxton via Birmingham where, on 16 May, he saw Heartbreak House at the Repertory Theatre (Conolly, 50–1). Nancy Astor's visit with Charlotte on 21 May was a success; in a 23 May letter to her housekeeper, Clara Higgs (1874–1948), Charlotte reported: 'Lady Astor's visit gave me the greatest pleasure and did me good. She was so sweet and loving and helpful. And she says she will drive over from Cliveden to Ayot to see me when I get back!' (Chappelow, 69).

Dearest Nancy

I have just driven Charlotte round the dales for nearly an hour – her first outing – and she seems none the worse.

Nottingham is 50 miles off; so we must allow 2 hours each way and save what we can on it. The car will aim at reaching the County Hotel before 10.30 at the latest. The station here is within a few steps of the hotel gate. Your train starts at 2.25, and reaches St Pancras at 6.15. Lunch at 1.15 will leave time for the most excessive overeating.

eternally
G.B.S.

23 / To Nancy Astor Ayot St Lawrence, Welwyn, Herts.
9th August 1930

[ALS: Reading, Grigg (e), Holroyd (e), Sykes (e)]

Shaw spent part of July at the Old Vic in London rehearsing his plays for the second Malvern Festival, for which he left on 10 August, returning on 25 September. In a separate 9 August letter (Reading), Charlotte reassured Nancy Astor that they already had a set of the first five volumes of the Collected Edition to give to her. The ellipsis in the final line is Shaw's.

Harpy

Where do you think I can get a set for you? You would have to sell Cliveden to buy one.

However, I'll give you mine. Charlotte is having the first volume (only

5 are yet issued) sent to Malvern so that I may autograph it. I particularly want you to read the autobiographical preface to this first volume. It is all you will be able to get through, as the rest of the five – novels written when I was an infant of 23–28 – would bore you worse than the Intelligent Woman's Guide.

We are packing, and intend to start tomorrow (Sunday) morning for Malvern, where our address will be The Malvern Hotel, Great Malvern, Worcs. I wrote this to you before; but you have probably lost it.

The Festival begins on the 18th. There will be a new play about Elizabeth Barrett Browning by Rudolf Besier, and 5 plays by me. 2 of them are little ones; but one of these has Queen Elizabeth in it. The 3 full length ones are The Apple Cart (by the provincial company, which I have never seen), Candida (Phyllis Neilson Terry's debût as a Shavian actress: she's charming, but may play the devil with it at the last moment), Getting Married (a ghastly business) and my masterpiece Heartbreak House (loathed by Charlotte) with Cedric Hardwicke as the centenarian captain (fine). Why not come and improve your just-beginning-to-grow mind ... That is all I have room for.

G.B.S.

The **set** was Shaw's *Collected Edition*, the **first volume** of which was *Immaturity*, the others being *The Irrational Knot, Love Among the Artists, Cashel Byron's Profession,* and *An Unsocial Socialist.* The **new play** by Rudolf Besier (1878–1942) was *The Barretts of Wimpole Street.* In addition to his own plays Shaw names above, the festival included *Widowers' Houses, The Admirable Bashville,* and *The Dark Lady of the Sonnets* in which **Queen Elizabeth** I appears. The **provincial company** was the Birmingham Repertory Theatre company. Shaw's remark is somewhat puzzling because he had seen the Birmingham company on numerous occasions; possibly he had yet to see the particular cast for the 1930 Festival production of *The Apple Cart.* **Phyllis Neilson-Terry** (1892–1977) performed two Shavian roles in her career, Candida at this festival and Epifania in a 1944 revival of *The Millionairess.* (Sir) **Cedric Hardwicke** (1893–1964) performed Captain Shotover in *Heartbreak House,* the Bishop of Chelsea in *Getting Married,* Lickcheese in *Widowers' Houses,* and Edward Moulton-Barrett in *The Barretts of Wimpole Street.*

24 / To Nancy Astor   Ayot St Lawrence, Welwyn, Herts.

5th January 1931

[APCS: Reading]

A portrait by photographer Olive Edis (1876–1955) of Shaw at his desk is on the reverse of the postcard. In addition to an invitation to Cliveden that Shaw here rejects, Nancy Astor wanted the Shaws to 'come out to St. Moritz. [Shaw] would love walking about in the sun' (letter to Charlotte Shaw, 7 January 1931 [Reading]). Apart from the pressure of work, Shaw had a legitimate reason for refusing: on separate occasions in late October 1930 Charlotte had hurt her ribs and then fell and broke bones in her shoulder and pelvis. The Shaws had also not passed Christmas at Cliveden in 1930, a fact Charlotte bewailed in a 2 January 1931 letter to Thomas Jones (NLW, Class W, vol. 17, f. 185).

Get away from this crush of work to Cliveden! Impossible. Just look at me.

Imagine Charlotte getting well, and then finding all her overworked sound limbs going back on her and crippling her worse than ever! She can't walk 10 yards: I have to run her about in the little car every sunny day.

Sir James Sexton! Yes, I should think I DO know that old hero. He's the best of the bunch.

Tons of love –

G. Bernard Shaw

Sir James Sexton (1856–1938), known as 'the Dockers' M.P.,' was a founding member of the Independent Labour Party and MP for St Helens (1918–31).

25 / To Charlotte F. Shaw [*no address*]
15th April 1931

[TLU (c): Reading]

On or about 25 February 1931, Nancy Astor gave a luncheon at her St James's Square home for silent movie star Charlie (Sir Charles Spencer) Chaplin (1889–1977). Also invited were Shaw, the English pilot Amy Johnson (1903–41), who had achieved fame by flying from England to Australia in May 1930, Lloyd George, and others (Chaplin, 336–8). Nancy, Shaw, and Chaplin attended the London premiere at the Dominion Theatre of Chaplin's film City Lights *on 27 February. Shortly after, the Shaws sailed on the Hellenic Travellers Club cruise 3 March–1 April 1931, then spent three weeks in Venice, followed by a stay in Paris (24 April–6 May). Also on the cruise was Violet Markham (Mrs James Carruthers, 1872–1959), the liberal activist and public servant, who reported to Thomas Jones: 'As for G.B.S. I can only describe him as a perfect scream. I wonder that his cheek is not worn out with having his tongue tucked into it. He and his wife talked the most advanced Communism. Russia was the only country to live in, etc., but as against this they travelled in the greatest luxury I think I have ever met on a tour of this kind. Between them they had four or five cabins'* (Jones, Diary, 7). *During this vacation 'between Corsica and Sardinia on March 5 Shaw began ...* Too True to be Good. *On June 30 at Ayot ... he finished it'* (Rattray, 239).

Dearest Charlotte

I am so glad that you are staying on and that there is a better report of G.B.S.'s cough. Do keep him away as long as you can, and as long as you are both enjoying it. There is really nothing to do here now.

Waldorf has taken Wiss, David, Michael and Jakie to Paris today, I have had to stay behind for the Vote of Censure in the House tomorrow. David is off to Germany for four months before going to Oxford [University]. Michael and Jakie are going into a French family for a couple of weeks before school starts, and I am joining Wiss in Biarritz on Friday. Waldorf is just seeing some studs and returns at the weekend.

Never in your life have you seen anything worse than Arthur Greenwood and Susan Lawrence on Housing and Slum Clearance in the House of Commons yesterday. The most reactionary Conservatives in the world couldn't have done worse than that couple have in the Ministry of Health, and I happen to know from the inside that they are breaking the hearts of some of the go-aheads in the Ministry. I made a stirring speech yesterday begging the Government to change the Minister. They ought to have done it long ago. There are few people who can do that kind of work and drink.

Do come to Wiss and me at Biarritz. I arrive there on Saturday morning and we stay for ten days, and if you would come to us it would be such fun. Write me to The Hotel du Palais. I wanted to have Wissie for a little while by herself, now that we have disposed of all the boys!! Do come.

I forgot to tell you that Waldorf, David, Bill, Philip Kerr, Margaret Wintringham and I went to see St Joan last night. I really think this is better than the last production. I am certain that Sybil Thorndike is better, we were all struck by that.

[Nancy Astor]

Wiss was Phyllis 'Wissie' Astor. **Michael** Astor (1916–80), the Astors' third son, served in the Second World War, was MP for Surrey (Eastern Division, 1945–51), and author of a revealing memoir, *Tribal Feeling* (1963). John Jacob **'Jakie'** Astor (1918–2000, knighted 1978), the Astors' fourth and youngest son, served conspicuously in the Second World War, rising to the rank of major. From 1951 to 1959 he was Conservative MP for his mother's former seat, Plymouth (Sutton). On 16 April 1931 Stanley Baldwin (1867–1947), Conservative MP and thrice Prime Minister, moved a **censure** motion that condemned the government for failing to carry out its election pledges over unemployment. The motion was defeated by 305 to 251. Nancy's only contribution to the debate was a series of interruptions that caused the Speaker to threaten to remove her from the Commons. **Waldorf** Astor was a keen horse breeder. **Arthur Greenwood** (1880–1954) was a long-serving Labour MP and Minister of Health (1929–31). **Susan Lawrence** (1871–1947) was Labour MP for East Ham North and Parliamentary Secretary to the Ministry of Health (1929–31). During the debate on **housing** (see *Hansard*, vol. 251, cols. 38–163) Nancy remarked: 'Fancy a Socialist Minister of Health being satisfied with a policy under which the Department has built a less number of houses than the reactionary Tory Government which preceded the present Government!' (col. 76). She also took the opportunity to advocate the 'provision of open-air nursery schools' (col. 78), one of her pet projects. William **'Bill'** Waldorf Astor (1907–66), 3rd Viscount Astor, was the Astors' eldest son. He was elected Conservative MP for East Fulham in 1935, served in the Second World War, and achieved unwanted notoriety through his peripheral connection to the 'Profumo Scandal' (see Irving, passim). **Margaret Wintringham** (d. 1955) had been the Independent Labour MP for the Louth division of Lincolnshire (1921–4). *S[ain]t Joan* was revived at the Haymarket Theatre on 6 April 1931; **Sybil Thorndike** (1882–1976) played Joan, a role she had made her own and reprised several times since the play's English premiere on 26 March 1924 at the New Theatre.

26 / To Nancy Astor   Hôtel Lotti, 7–9 Rue de Castiglione, Paris
2nd May 1931

[APCS: Reading]

A photograph of the Hôtel Lotti is on the reverse of the postcard. Shaw's opening sentence again guys Nancy Astor's Christian Science beliefs.

Charlotte is suffering from the delusion which doctors call congestion of the lungs. She is over the worst of it; and, with a doctor and a Scotch nurse to console her, is comparatively happy, and may be able to travel back by Tuesday or Wednesday. I *must* be in London on Thursday even if I have to fly over and return. My curse on the wretch who invented holidays!

G.B.S.

27 / To Waldorf Astor   Ayot St Lawrence, Welwyn, Herts.

27th June 1931

[ALS: Reading, Letters (e)]

The genesis of the trip to Russia in July 1931 (which included Shaw, Waldorf, Nancy, and David Astor, Philip Kerr [see Letter 20], Charles Tennant [d. 1942], a Christian Scientist, and Gertrude Ely [1876–1970], one of Nancy's American friends) is somewhat uncertain. Sykes (325) indicates that Russian diplomats in London were the source of the invitation for the visit; Pearson (325) claims that Philip Kerr and Waldorf Astor had thought it up. Evans (127–9) provides an even-handed discussion of the possibilities. Shaw himself maintained that 'the Astors suddenly took it into their heads to see for themselves whether Russia is really the earthly paradise I had declared it to be; and they challenged me to go with them' (Laurence, Letters, 242). Interestingly, as recently as 5 July 1928, Shaw had rejected the idea of going to Russia himself 'because people were expecting miracles from Soviet Communism' (ibid., 104), so it may have been the Astors' paradoxical presence that convinced him to go in 1931. On 20 April 1931 T.E. Lawrence had written to Charlotte Shaw that Nancy Astor was babbling about both Shaws going to Russia and expressing his concern that such a long journey in the summer heat might kill Charlotte (BL 45904, f. 144v). In the incomplete draft of her (not entirely reliable) memoirs (Reading), Nancy wrote: 'The Press made much of our visit and many legends have grown up about it. There was however nothing political nor conspiratorial about it. We all needed a holiday. We were all intensely interested in Russia and we wanted to see the country for ourselves.' Shaw certainly enjoyed helping to arrange the trip, which was scheduled to depart on 18 July. The trip has been recounted thoroughly in several sources, including Shaw's own perspective in letters to Charlotte (who did not go) in Laurence, Letters (243–59), Evans (passim), Holroyd (233–48), Pearson (318–32), and Sykes (325–45).

My dear Waldorf

The enclosed has been requisitioned by your secretary. According to p. 15 it is valid for all Europe, including the U.S.S.R., as far as the F.O. is concerned.

I have written to Sokolnikoff, asking him to order his consul to rush our papers through instantaneously. We shall need entry visas for Latvia, Lithuania, and Poland (unless we pass across the Corridor in a sealed waggon). I dont think Holland & Germany now bother about them. I have told S that we shall expect a salute of at least 101 guns on our arrival in Moscow, and that as we wish to see the torture chamber of the Tcheka he should warn them to have a victim or two ready, so that we may witness the process.

The worst snag in the scheme is the season. Does Nancy stand heat well? A railway journey through central Europe in July or early August is a test for the heat resistance of Beelzebub. September is the proper time. Even the nights are not cool now.

We must not burden ourselves with evening dress. It is not actually contraband; but it is in bad taste, and extremely suspicious. Gordon Selfridge went to the opera attired as for Covent Garden, and, being not only the sole person in the theatre in that condition but in all Russia, distracted the attention of singers, orchestral players, conductor and audience to such an extent that the performance was wrecked. He did not enjoy his success as I should have done.

Have you considered the alternative of flying?

The Intourist people want to take us to central Asia.

ever

G.B.S.

The **enclosed** was probably Shaw's passport. The **F.O.** was the British Foreign Office. Grigory Y. **Sokolnikoff** (1888–1939) was a Russian lawyer, economist, and Ambassador to Britain (1929–33). The **Tcheka** (Cheka or Vecheka) was the Russian political police agency until 1922. It underwent several reincarnations before becoming the KGB in 1954. The American **Gordon Selfridge** (1858–1947), who founded his famous London department store, Selfridge's, in March 1909, is credited with coining the phrase 'The customer is always right.' He visited Russia in 1925.

28 / To Waldorf Astor   Ayot St Lawrence, Welwyn, Herts.

28th June 1931

[ALCS: Reading]

On the same date, while Shaw was revelling in the organizational details of his forthcoming trip, Charlotte confided her apprehensions to Nancy Astor as well as her relief that Nancy was going: 'But Nancy, I trust you. You will take the right sort of care of him & not let him do too much! It will be difficult: but if anyone can keep him in hand, you can! We will talk of it' (Holroyd, 233). Nancy replied (30 June 1931, Reading): 'I know what you mean about G.B.S. and I do feel the responsibility of it. I can't guarantee as to his food, but I do guarantee that he won't do too much. How I wish you were coming! And yet I know that you were

*wise in not doing so, but you would make just the whole difference to the trip. Tell
G.B.S. that I am assured that it is no hotter in Russia than it is here today.'*

I have just lunched with a timber industrialist who has to frequent Russia
on business. He recommends long sea by opportune tourist steamer (if
available) to Reval and Leningrad. If Moscow is the first objective over-
land, then fly to Brussels (leaving London at 15 or 3 p.m.), catching the
Nord Express for Berlin about 19 (7), spending the night in the train
and the day in Berlin, and then catching the Moscow Express via Warsaw. He denounces the Latvia route as wretched. If we left London on
Saturday afternoon by this route we could be in Moscow on Tuesday
morning, having slept 3 nights en route. Time from Berlin to Moscow 36
hours. Dust on the Russian dirt track so frightful that windows cannot be
opened. No water sometimes. Cotton gloves and pullovers needed as
naked fingers make everything filthy. This is the very worst time of year.
Leningrad to Moscow 12 hours by night. Nijni not very far from Moscow.
Long sea means five days. Straight through to Moscow without a break
very trying. Flying the whole way feasible; but my timber man has no
experience of it. He is strong for Brussels, Berlin, Warsaw, Moscow, if
Leningrad will not serve our turn.

G.B.S.

The **timber industrialist** is unidentified. **Nijni**-Novogorod lies between Moscow and St
Petersburg.

29 / To Waldorf Astor Ayot St Lawrence, Welwyn, Herts.
1st July 1931

[ALS: Reading]

A penny steamer wouldnt do; but there might [be] an Orient or P. & O.
liner doing a cruise to Leningrad: they go everywhere now to save eating
their heads off.

Intourist insisted on shaking hands with me all round most enthusiastically; so I can act as intermediary if necessary.

Let us take a barrel of oranges and do a ten days fast on the juice. 75%
of what we usually eat is probably just right for us.

G.B.S.

P. & O. was the Pacific and Orient Steamship Company.

30 / To Waldorf Astor Ayot St Lawrence, Welwyn, Herts.

6th July 1931

[ALS: Reading]

While Shaw's concern here for his creature comforts is understandable (especially given his age), it hardly accords with the image of him as a Communist hero: 'He was, moreover, very wealthy and lived like a bourgeois. A friend of reactionaries and capitalists, he traveled in the company of British aristocrats and rich Americans' (Geduld, 14). (See also Violet Markham's similar criticism of Shaw, headnote to Letter 25.)

I forgot to say that Sokolnikoff's instructions are to send all the passports to him at 13 Kensington Palace Gardens W.8. He will put them through for us without delay.

If possible I want single berth sleeping car accommodation for myself, because I cannot sleep in a train unless I read and sleep in two-hour shifts; and this involves monkeying with the lights in a manner too disturbing for the feelings of a second passenger. I dont care what it costs if it is practicable.

This is of course for whoever is in charge of the arrangements. You said who, but I forget.

G.B.S.

Ann Molesworth Kindersley, Waldorf Astor's secretary, who was handling the arrangements, replied to Shaw on 7 July: 'I have ordered you a separate **sleeping** compartment, but regret to say that for this you will have to pay about £18 extra. However, I agree with you that to have a compartment to yourself is worth almost anything. There are no single sleepers on the Russian railways' (BL 50520, f. 82).

31 / To Nancy Astor [*no address*]

15th July 1931

[Fox]

The Russia trip was almost scuppered a few days before the scheduled 18 July departure date by the arrest of Robert 'Bobbie' Gould Shaw (1898–1970), Nancy's son by her first marriage, for a homosexual offence. Although the police gave Bobbie the opportunity to make a discrete escape to France, he chose to face prosecution, a course of action recommended by Philip Kerr (14 July 1931 letter to Nancy [Reading], quoted in Sykes, 326–7). Kerr broke the news to Shaw on the morning of 15 July, along with the Astors' decision not to go to Russia: 'And now they have had to change their plans and nothing is left of the proposed party but myself, the Marquess of Lothian (Phil Kerr) and Tennant' (16 July 1931 letter to Horace Plunkett; Laurence, Letters, 242). No sooner had Shaw written that than the Astors changed their minds again: 'PPS It now seems possible that the Astors will be able to come on Saturday after all' (ibid., 243). So the trip went ahead and, thanks to the Astors' influence, news of Bobbie Shaw's case was suppressed by the press. Shaw returned to the topic of Bobbie's homosexuality after his 1932 South Africa visit (Letter 40).

Dearest Nancy

Why is Providence so jealous of your high spirits that it deals you these terrible BIFFS at your most hopeful moments? What can one do to comfort you?

I hope the Press will have the decency to say nothing about poor Bobbie's step-connexions. In his case I think I should plead technically Guilty, admitting the facts but not the delinquency. The natural affections of many men, including some very eminent ones (Plato and Michael Angelo, for instance) take that perverse turn; and in many countries adults are held to be entitled to their satisfaction in spite of the prejudices and bigoted normality of Virginians and Irishmen like our two selves. Bobbie can claim that he has to suffer by a convention of British law, not by Nature's law. At the other side of the channel there would be no case against him, and no disgrace attached to him.

I must go to Russia, sadly enough now. If I did not, people would ask why; and that must not be.

Oh Nancy, Nancy, something is wrung in me by your sorrows. I suppose you would call it my heart.

Better tear this up

ever & ever
G.B.S.

32 / To Waldorf Astor Malvern Hotel, Malvern
21st August 1931

[ALS: Reading]

Shaw and the Astors returned to London from Russia on 2 August, their visit stirring up considerable interest and controversy (see Sykes, 343–5). Shaw asked

Molly Tompkins: 'Have the Italian papers reported me as disappointed with Russia and unhappy about it? If so, their mendacity is colossal. Here the scandal is that I am boosting Russia to the skies; my visit now seems like an extraordinarily jolly dream: never in my life have I enjoyed a journey so much. You would have been disgusted at my reception as a Grand Old Man of Socialism, my smilings and wavings and posings and speech makings; but it made things very smooth for us all' (letter, 13 August 1931, Tompkins, 150). Winston Churchill (1874– 1965) launched a notable attack on Nancy and Shaw in '"Personalities": No. 4. Lady Astor and G. Bernard Shaw,' Sunday Pictorial, *16 August 1931 (reprinted as part of Churchill's chapter on Shaw in* Great Contemporaries *[1937]). While Churchill paid tribute to Shaw as a profound, original thinker, he also deemed him little more than a paradoxical jester. Nancy was contradictory: 'She denounces the vice of gambling in unmeasured terms, and is closely associated with an almost unrivalled racing stable. She accepts Communist hospitality and flattery, and remains the Conservative member for Plymouth.' Shaw attended the third Malvern Festival from mid-August to mid-September.*

My dear Waldorf

The enclosures explain themselves.

The reply to Churchill will appear on Sunday next in London, in the Sunday Pictorial, and simultaneously in all the papers covered by the North American Newspaper Alliance, which has purchased the world rights (first serial) from me for 200 guineas, and may therefore be depended on to push its circulation from this to Japan both ways round. So Nancy is avenged: he will think twice before he again implies that she is a tote fiend.

You will notice that I have given away the Churchillian bit of our interview with Stalin. I have not done so without careful consideration of Stalin's probable wishes. I feel quite sure that he wants his reasons for maintaining a heavy armament to be well known. And he will certainly not dislike the publication of our personal impressions as long as they are credibly complimentary. Observe the touch about Louis XIV. Well, he deserves it.

I have waded through some billions of press cuttings – previously weeded by Charlotte – elicited by my two lectures at Digswell and Rowledge and my two letters to The Times. I still have a couple of articles to give to the N.A.N. Alliance and to Hearst for his magazine.

Phil has had a copious press for his Cambridge lecture; and there is great curiosity to hear Nancy's account. Nothing under 500 guineas for the world rights, I should say. Hopes of unseating her run high in Plymouth; and the American publishers say that I have ruined myself for ever; but we shall see.

I am guessing that you are in Jura. Tell Nancy I wish I were there to help her with the boots and the washing up.

Our love to everybody.

G.B.S.

The **enclosures** included Shaw's typescript 'What Stalin Thinks of Mr Churchill' (written 18 August 1931), his **reply** to Churchill's *Sunday Pictorial* article, published as 'G. Bernard Shaw Replies to "Personalities" Article,' *Sunday Pictorial*, 23 August 1931. Shaw dismissed the notion that Nancy was a **tote fiend**: '... her husband breeds horses but never bets on them. I should not myself say that this amounts to gambling; but Mr Churchill no doubt argues that a lady who goes to Russia and actually discusses him with The Monster Stalin is capable of anything.' Shaw's **Churchillian bit** reads: 'We could not pretend that Mr Churchill is, in respect to Russia, the only fool in England, or that Russia can with any prudence disband a single Red regiment whilst there is a daily possibility of Mr Baldwin coming into power and including Mr Churchill in his Cabinet.' Joseph **Stalin** (1879–1953), Soviet dictator, was Secretary of the Communist party (1922–53) and Premier (1941–53). In his typescript Shaw wrote that '**Louis XIV** would have called him [Stalin] wellbred.' On 5 August 1931 Shaw had delivered a lecture to the Independent Labour Party National Summer School at **Digswell** Park, Welwyn (reprinted in Laurence, *Platform*, 218–26, and reported as 'Mr Shaw's Comparison: "Intellectual Superiority of Russian Statesmen,"' *The Times*, 6 August 1931). His lecture at **Rowledge** in Surrey has not been identified. Shaw's **two letters** to *The Times* were 'Mr Shaw on the Soviet Fabianism in Action' (13 August 1931) and 'The Soviet System: Mr Bernard Shaw's Rejoinder' (20 August 1931). William Randolph **Hearst** (1863–1951) was the American publisher of numerous newspapers and magazines, including *Cosmopolitan*, to which Shaw contributed 'What G.B.S. Found in Red Russia,' vol. 92 (January 1932), 42–5, 134–6. On 5 August 1931 **Phil**ip Kerr gave a lecture at the Liberal Summer School in Cambridge, reported as 'A Liberal's Impression of Russia,' *The Times*, 6 August 1931. Waldorf Astor greatly enjoyed his retreat, Tarbert Lodge (which can still be rented), on the Isle of **Jura** in the Inner Hebrides of Scotland, although Nancy disliked its isolation. Ironically, given Nancy's teetotalism, Jura is known for its malt whisky.

33 / To Nancy Astor   Malvern Hotel, Malvern
                                        2nd September 1931

[ALS: Reading, Holroyd (e), Letters (e)]

Britain experienced severe economic difficulties in 1931 (as did numerous countries), including a large budget deficit, which was to be cut by reducing the unemployment benefit or 'the dole' by £67 million. (The benefit was funded by a national insurance scheme, which, in 1931, was paying out considerably more than it was collecting.) Divided on this issue, the Labour Cabinet resigned on 22 August 1931 and a National Government was formed. This coalition was led by Ramsay MacDonald who, regarded as a traitor to the cause by fellow Labour colleagues, was expelled from the Labour Party.

My dear Nancy

Do not commit yourself too hastily about this political crisis. They none of them know exactly what they are doing. It happens from time to time that our MPs, in their hopeless class ignorance of what the proletariat is feeling, approach a measure in the most superior confidence that it is sound, necessary, and popular. Suddenly their agents and local supporters send up frantic warnings that their seats will be lost if they vote for it. They in turn rush to the whips, who carry the alarm to the Government, and there is an eleventh hour stampede.

I shall not be in the least surprised if something of the sort happens when the question of cutting 1s/9d off the 17/- dole reaches the agenda. The swiftness with which the sword of Damocles fell on Macdonald's neck at Seaham has made it clear that neither he nor any of those who have taken office under him will be able to face a Labor constituency for a long time to come. But every constituency today is a Labor constituency. Conservatives get returned only where the proletarians and the tradesmen depend on the incomes of the rich for employment. Their interest is to maintain property and live on it at one remove. But on this question of insurance and dole (they may all be on it tomorrow) and wages, their interest is *not* that of their masters. Lee and Arthur and the rest will vote to maintain you in Cliveden, St James's Square and Rest Harrow; but they wont vote for a cut in wages or insurance.

A rot may therefore set in at any moment in the Conservative ranks. The whips may tell Baldwin that seats will be lost in all directions if the matter is allowed to come to an issue, and that pressing it will make a present of the next election to Henderson. They may even report that they cannot be sure of bringing a majority up to the scratch on a division.

In your place I should be strongly tempted to tell the whips that you do not know how you are going to vote, as you do not feel like losing your seat to save Macdonald's face.

The bankers are the most Godforsaken fools. They have humbugged Macdonald and Snowden into committing political suicide and thus making dreadful examples of themselves to Labor leaders who sit on the horse's head instead of riding it hard. The measures they demand will not be of the least use; and the Labor Party will be reinforced and driven to the Left. When they threaten you with the pound sterling you must say no word to indicate a doubt; but put your thumb unto your nose and spread your fingers out. Giving one and ninepence of an unemployed man's purchasing power to Lord Howard de Walden wont save it.

Enough of this political twaddle. Dont worry about the sorrows and terrors of the poor things in Russia who are still foolishly trying to be ladies and gentlemen: it does not hurt them half as much to be governed by Communists as it hurts you to be governed by distillers and brewers and publicans and doctors and 'forty millions, mostly fools.' So buck up, and preach The Revolution. That trip to Russia would have doubly endeared you and Waldorf to me had that been possible.

My namesake's health is evidently being benefited. Curiously, that always happens.

I was tempted to fire a broadside into the Plymouth papers, but was afraid of doing more harm than good.

Bless you, dearest Nancy, and goodnight
G.B.S.

Ramsay MacDonald became Labour MP for **Seaham** after it had been represented by Sidney Webb from 1923 to 1929. With MacDonald's expulsion from the Labour Party, the Seaham Labour Party asked him to resign, which MacDonald refused to do. In the October 1931 general election MacDonald's vote was reduced by 80 per cent, and he lost the seat in 1935 to Emanuel Shinwell (1884–1984), who then held it for thirty-five years. Edwin **Lee**, the Astors' butler, was considered one of the best butlers, if not the best, in England and had served the Astor family since 1913. **Arthur** Bushell, a valet at Cliveden, achieved some notoriety for his 'drag' turns at parties for the Cliveden servants; Nancy was not amused when, at one such occasion, he displayed a pair of green knickers with a Union Jack sewn on them (Rose, 123). Arthur **Henderson** (1863–1935), a Labour MP, was Foreign Secretary (1929–31) and briefly party leader in 1931. Philip **Snowden**, created Viscount in 1931 (1864–1937), was variously a Liberal and a Labour MP who served as Chancellor of the Exchequer (1924, 1929–31). Thomas Evelyn Scott-Ellis, 8th Baron **Howard de Walden** (1880–1946) was a millionaire landowner whose circle included numerous artistic figures. Shaw's phrase **'forty millions, mostly fools'** reworks Thomas Carlyle's (1795–1881) 'The practice of modern Parliaments, with reporters sitting among them, and twenty-seven millions mostly fools listening to them, fills me with amazement' (*Latter Day Pamphlets: No. 5 The Stump-Orator* [1850]). Shaw's **namesake** was T.E. Lawrence, now Shaw.

34 / **To Nancy Astor**   4 Whitehall Court SW1
                                                      10th October 1931

[ALS: Reading]

Parliament was dissolved on 7 October 1931, with a general election called for 27 October. Ramsay MacDonald carried the day and formed a coalition National Government that was supported by 521 MPs (fulfilling Shaw's prediction in this letter of a landslide victory). Labour garnered just 52 seats, Liberals 37, and other parties 5. Possibly because of the strain and difficulties caused by Bobbie Shaw's imprisonment and a sense of her own diminished effectiveness, there was some doubt whether Nancy Astor would stand for re-election (Jones, Diary, 14, 16–17). However, she did and she increased her majority at Plymouth to 10,204, the highest of her seven parliamentary contests.

My dear Nancy

Read the enclosed when you have a spare moment. It is one of the bulletins of the Second International, which is hostile to the Soviet and to its pet International – the Third.

Mrs Cecil Chesterton's 'My Russian Venture,' just published by Harraps, is interesting to us, because she kept off our tracks and vagabonded about seeing what we did not see.

I am broadcasting to America tomorrow (Sunday) on Russia.

The election is a frightful gamble, though your people dont know it. The Labor people think that the cry for a National Government, being pure bunk, will carry the day and cost them 50 seats. I am not so sure: a landslide the other way is quite on the cards. For the first time since the eighties the police are breaking people's heads every day. A snapshot of a mounted policeman prancing on an unemployed demonstrator appeared in another paper with the tramplee carefully blocked out.

I strongly advise you to say that you dont believe in wage cutting and that the call for a national government is really a call for a strong government with no opposition that the guillotine cannot deal with, and that no woman can stand the silly way the men waste time when Rome is burning. The official program and the official phrases are not good enough for this election; and Tariffs are fatal at a seaport. It is no use letting fools pull your strings: you must go for a personal success and damn party politics.

I had it out with Londonderry at Lady Lavery's yesterday. Charlotte says I behaved disgracefully. Ramsay, as usual, let him make a speech in defence of the gold standard without warning him that its abandonment was already settled.

I think I shall write an election song about The Man That Broke the Dear Old Bank of In–gland.

Bless you from my heart
G.B.S.

The **enclosed** has not been identified. The **Second International** was a federation of socialist parties formed in 1889, which, in the 1930s, opposed fascism and German rearmament as well as the Soviet-dominated **Third** International or Comintern. The latter was founded in 1919 to promote world revolution. **Mrs Cecil Chesterton** (née Ada Eliza Jones, 1888–1962), was a journalist, dramatist, and founder of the Cecil Houses for homeless women. Her book *My Russian Venture* was published in 1931. Shaw's broadcast to **America** on 11 October 1931 (which Charlotte found very amusing) was full of praise for Russia; it compared Russia's budget surplus with America's deficit and noted Russians' pity for Americans being capitalists, not communists. It was printed as 'Shaw Twits America on Reds' "Prosperity,"' *New York Times*, 12 October 1931 (reprinted as 'Look, You Boob! A Little Talk on America,' in Laurence, *Platform*, 226–34). Nancy Astor had already decided against **wage cutting**: in her election leaflet, in the form of a letter dated 9 October 1931 (NLW, Class Q, vol. 2, f. 16), Nancy criticized the former Labour Cabinet's proposed 'cuts in the pay of teachers, of the Navy, and Army, of the Police, of Civil Servants, of the Dockyard.' She endorsed **Ramsay** MacDonald, now leader of the small National Labour Party: 'Let us take the higher ground. Put aside personal likes and dislikes. Drop Party politics. Think only of the Nation and support the National Government.' Charles Vane-Tempest-Stewart, 7th Marquis of **Londonderry** (1878–1949) had been a Conservative MP since 1906 and was Secretary of State for Air (1931–5). Hazel **Lady Lavery** [née Trudeau] (1887–1935), an American beauty, was married to the Irish painter Sir John Lavery (1856–1941). A run on the pound sterling in 1931 led Britain to abandon the **gold standard**, the monetary system whereby a currency was valued in gold, for which it could be exchanged. The lyrics and music for the popular song '**The Man That Broke** the Bank at Monte Carlo' (1892) were written by Fred Gilbert (d. 1903).

35 / To G. Bernard Shaw   [3 Elliott Terrace, The Hoe, Plymouth?]
13th October 1931

[TLU (c): Reading, Sykes (e)]

Dearest G.B.S.

I loved your enclosures. It is very disturbing this about Russia, and I am afraid I believe that most of it is true. The more one thinks of it, the more natural it is with community farming even with the Russians. So far it hasn't come up in the election. If you could come down here and hear the Socialists' twaddle, you would vote for me gladly, and no doubt you would come out and help me. The first two or three days I was not feeling my usual lively self, but am quite all right now.

What really discourages me about Ramsay is his lady friends!!! I should have liked to hear you go at Charlie Londonderry, which is another discouraging thing. Waldorf and I laughed heartily at the Marquis's not knowing. Talking of Marquises, do see Philip [Kerr] sometime.

[Nancy Astor]

36 / To Nancy Astor
4 Whitehall Court SW1
28th November 1931

[ALS: Reading, Holroyd (e), Letters, Sykes (e)]
The Shaws sailed for South Africa on 24 December 1931 and did not return to England until 4 April 1932. Charlotte Shaw, in a letter to Nancy Astor dated 29 November 1931 (Reading), also suggested that Nancy and her son, Bobbie (now released from prison), might join her and G.B.S. on their South Africa trip.

Dearest Nancy

Charlotte and I have just, in a moment of insanity, taken our passages for the Cape on Christmas Eve, as the most comfortable of the Union Castle liners, the Carnarvon, sails on that day. Charlotte wants sunshine; and I, who have been working like fifty plantations of niggers since our return from Russia, will be the better for a break in my routine. The Madeira Cape route is much the shortest journey – three days – from Southampton to assured calm and summer.

You ought to see the Empire which you govern. The parliamentary Whip will be quite independent of you for five years to come. Why not come to the Cape with the whole Astor-Shaw tribe, Charles Tennant, Phil [Kerr], old Uncle Tom Cobley and all. Phil could leave the Lords to an understudy: he is wasting his time as completely as Gandhi; for while they are playacting at the Round Table the real conflict of competitive murder is going on in India. If the Indians can create a situation in which, as in Ireland under Collins, the situation of the garrison becomes unbearable, then India will win. Nothing else will produce anything but Coercion Acts and martial law.

I must post this before eleven or it will not reach you until Monday. Probably it wont anyhow.

with undying affection
G.B.S.

'Old Uncle Tom Cobleigh [**Cobley**] and all' is the last line of the refrain to the ballad 'Widdicombe Fair.' Mohandas Karamchand 'Mahatma' **Gandhi** (1869–1948), whom Nancy Astor had met on 6 October (Jones, *Diary*, 15) and Shaw on 6 November 1931, was leader of the Indian National Congress. In 1930–2 he attended three **Round Table** conferences in London that sought agreement on constitutional changes in India. The conferences resulted in the India Act of 1935, which provided for considerable self-government in India; however, full independence was not achieved until 1947 when the separate nations of India and Pakistan were created. Michael **Collins** (1890–1922) was an Irish nationalist who fought in the 1916 Easter rising against the British in Dublin. He became a key figure in the Irish Republican Army and its guerilla tactics against the British (1919–21). Shaw met Collins on 20 August 1922, two days before he was killed by Republicans for signing a peace treaty with Britain (Holroyd, 62).

37 / To Nancy Astor　　　　　　　4 Whitehall Court SW1
10th December 1931

[ALS: Reading, Holroyd (e)]

Nancy Astor was unable to accept Shaw's invitation: she scribbled 'I can't go!' at the top of Shaw's letter.

Dearest Nancy

If you are in town Thursday next, the 17th, there are two things you might do.

1. Go to Colnaghi's to see me at full length in bronze. Troubetskoy should have done you: he has the noble touch.

2. Spend five hours, from 5.30 to 10 or thereabouts at Whitehall Court to hear the new play and dine before the last act so as to give me a rest. We have asked Barry Jackson and Ayliff (professionally), Dean Inge and Mrs Inge (he is so deaf that he cannot hear in a theatre) and Lady Rhondda. Our table will hold only eight, and the one vacancy will be kept for you if you will come.

Let us know as soon as you can.

sempre a te
G.B.S.

Colnaghi's was a London art gallery, originally the House of Paul (1751–1833) and Dominic (1790–1879) Colnaghi and Co. Prince Paul Troubetskoy (1866–1938) was a Russian-born sculptor who made a bust of Shaw in 1908, a statuette in 1926, and a full statue in 1927. Shaw's new play was *Too True to be Good*. William Ralph Inge (1860–1954), Dean of St Paul's Cathedral (1911–34), was the model for the Elder in Act 2 of *Too True to be Good*. In Act 2 of *The Simpleton of the Unexpected Isles* (1935) the Angel reports he announced Judgment Day to Inge 'in a dream, and asked him whether the English would appreciate the compliment. He said he thought they would prefer to put it off as long as possible, but that they needed it badly and he was ready.' Inge's wife was Mary Catherine Inge (1880–1949).

38 / To Nancy Astor   Union-Castle Line, RMMV *Carnarvon Castle*
27th December 1931

[ALS: Reading]

Accounts of the Shaws' South Africa journey are related in Holroyd (271–84), Pearson (359–63), and Shaw's letters (Laurence, Letters, 269–80).

Dear Nancy

On Christmas day an enormous bale was delivered to Charlotte. I swore at the folly of inconsiderate people who would not remember that our luggage was packed to the last corner, and that another article to carry would wreck us. On unpacking the thing I expatiated further on your extravagance and absurdity in sending us a rug when you knew quite well that we were already provided with all such necessaries. However, I found your rug much more comfortable than my own; and Charlotte has not seen it since. We had a row because I had soullessly thrown the card with your message away with the wrappings, and she wanted to clasp it to her bosom for a while.

We have had practically smooth water since Southampton, and have got over our irreducible minimum of qualmishness. It was an unspeakable relief to get away; for we were both fearfully overdone. After a day or two our pep was restored and our youth returned. This morning, the tide turned as we struck the edge of the tropical heat, and we began going limp. Still, its pleasant; and I still have energy enough to write you this wave of the hand before the post is closed for Madeira, where we stop tomorrow to send back a mail bag.

And now the dressing bugle reminds me that I have not time to finish this letter, which is not yet even begun. I wanted to discuss all your affairs in my usual interfering manner. Well, it can't be helped.

If Phil [Kerr] has not started, and you happen to see him, give him my love and thanks for the introductions.

I am loth to stop, but must. Half a sheet is better than no letter.

sempre a te
G.B.S.

In a letter to Charlotte Shaw (23 December 1931, BL 56492, ff. 227–9), Philip Kerr enclosed **introductions** to several South African politicians, including Sir Patrick Duncan (1870–1943), Sir Lionel Phillips (1855–1936), Basil Kellett Lang (1878–1944), and Lieut. Col. Hon. Frederic Hugh Page Creswell (1866–1948).

39 / To Nancy Astor
The Royal Hotel, Knysna,
C[ape] P[rovince], South Africa
18th February 1932

[ALS: Reading, Ervine (e), Holroyd (e), Pearson (e)]

Shaw was, at best, an indifferent driver: at times he confused the brake pedal with the accelerator. He sent a similar, but shorter, account of his car accident to Lady Rhondda (Laurence, Letters, 276–7), and told T.E. Lawrence to 'make Lady Astor shew you the letter I am sending by this mail detailing the consequences to poor Charlotte' (Dunbar, 280). While Charlotte was incapacitated, Shaw wrote The Adventures of the Black Girl in Her Search for God, *which he completed in eighteen days and which was published on 5 December 1932. It proved to be a popular, if controversial, work.*

Dearest Nancy

We are laid up here in a deuce of a mess. I have simply pollywogged poor Charlotte. On the 10th we were motoring hither from a pleasant seaside place called Wilderness on our way to Port Elizabeth. I was driving; and I negotiated several mountain tracks and gorges in a masterly manner. Then, unhappily, we came upon what looked like half a mile of straight safe smooth road; and I let the car rip. Suddenly she twisted violently to the left over a bump. I twisted her violently to the right, and, rising with all my energy to the sudden peril, stood on the gas hard as I held the wheel in a grip of iron. The car responded nobly. She charged and cleared a bank with a fence of five lines of barbed wire; carried the wires to a bunker (a sunken path) three feet deep; banged her way through; and was thrashing down a steep place to perdition when at last I transferred my straining sole from the accelerator to the brake and stopped her with the last strand of barbed wire still holding, though drawn out for miles.

Except for a few negligible knocks I was not hurt, nor the man beside me, nor even the car. But oh! poor Charlotte! When we extricated her crumpled remains from the pile of luggage which had avalanched her I feared I was a widower until she asked were we hurt. Her head was broken; her spectacle rims were driven into her blackened eyes; her left wrist was agonizingly sprained; her back was fearfully bruised; and she had a hole in her right shin which something had pierced to the bone. And there was fifteen miles to go to reach this hotel.

That was eight days ago. The bruises and sprains do not worry now; but she is still flat on her back with the shin hole giving no end of trouble. She put up a temperature of 103 yesterday (my heart jumped into my mouth) but today the wound took a favorable turn, and the temperature is down to 100. She is very miserable. By the time this reaches you I hope to have her at Wilderness recuperating; and you may assume that all is well again unless I have cabled in the meantime.

I have cancelled all my arrangements so as to leave her mind quite easy as to having to travel, and shall keep her in this climatic paradise (in which she blossomed like the rose until the mishap occurred) until she is well enough to propose the return journey herself. At best we might reach Southampton on the 11th April in the Warwick Castle; but I am not too sanguine about that. I shall not be surprised if we have to wait for the Carnarvon Castle, which will not arrive until the 2nd May. Still, if the improvement since yesterday in that damned wound continues and she gets on her feet again, the rest of the recovery may be fairly rapid.

The doctor and nurse, though ignorant of C.S. [Christian Science] except by hearsay, are in other respects treasures. Last night I woke up and found myself happy and perfectly callous. I concluded that the danger was over; but Charlotte was extremely indignant. She does not know how serious the thing *might* prove; but I do.

By a miracle the accident has not got into the papers. It would bring a deluge of inquiries, and for other reasons should be kept as secret as possible. So keep it within our more intimate circle.

Up to the moment of the catastrophe the trip was a great success. For sunshine, scenery, bathing, and motoring, the place is unbeatable. In Cape Town I did a stupendous lecture on Russia, speaking for an hour and three quarters without turning a hair, at the City Hall, and enriching the local Fabian Society beyond the dreams of avarice. I also made the first broadcast to be relayed all over the Union of S.A.

The two political parties, Nationalist (in office) and South African (Opposition) keep going with a sham fight about the Gold Standard, which neither of them understands. The real difference is a racial feud between Dutch and English which we know nothing of in England; but which is quite venomous here.

Phil [Kerr] can do no good in India. Our Diehards, like Macbeth in the musical version, 'will spill much more blood, and become worse! – worse!! – worse!!! – to make their title good.' And in the end they will be beaten by the Indian Collinses whilst they are keeping the pacific Gandhi carefully locked up. Bill may pick up some personal experiences in Manchuria; but why doesnt he try a few months in Geneva? – or has he perhaps done that already?

sempre a te, carissima Nancy
G.B.S.

On 1 February 1932 Shaw gave a **lecture** to the Cape Fabian Society entitled 'The Rationalization of Russia,' and gave his nationwide **broadcast** on 6 February 1932 (Gibbs, 285–6). Shaw's reference to a **musical version** of *Macbeth* is possibly to the 1847 opera by Giuseppe Verdi (1831–1901). On the **Indian Collinses**, see Letter 36. **Bill** [William Waldorf] Astor, who spent much of 1932 in the Far East, was currently secretary to Lord Victor Alexander George Robert Bulwer-Lytton (1876–1947), who was in charge of a League of Nations enquiry into Japanese aggression in Manchuria. Lytton's 1932 report, which condemned Japan's aggression against China, was praised widely, but ignored by governments. Charlotte Shaw read the report during the Shaws' 1932–3 around-the-world tour (see Letter 44).

40 / To Nancy Astor 4 Whitehall Court SW1
15th April 1932

[ALS: Reading, Fox (e), Letters, Sykes (e)]

Within days of his return from South Africa Shaw wrote this lengthy and sympathetic letter about Robert Shaw's homosexuality, which had continued to trouble both Nancy Astor and her son after his release from prison (see Fox, 379–83, and Letter 31). Nancy's reply, if any, appears not to have survived.

My dear Nancy

I find myself troubled from time to time when I think of the case of our friend [Robert Shaw] who got into difficulties just before our trip to Russia. I wonder has he ever studied his own case scientifically and objectively. A man may suffer acutely and lose his self-respect very dangerously if he mistakes for a frightful delinquency on his part a condition for which he is no more morally responsible than for color blindness. Also, his relatives may suffer just as cruelly from the same mistake.

During the last fifty years there has been a very large output of elaborate studies of the subject in Germany and to a less extent in England. It has been quite conclusively established that the curious reversal of the normal course of attraction is an entirely natural and genuine phenomenon which is so far from being associated with general depravity of character that some of the greatest men have experienced it (Michael Angelo, for example) and some silly-clever intellectuals actually affect it as a symptom of mental superiority though they are really quite normal.

When I was young and ignorant I had the usual thoughtless horror of it; for though I had absolutely no scruples or reticences where women were concerned, any sort of sexual relation within my own gender was repugnant and impossible: in fact I never thought of such a thing and did not want to hear about it. The subject was at last forced upon me by a special friendship which I formed with a married couple who had also a special friendship with Edward Carpenter, with whom our Socialism had brought me into contact.

When I read Carpenter's Towards Democracy, which made a very fair shot at being a great poem in the manner of Walt Whitman, I at once perceived that it was womanless, and that all Carpenter's ideals of noble companionship were unisexual.

Now in our friends the married couple the man was normal; but the woman, who was affectionately fond of all three of us, and a quite good, sincere, innocent person, would not allow her husband his conjugal rights, and was always taking wild sentimental fancies to women whom she took for persecuted angels, and whom I had to unmask as liars and humbugs. At last she was troubled and on the verge of a nervous breakdown, and couldnt tell why. I told her to go and get a job in a factory, as factory girls cannot afford nerves and havnt time for them; and to my astonishment and dismay she took me at my word and went and did it. The result was excellent, though of course, being a lady, she very soon got pushed up into literate and managing work.

But she also found salvation by learning what was really the matter with her. I presume that it was Carpenter who enlightened her: anyhow she told me with great exultation one day that she had discovered the existence of the Urnings; that she was herself an Urning; and that she was very proud of it and understood everything that had puzzled and worried her before. And so she dropped the factory and sublimated her desires into harmless raptures about music and poetry and platonic adorations of Carpenter and of me and of all the nice people she came across.

This gave me a serious and humane view of the subject. It was clear that Carpenter, understanding his condition scientifically and poetically, was not degraded by it. It was equally clear that the lady, when he enlightened her, at once passed from a state of mind that threatened her reason and destroyed her happiness to ease of mind and a new and respectful interest in herself. Neither of them were in the least danger of falling into the debauchery which is a possibility of their condition exactly as it is a possibility of the normal condition.

Carpenter, being dead, yet speaketh, as you may see from the enclosed memoir and catalogue. Do you think he could be of any use in the case of our friend? However helpful his mother may be to him in some ways it is practically impossible for a man to discuss his sexual life with his parents, just as it is impossible for them to discuss their sexual lives with him. The attempt may be nerve shattering on both sides. Yet the first need is for free healthy discussion. When my late woman friend (she is dead) got enlightened she at once began to talk eagerly and interestedly and happily to me about the Urnings and herself with a quite wholesomely shameless objectivity. Now what you tell me about our friend makes me suspect that he has not reached that point and is still struggling with mischievous and tormenting shames and reticences. At all events I will chance this letter to you and leave the matter to your judgment; for in this matter Mrs Eddy, bless her, is no use; and the Bible, with its rubbish about Lot's wife, is positively dangerous.

I have written a most frightfully blasphemous religious story called The Adventures of the Black Girl in her Search for God which you will perhaps like better than the play. Both of them can be read only to a very select and intimate audience: no American ambassadors and frivolous ladies and so forth.

I shall be rehearsing like mad all next week, making lunches at fixed hours impossible; so I may not see you quite so soon as I could desire.

ever your
G.B.S.

The **married couple** was Henry S. Salt (1851–1939), a schoolmaster, writer, and secretary of the Humanitarian League, and his wife Kate (d. 1919), who had been Shaw's secretary in 1898. Edward **Carpenter** (1844–1929), socialist and moral reformer, supported various progressive causes aimed against middle-class conventions. His four-volume Whitmanesque poem, *Towards Democracy*, was published between 1883 and 1902. American poet **Walt Whitman** (1819–92) believed in democratic equality and individual rights. His major work, with its hints of his own likely homosexuality, was *Leaves of Grass*, first published in 1855 and enlarged in eight subsequent editions. **Urning** and Uranian were terms devised in 1862 by Karl Heinrich Ulrichs (1825–95) to describe homosexuals. The **enclosed memoir** was *Edward Carpenter: In Appreciation* (1931), a collection of articles by various authors, edited by Gilbert Beith. Mrs Mary Baker **Eddy** (1821–1910) was the American founder of Christian Science. In 1875 she published *Science and Health with Key to the Scriptures*, which Nancy Astor read daily. In Genesis 19:26 **Lot's wife** 'became a pillar of salt' for looking back on the sinful cities of Sodom and Gomorrah (presumably Shaw did not intend a pun on Henry Salt's name, which is not mentioned in this letter). Shaw was **rehearsing** *Heartbreak House*, which was revived at the Queen's Theatre 25 April 1932.

41 / To Nancy Astor   Ayot St Lawrence, Welwyn, Herts.
                                                            1st May 1932

[ALS: Reading]

Although the references in this letter are indeterminate, Shaw reveals his supportive nature towards Nancy Astor.

My dear Nancy

The arrangement now stands that we dine with you on Thursday. But we – you and I – must contrive to have a quiet word together if there are other guests.

The fate of your clause infuriated me. These are the little incidents that hurl me back on Karl Marx and his central warning that Capital in pursuit of profits has no conscience and will commit any atrocity for the sake of another farthing an hour. You did well to crack the official insect between your finger and thumb.

ever

G.B.S.

The nature of Nancy Astor's **clause** (presumably in a bill in the House of Commons) has not been determined. **Karl Marx** (1818–83) published the first volume of *Das Kapital* in 1867, which Shaw had read in French and English translations in the 1880s.

42 / To Nancy Astor   Ayot St Lawrence, Welwyn, Herts.

27th June 1932

[ALS: Reading]

Shaw was preparing for another Malvern Festival, which he attended 25 July– 25 August 1932. T.E. Lawrence, the model for Private Napoleon Alexander Trotsky Meek in Too True to be Good, *joined the Shaws at Malvern for two days. He told Nancy Astor he was wowed by the play (5 September 1932 letter, Reading). The nature of Nancy's invitation (which Shaw declines) is unknown; however, the Astors spent the autumn of 1932 in the United States.*

The proposed elopement is, alas! impossible: I have to rehearse the new play at the Old Vic on Saturday morning. I should dearly like to go; and I greatly need a change; but the rehearsals and a broadcasting job ('Rungs of The Ladder') and other engagements have tied me up almost until we go to Malvern.

However ——————

G.B.S.

The **new play** was *Too True to be Good*, performed at Malvern on 6 August 1932. Charlotte Shaw told Nancy Astor the play was forceful but she lamented the 'torrent of vulgar abuse & drivel!' from the press (Holroyd, 269). The play's transfer to London's New Theatre on 13 September 1932 also received poor notices and the production ran for only 47 performances. Shaw's **broadcasting job**, a talk on parents and children, was given on 11 July 1932, and published in *The Listener*, 20 July 1932.

43 / To Nancy Astor   *Empress of [Britain]*, Bombay
                                                  13th January 1933

[APCS: Reading, Holroyd (e), Letters, Pearson (e)]

The Shaws began their luxury around-the-world cruise on the Empress of Britain
*at Monaco on 16 December 1932, returning to Southampton on 19 April 1933.
They visited Naples, Athens, Haifa, Luxor, India, Colombo, Singapore, Hong
Kong, China, Japan, Honolulu, San Francisco, Los Angeles and New York.
(Their journey is recorded by Holroyd, 284–314; see also, Kay Li, 'Globalization
versus Nationalism: Shaw's Trip to Shanghai,'* SHAW: The Annual of Bernard
Shaw Studies 22 *[University Park, PA, 2002], 149–70.) In his 10 March 1933
letter (Reading), T.E. Lawrence told Nancy Astor he thought that Shaw had left it
too late in life for world travels and that Shaw was blind to reality because he was
feted too much. On the reverse of the postcard is a portrait of Shaw with his hostess,
'Atizabegum,' on the deck of a ship.*

Dearest Nancy

This is my latest conquest.

We are alive; but that is all. We started tired to death, hoping for rest;
but this ship keeps stopping in ports where the water is too filthy to
bathe in and shooting us ashore for impossible excursions to see the
insides of railway carriages, and be let out, like little dogs, for a few
minutes exercise and a glimpse of a temple or a hotel meal or a cobra-
mongoose fight. We absolutely refused, and were roasted for a week at
Luxor and are now roasting at Bombay for another week.

The Begum on the other side, a lion huntress acharnée, concentrated
all the native nobility on me at a grand reception full of Nizamesses and
Indian highnesses; and oh my! can't they dress, these native plutocrats.
The place blazed with beauty. The British are right to boycott them
(there was only one white real lady, spouse of a Chief Justice); for the
dusky damsels would not leave their daughters an earthly.

I have been hung with flowers in the temples and drenched with
rosewater and dabbed with vermilion in the houses; and the ship is
infested with pilgrims to my shrine. Charlotte and I curse the day of our
birth and the hour of our sailing incessantly. Our sole comfort is to think
of THEE and wish we were within reach of you.

                                                  G.B.S.

44 / To Nancy Astor　　　　　　　　　*Empress of Britain*, Pacific Ocean
21st March 1933

[ALS: Reading, Holroyd (e)]

Dearest Nancy

It was a great joy to get two long letters from you at Honolulu, & have
your news. I do feel badly about not writing. If you could be with us for a
day or two you would understand. And yet it is not the conditions – it is a
sort of worthlessness that comes over one in this vagabond life. How we
shall ever settle down again – I dont know! But 'love failing' – no – dear
one – that I truly believe is one thing that *wont* happen – ever.

I am lying on my back in my bunk & writing this now, because I have
just realized that after San Francisco, where we arrive the day after
tomorrow I cant write any more, as our ship will go as fast as the letters!
So this is a last chance.

It has been a very mixed business, this trip. Some of it we have really
enjoyed wonderfully – we have seen some glorious places & made some
delightful friends & learned quite a lot of things. On the other hand the
discomfort & over-fatigue & strain of great heat & great cold has been
serious – our journey has, emphatically, *not* been a rest.

I dont think it is any more trying to go back over our travels & tell you
now but if you want to hear I can tell you all about it – & should love to –
dear Nancy, when we meet.

Tell Bill [Astor] I have fallen in love with China, & am now passion-
ately excited about the war & the whole question – & hate the Japanese –
& have read the Lytton report from end to end with avidity! I shall love
to talk to him. We met lots of people he knew there.

China is wonderful. I felt *at home* there – I belonged there!

Now we are to go straight from the ship, on Friday morning, in an
aeroplane, to [Randolph] Hearst's ranch, San Simeon. I do wonder what
it will be like. Later he flies us to Los Angeles where we rejoin the ship.

I must tell you that I have been worried the whole time by the thought
of that accursed lecture coming in New York. And, darling, I must tell
you, quite straight, I have been just a bit sore about you pushing it on.
When we spoke together I made sure you would keep it quiet that we
were touching at New York. It was when he got your letters he suddenly

decided to say he would do it for you – I think. Nancy I do not feel he is up to it. It will be a terrible strain after all the exertions & fatigues of this amazing journey. And it is going to be so hot again at Panama. Well: we must hope for the best. Of course he will 'get through.' But I cant believe he will do himself justice. I have put it out of my mind, quite, now, till the time comes.

I think it's grand about David [Astor]. I believe that boy will do great things some day. He certainly is one of the most charming people I ever met.

Too bad about Wiss [Phyllis Astor]. Poor darling what a lot she has gone through. But I have known people so much better & stronger after having their appendix out. How splendid if she could be spirited over here: only I know two days on the ship would bore her to death. Our passengers are not an exhilarating crowd.

I often think of our Wednesday evening services & wish I could fly over & join you. Well, it's not so long now. The 19th April we are due back.

Do you know, when I came away, I did not think we should come back alive. Now, somehow, I think we will. Really, I am longing to see you again – & just 2 or 3 other people – That's all!!

It is so nice of you to cheer up T.E. [Lawrence]. I am sure he is sometimes very sad. I have not written to him either – I have not written to anyone. I couldnt somehow. I expected to see T.E.'s mother & brother in China, but they didnt turn up. The conditions were impossible. At Shanghai we lay far out at sea, & it was a journey to get ashore. At the port for Pekin we were ice bound, & had to smash [our] way to shore in the heavy ice-breaking steamer that took us off the ship, at the pace of about a mile an hour. Inland all the lakes & rivers were frozen *solid*! We flew over the Great Wall & the country round Pekin. The 'plane was warmed, but the thermometer outside registered 67° *of frost* – of course we went high up.

22nd March

GBS tells me to say he has not written because he has been so busy making plays! He has written one (short) & nearly finished another, long, political one! I am to tell you nothing about them as he wants to tell you himself & read them to you. But please keep this to yourself until we get back. No one else has been told.

He sends his love – his *best*.

My thoughts & remembrances to them all & my true love to you, dearest.

Charlotte

For the **Lytton Report**, see Letter 39. On 11 April 1933 Shaw delivered a **lecture** at the Metropolitan Opera House, New York, entitled 'The Future of Political Science in America,' which was critical of American capitalism and culture. The lecture was also broadcast on radio by the National Broadcasting Company. **T.E.'s mother & brother** were Sarah Lawrence (1861–1959), who had been a missionary in China since 1922, and Dr Montague Robert Lawrence (1885–1971), a medical missionary. Shaw's **short** play was *Village Wooing* (first performed at the Little Theatre, Dallas, 16 April 1934), the **long** one was *On the Rocks* (first performed at the Winter Garden, London, 25 November 1933).

45 / To Nancy Astor   Ayot St Lawrence, Welwyn, Herts.
24th April 1933
[ALS: Reading]

Dearest Nancy

I have been so tired I thought I would die! Both of us came back utterly exhausted. The lecture in New York, though a real success, flattened us out: & a very bad passage back extinguished us. Now, after a day's real rest here we are beginning to perk up a little.

You know we had only 24 hours in New York, so we couldnt see your sister [Irene Gibson] which we regretted very much. It was all the most amazing rush. We were nearly torn to pieces by wild journalists. But it must be told: it can't be written.

We are both longing to see you again, but we know you are away for Easter. Loved your letter from Brioni.

Looking forward eagerly to a meeting, & with the best of love – ever

Charlotte

46 / To Nancy Astor   4 Whitehall Court SW1
12th May 1933
[ALS: Reading, Masters (e), Sykes]
Quite why Waldorf Astor and Shaw concocted the idea of displaying a sculpture of Nancy in the Palace of Westminster (Masters, 179) is puzzling since the picture by Charles Sims (1873–1928) of her historic introduction into the House of Com-

mons was withdrawn from the palace in 1924, after only a few months, because of strenuous objections (see Sykes, 277–8). Perhaps Waldorf and Shaw thought Nancy's increasing longevity as an MP and her support of the government made the time more propitious; however, the plan was ultimately dropped. There is a photograph of Nancy, the bust, and Strobl in Sykes (following 256).

My dear Nancy

You must go to de Strobl's studio and give him one real sitting: that is, you must behave exactly like a professional model with her livelihood (half a crown an hour) at stake. The bust is a beautiful work: you will never get anything like it brought into existence again in point of beauty and refinement; but it lacks the final touch which will completely identify it with you. Charlotte made him do something to the eyes which brought it nearer; but it will only be a 'Bust of a Lady' unless you do your clear duty as a civilized woman (as distinguished from a Virginian savage) and take the work quite seriously for an hour or two.

He says the conditions under which he has worked have been frightfully distracting, difficult, and distressing, as you are incapable of stillness and silence. I suggested chloroform; but I now appeal to one of your several better selves. He is a very fine workman and should be treated with genuine respect. And he is too amiable to resort to the poker or the broomstick, which is what you deserve. Unless you enable him to superfinish that bust angels wont never love you. Nor will

GBS

Zsigmond Kisfaludi-**Strobl** (Sigmund de Strobl, 1884–1975) was a Hungarian sculptor who had sculpted Shaw in 1932. On returning to Hungary, a customs official refused to allow Strobl to pass until he had seen Shaw's head (21 October 1932 Strobl letter to Shaw, BL 50520, f. 172). Shaw's comments on Strobl's bust of him are in Laurence, *Letters*, 486–7.

47 / To Nancy Astor   4 Whitehall Court SW1
9th June 1933

[ALS: Reading]

My dear Nancy

I saw the bust in de Strobl's studio the other day; and it is now quite a different affair, so good and so serious that it MUST go to Westminster as the memorial of the first woman to sit in the House.

How is that to be worked? If it cannot go on the estimates or on the Secret Service Fund, Waldorf must present it on the understanding that it will be graciously received. I'll go halves with him in the price – though it should be done by penny subscription from all the women in the Kingdom.

If Queen Mary will unveil it I'll give her an autographed copy of The Black Girl, and a box for the first night of my new play.

sempre a te, Nancy
GBS

Queen Mary of Teck (1867–1953) was the wife of King George V (1865–1936). By his **new play** Shaw probably means *On the Rocks*, although he was still completing both it and *Village Wooing*. In his 22 December 1933 letter to his Austrian-born German translator Siegfried Trebitsch (1869–1956), Shaw wrote: 'You suggest Mrs Baker-Eddy as a future heroine. But she is in On the Rocks as the lady doctor!' (Weiss, 339). Were this known to Nancy Astor, a Christian Scientist, *On the Rocks* would be of special interest.

48 / To Nancy Astor

Malvern Hotel, Malvern
25th August 1933

[TLS: Reading]

In 1933 Lord Riddell of Walton Heath (George Allardice Riddell, 1865–1934) published his War Diary 1914–1918, *which renewed a controversy created in 1917 when Henry Petty-Fitzmaurice, 5th Marquess of Lansdowne (1845–1927), suggested a compromise peace with Germany. Lansdowne's proposal had been made in a 29 November 1917 letter to the* Daily Telegraph, *and correspondents in* The Times *in 1933 argued over whether Lord Balfour, who had been Foreign Secretary from 1916 to 1919, knew of Lansdowne's letter before its publication.*

Dearest Fancynancy

The enclosed cutting from The Daily Telegraph may amuse you. I sent it to The Times in the first instance, of course; but Geoffrey [Dawson] is such a stupendous simpleton that he hasnt noticed that anything has happened since 1917, and rejected it on the ground that it had 'little or no bearing on the only point raised in the correspondence' and 'would only have confused the issue.' He did not even know that the issue raised by the correspondence was not whether Lansdowne had shewn his letter to Balfour or not, but whether he was a statesman who had grasped the situation when all the rest were drivelling about Lenin being in the pay of the Kaiser, or an intimidated old dotard who wanted to knuckle down to Germany.

It ended in my telling Geoffrey that he is the world's worst journalist (which is what makes him an ideal Times editor) and repeating history by sending the letter to the D.T.

In the meantime I sent the letter to the present Marquess, who said that he had been against his father like everyone else in 1917, but that he was all for publication.

I dont think I have anything else that Charlotte has not told you. My oration at the Metropolitan Opera House in New York is being published as a two shilling booklet by my publisher (not by me) next Tuesday; and to my great surprise he has sold 20,000 before publication. The public must think that it is another Black Girl, who has passed her hundred thousandth.

I am slaving at getting my new play ON THE ROCKS ready for the stage; and the title reminds me of something. The world is really sufficiently on the rocks to make it advisable to insure our widows and orphans of the plutocracy against revolutionary onslaughts on property. Some time ago, having ten thousand pounds to spare, I bought an annuity for Charlotte from one of the big Canadian Insurance companies. Roosevelt has entered on a path which may lead him to an attack on ground rents and absenteeism. Already the taxation is much heavier than would have been thought possible when we formed our political habits of mind. Possibly you and Waldorf may have considered this: but you keep such bad political company that the risk may not have seemed worth insuring. If so, spend your next savings not on good works but on Canadian annuities (joint ones) and see that the infants are brought up either to professions or to the fried fish shop business, which is much more lucrative.

Forgive this intrusion into your private affairs. It is a weakness of

your devoted

G.B.S.

The **enclosed cutting** was 'Mr Bernard Shaw and Lord Lansdowne: The Peace Letter,' *Daily Telegraph*, 24 August 1933 (reprinted in Laurence, *Agitations*, 291–2). Vladimir Ilich **Lenin**

(1870–1924) was founder of the Russian Communist Party and the Comintern. **Kaiser** Wilhelm II (1859–1941) was, until the end of the First World War, Emperor of Germany and King of Prussia. The **present** (6th) **marquess** was Henry William Edmund Petty-Fitzmaurice (1872–1936). For details of Shaw's New York **oration** see Letter 44; it was published on 29 August 1933 as *The Political Madhouse in America*. On 27 August 1933, Thomas Jones reported that 'after dinner, each evening [at Gregynog Hall in Wales], G.B.S. is reading to us his new *On the Rocks*' (*Diary*, 112). Shaw wrote to his accountant, Stanley Clench (1893–1961), on 6 July 1932 to arrange for Charlotte's **annuity** (Laurence, *Letters*, 300). Immediately after his inauguration as President on 4 March 1933, Franklin Delano **Roosevelt** 'F.D.R.' (1882–1945) launched his 'new deal,' which aimed at stimulating the economy, reducing unemployment, and helping the poor.

49 / To Nancy Astor   4 Whitehall Court SW1
                                                            5th October 1933

[ALS: Reading, Pearson (e)]

Nancy Astor was antifascist, while Shaw admired Mussolini (among other dictators). So her invitation for Shaw to meet the antifascist Carlo Rosselli is, perhaps, curious. Rosselli was well known to Nancy ('In Europe Rosselli could count on the support of … Lady Nancy Astor') as well as the Fabians: '[Rosselli's] Anglophilia was furthered by a trip to England in the summer of 1923, where he met G.D.H. Cole, R.H. Tawney, the Webbs, and members of the Fabian Society' (Pugliese, 5, 60).

Alas! dearest Nancy, Charlotte's abed in Ayot with a cold and cannot come up to town this week; and I cannot give you a lunch here tomorrow because I have a lunch at the Carlton with Mrs Phillimore to meet Zilliacus (secretarying Henderson at Hastings for the League of Nations) who is returning to Geneva on Saturday, and whom I *must* see. This is heartbreaking; but it can't be helped.

As to the man with 'a profoundly liberal mind: an English mind' he must be as great a curiosity as a man with a profoundly peaceful mind: a tiger's mind. All these anti-Mussolinians are idiots.

I have a lady coming to see me here at 5.30 tomorrow. From after lunch until then I am free if I can be of any use; but I dont see how we can work up a tea party for Rosselli's curiosity.

Many blessings on you from your

                                                            G.B.S.

The **Carlton** Club (in St James's Street) was founded in 1832 by Tory MPs. Mrs **Phillimore** was possibly Lucy 'Lion' Phillimore, Fabian and social worker, and a friend of Charlotte

Shaw. She married Robert Phillimore (1871–1919) in 1895 and was still alive in the mid-1940s. Konni **Zilliacus** (1894–1967) worked for the Information Section of the General Secretariat of the League of Nations (1919–39). He became a Labour MP in 1945. Arthur **Henderson** was president of a disarmament conference that had opened in Geneva in February 1932. Beatrice Webb believed his 'guileless and naive' tactics had dragged out the conference over 'two long years' (Mackenzie, *Diary*, 309). Benito **Mussolini**, 'Il Duce' (1883–1945), was the Italian Prime Minister and fascist dictator (1922–43). Earlier he had been a socialist. According to Shaw's engagement diary, the **lady coming** was the American actress Mary Lawton (d. 1945). Carlo **Rosselli** (1899–1937) was founder of the liberal-socialist movement 'Justice and Liberty.' He fought in the Spanish Civil War (1936–9) and was assassinated with his brother, Nello (1900–37), in France on 9 June 1937 (Pugliese, 218–26).

50 / To Nancy Astor

The New Zealand Shipping Company's [RMS *Rangitane*] Passing Southampton or thereabouts 9th February 1934

[ALS: Reading, Letters (e)]

During November 1933 Shaw was preoccupied with the production of On the Rocks, *which he began rehearsing on 1 November. He, Charlotte, and Nancy Astor attended the first night at the Winter Garden Theatre on 25 November. Charlotte's enthusiastic impression of the reception of the play (Conolly, 60–1) was not shared by Beatrice Webb, who declared it was 'one protracted discussion ... by an aged cynic who [has] outlived his genius.' Nor could she understand why Shaw was 'always asserting that dictatorship is* good in itself *as a political system, even Hitler's medieval barbarism' (Mackenzie, Diary, 319). The general public was unresponsive:* On the Rocks *managed only 73 performances, its run ending on 27 January 1934. On 6 February 1934 the Shaws lunched in London with the Astors, David Lloyd George, and Elisabeth Bergner. Two days later they embarked on yet another extensive voyage, this time to New Zealand, sailing westwards via Jamaica and the Panama Canal. They arrived back in Plymouth on 17 May 1934 (see Holroyd, 314–20, for an account of the trip).*

Dearest Nancy

I find that we call at Plymouth for mails; so I am able to send this note to you to say that before leaving yesterday I saw Macdona, who is very anxious to redeem the catastrophe of On The Rocks by reviving St Joan with Liesl (*alias* Elizabeth Bergner). Obedient to your instructions I told

Macdona to go ahead, and wrote to Liesl recommending him to her. So if her present engagement does not go on for ever, or until my return, she may follow on with St Joan.

Sean is all right now that his shift from the Dublin slums to Hyde Park has shewn that his genius is not limited by frontiers. His plays are wonderfully impressive and *reproachful* without being irritating like mine. People fall crying into one another's arms saying God forgive us all! instead of refusing to speak and going to their solicitors for a divorce.

The sea has been flatter than the round pond; but Charlotte is not up yet (11 a.m.) and woke up only for a moment to tell me to send her fondest love to you.

She isnt lonely. Any woman married to me would be only too glad to be in that enviable state.

Pity you are not in Plymouth. I could wave to you.

> sempre
> G.B.S.

Charles **Macdona** (c. 1860–1946) was an Irish actor and manager who, in 1921, organized the Macdona Players, a touring group, in order to present Shaw's plays. Macdona had presented *On the Rocks* at the Winter Garden Theatre. Elisabeth **Bergner** (1897–1986), the Polish/Viennese actress, had performed St Joan in Berlin in 1924, a role she did not play in England until the 1938 Malvern Festival. Her first English appearance was in Margaret Kennedy's (1896–1967) *Escape Me Never* at Manchester in November 1933). **Sean** O'Casey's latest play was *Within the Gates*, produced at the Royalty Theatre on 7 February 1934. The O'Caseys accepted Nancy Astor's hospitality freely while the play was in rehearsal. Nancy also threw a first-night cast party.

51 / To Nancy Astor　　　　　　　Hotel Cargen, Auckland
[c. 18th] March 1934

[ALS: Reading, Holroyd (e)]

The Shaws arrived in Auckland, New Zealand, on 15 March 1934. From there they visited Rotorua, Wellington, and Christchurch (Gibbs, 295–7) before beginning their homeward journey on 14 April 1934.

Nancy dear, dearest –

Here we are at the antipodes standing, so to speak, at your feet. Well, it feels strangely like anywhere else! It is a gay-looking town – heaps of pretty bungalows with large bright gardens: practically no large houses.

Government Ho[use] is a medium-size quite ordinary country house. They gave us lunch & were *very* nice to us – really both of them quite charming. He [Viscount Bledisloe] spent quite a long time making out a route for us & we are going to do pretty well what he said. All the officials wanted us to 'star' in the towns, but as G.B.S. is already almost dead from 3 days here we resisted & Lord Bledisloe was awfully good about backing us up so we are going to spend nearly our whole time in the country. First a week at Rotorua where there are geysers, & a lot of nice forest drives: then a week (Easter) at Chateau [Tongariro] where there are snow mountains & deserts: then *perhaps* a week near Nelson in the fiords.

We had quite a good voyage though we did get dead tired of it at the end! The drawback was extremes of temperature: cold at the beginning & such, & dreadfully hot for a fortnight in the tropics. The ship is most comfortable a[nd] well-run, & now we have made friends on her for the homeward run. She sails from *Wellington* on the 14th April.

I think of you so often, & long for a chat. I got your cable saying you were going to Biarritz but of course they will send you this. I hope you will have nice weather there. I wish I could hear all your news.

We are both well – considering. G.B.S. is *marvellous*! The amount of interviewing, talking & public speaking he can do! We find a lot of interest here in Russia – he has been telling them about that.

Ever, dearest, with our united love
Charlotte

I long to know what happened to Sean's play.
We did such a wonderful drive yesterday into the 'Bush.' The Bush is not scrub but lovely mountain slopes covered with trees & tropical (*sub-*tropical!) vegetation – the great feature being the tree-ferns, which grow into forest-trees & crop up in groups all over the place. Such lovely waving fronds – enormous! Also the kauri trees, which rival the California sequoias.

Sir Charles Bathurst, Viscount **Bledisloe** (1867–1958) was Governor-General of New Zealand (1930–5). In 1898 he had married Bertha Susan Lopes. On **Sean's play**, see Letter 50.

52 / To Nancy Astor

The New Zealand Shipping
Company's RMS *Rangitane*
Wellington to London
28th April 1934

[ALS: Reading, Holroyd (e), Letters, Pearson (e)]

Two days before this letter, Shaw completed The Simpleton of the Unexpected
Isles, *which he read to Beatrice and Sidney Webb in early July: 'Another play of the
fantastic-ethical-sociological sort' (Mackenzie,* Diary, *334). On 27 April 1934
Shaw began writing what eventually became* The Millionairess.

My dear Nancy

If the engines dont break down again (the ship is too full) we should be
in the Thames on the 17th. But I am not sure. We lost a day in starting to
take a lot of what are called naval ratings. They turned out to be human
beings. Perhaps we shall dump them at Plymouth, though we do not stop
there officially.

When we are near enough to know with some sort of exactness the day
of our arrival I will send Miss Patch a wireless.

Although New Zealand actually has a law prohibiting the landing of
any person who has recently visited Russia I had the same Royal Progress
as we had in the U.S.S.R. After a week in Auckland I positively refused to
visit any other city except Wellington, from which I had to sail. Nevertheless at the last moment I made a dash south for Christchurch. The Mayor
waylaid us 30 miles out; and after a civic reception (broadcast) I returned
to Wellington a pitiable old wreck, and only escaped a second one by
inviting the Mayor to lunch and pleading extreme exhaustion.

I wish you and Waldorf had been with us. There is a municipal milk
supply in Wellington, and an amazing maternity welfare institution cen-
tering on a strange old genius, Sir Truby King, with the result that the
infant mortality rate in N.Z. is *less than half* the English rate. I wished
extremely you had been with me there. And the agricultural problems
would have filled all Waldorf's time. You both ought to have a look at this
queer Empire at close quarters. Tramping the deck for exercise and
playing childish deck games is not worse than the division lobbies.
The En-zeds [New Zealanders] are intensely imperial-patriotic, and call
England HOME. Their devotion takes the form of expecting us to

exclude all butter and wool except theirs; to wage tariff wars against all Powers refusing to do likewise; to fight all Asiatic States who demand access to the island which its piously Victorian but resolutely birth-controlling British inhabitants resolutely refuse to populate; and to allow all their exports freely into England whilst they pile up protective duties against us and buy freely from Czechoslovakia, China, and anywhere else where we are undersold.

If England makes an alliance with Japan, which lots of our Diehards are quite capable of doing, the United States will have to make a counter-alliance with Russia; and then Australasia will have to chuck the silly Empire and join the U.S.A. Likewise Canada. But you have to get into the Pacific to realize how possible this is. If Russia were to relapse into predatory Capitalism and Communism to be rooted out of China, a dangerous situation would develop with terrific rapidity. Consequently it is our business to back up Communist Russia and China for all we are worth. But people think I say this because I am a Communist, whereas it is the most obvious Conservative Balance-of-Power diplomacy. I must therefore leave it to you and Waldorf to wave the red flag.

I am flying this letter from Panama to New York; but it wont reach you more than a few days ahead of ourselves. Charlotte is longing to see you. I am moderately eager myself.

sempre a te

G. Bernard Shaw

Daniel Giles Sullivan, MP (1882–1947) was **mayor** of Christchurch (1931–6). Shaw's **broadcast** was 'Shaw Speaks to the Universe' (12 April 1934). When their children were growing up, the 'Astors traveled on the train with their own cow for their children's **milk**' (Fox, 182) in order to ensure a safe supply. Sir Frederic **Truby King** (1858–1938) received his medical education at the University of Edinburgh and was concerned with public health. He founded the Society for the Promotion of the Health of Women and Children (the 'Plunket Society').

53 / To Nancy Astor   Ayot St Lawrence, Welwyn, Herts.

3rd October 1934

[TLS: Reading, Pearson (e)]

After his trip to New Zealand, Shaw spent 22 July–16 September 1934 at the Malvern Festival. He was currently working on a screenplay for Saint Joan *(see endnotes, Letter 65) and so had no time for Nancy Astor's invitation.*

My dear Nancy

It's not possible: I'm working 'gainst time, Sundays and weekdays.

As to your list of guests, you want to frighten me away. Marie doesnt want to meet that old lot. Cant you collect a few young artistic disreputables for her?

Why not bring her to see me? I'm not proud; and I can put the shyest of queens at her ease in two minutes. But when I am counting the remaining hours of my life to clear up my work I can't give queens three days in a country house and never catch a glimpse of you except at meal times.

Last time I came across Marie Carmen Sylva was at the Gare de Lyon, where up to the final moment I thought the grand reception was all for ME.

Read the autobiographies of Inge (called Vale) and H.G. Wells. Jakie [Astor] will think the latter a scream.

ever and ever

G.B.S.

Shaw appears to have conflated Queen **Marie** of Romania (1875–1938) with her mother-in-law, Queen Elisabeth of Romania (1843–1916) who, as **'Carmen Sylva,'** wrote poems, short stories, novels, and fairy tales. Queen Marie had been a rival for Waldorf Astor's affections for some years before his marriage to Nancy in 1906 (Sykes, 84–6, 105–6). Dean **Inge**'s *Vale* was published in 1934, as was the two-volume *Experiment in Autobiography: Discoveries and Conclusions of a Very Ordinary Brain (Since 1866)* of **H.G. Wells** (1866–1946).

54 / To Nancy Astor   Ayot St Lawrence, Welwyn, Herts.
31st October 1934

[ALCS: Reading, Sykes (e)]

Shaw has pasted on to the postcard a newspaper photograph of him escorting a woman, to whom he refers in his last two lines.

I am sorry that luncheon this week is impossible. On Thursday we have people to talk about rehabilitating Roger Casement!!

On Friday I have a man's lunch at Sir Robert Hadfield's to meet General Smuts.

Dull, but inevitable.

We are not, as you might suppose, getting married; but it very nearly came to that.

Aint she lovely?

G.B.S.

Sir **Roger Casement** (1864–1916) was an Irish nationalist who sought German aid against British rule and was executed for high treason. In a 19 November 1934 letter (Laurence, *Letters*, 387–9), Shaw discusses the Casement issue in the context of a book by Dr William J. Maloney (1881–1952) then circulating in manuscript and published in 1936 as *The Forged Casement Diaries*. **Sir Robert Hadfield** (1858–1940), a metallurgist and industrialist, lived at 22 Carlton House Terrace. Shaw had previously met the South African statesman Jan Christian **Smuts** (1870–1950) during his 1932 South Africa trip. The **lovely** lady in the clipping pasted to Shaw's card was Lady Mary Lygon (1910–82), a close friend of novelist Evelyn Waugh (1903–66) and the subject of the thirteenth of Sir Edward Elgar's (1857–1934) 'Enigma Variations' (1899). Shaw was a friend and admirer of Elgar.

55 / To Nancy Astor   4 Whitehall Court SW1
16th January 1935

[ALS: Reading]

On 24 November 1934 Shaw suffered a minor heart attack and, in early January 1935, Charlotte reinjured the wound she had sustained in South Africa and developed blood poisoning. Thus, a planned eight-week trip to South America had to be cancelled. Nancy Astor went on a skiing holiday to St Moritz, Switzerland, and attempted to persuade Shaw to visit her there (see Letters 56 and 57).

Charlotte did not realize that you were going away so soon, and reproached me for letting you depart without a word from her.

Nevertheless it was better as it was.

She now knows that the voyage on the 26th is cancelled. She did not know this before. She is decidedly not worse; but I wish she were happier.

She sends all sorts of messages.

Bon voyage!

G.B.S.

56 / To Nancy Astor   4 Whitehall Court SW1
26th January 1935

[ALCS: Reading, Holroyd (e)]

[Charlotte] Recovering, but slowly. Fearfully difficult as the temperature falls. Her niece wanted to see her yesterday. I conveyed the application. The reply was 'I can scarcely bear to see YOU much less anyone else. Tell her to &c. &c. &c. &c.' However, the return to reasonableness is unmistakeable these last few days; and by the time you return I hope she will be almost normal.

It would do me a lot of good to join you; but I cannot pretend that there is anything wrong with me; and to leave her, even for a week end at Ayot, is still out of the question.

Pleasant to think of you in the sunshine on the outside edge.

G.B.S.

Charlotte Shaw's **niece** was Mrs Cecily Charlotte Colthurst, who received £20,000 in Charlotte's will.

57 / To Nancy Astor   4 Whitehall Court SW1
2nd February 1935

[TLS: Reading]

Dearest Nancy

I am too old for St Moritz: at my age bones are brittle: they break easily and mend with difficulty. There is nothing to be done at St Moritz but learn to ski and try to skate again after forty years' disuse of that dangerous practice. Besides, I can't get away. Charlie* is ill; the faithful Patch is prostrate; her deputy has flopped senseless and been three weeks in bed without the power to rise and fly to my assistance; and I must stick here until the muddle clears up; for the mere office business of my place never stops, and though I neglect my private residence recklessly money comes in by every post and has to be acknowledged. So pity me and thank your stars that you are out of it all, bless you.

So Lloyd George has sold Phil [Kerr] by coming down to the right of the Labour Party, which is no use at all, instead of to the left of it, as we arranged with Stalin.

Claudette* improves daily. She can now walk once up and down the room with several persons holding her; but she still cannot see anyone except the waiter, the maid, the day nurse, the night nurse, the secretary, and

Yours affectionately,
G. Bernard Shaw

*The expressions Charlie and Claudette above mean Charlotte. My provisional secretary is not yet familiar with family names.

On his seventy-second birthday (17 January 1935) at the Drill Hall, Bangor, **Lloyd George** announced his proposals for 'national development' to stimulate an economic recovery. His speech, 'A Policy for the Nation,' was reported verbatim in *The Times*, 18 January 1935. Waldorf Astor advised Thomas Jones: 'Don't let [Stanley Baldwin] be frightened by [Lloyd George's] "programme"! It can be modified' (21 December 1934 letter, NLW, Class Q, vol. 1, f. 34).

58 / To Nancy Astor   Union-Castle Line, MV *Llangibby Castle*
In the Red Sea approaching Bab el Mandeb
8th April 1935

[ALS: Reading, Holroyd (e), Pearson (e)]

With Charlotte Shaw finally recovered from her blood poisoning, the Shaws set sail on 21 March 1935 for a voyage to South Africa via the Mediterranean, Suez Canal, Durban, and Cape Town. They arrived back in England on 10 June 1935. During the voyage Shaw revised The Millionairess, *which he had begun on 27 April 1934 during their New Zealand trip. 'I finished the Millionairess play in Mombasa and (having now three plays unpublished) am starting to work at prefaces. Beatrice will have to revise the Millionairess, as she has a scene in a sweater's den!' (20 April 1935 letter to Beatrice and Sidney Webb [Michalos, 226]). Shaw provided the gist of the play when he and Charlotte visited the Webbs on their return to England. Shaw's admiration for Russia's successes mentioned in this letter would seem to justify Beatrice Webb's observation: 'As a young social reformer, [Shaw] hated cruelty and oppression and pleaded for freedom. He idealized the rebel. Today he idealizes the dictator, whether he be a Mussolini, a Hitler or a Stalin, or even a faked-up pretence of a dictator like Mosley. He refuses to discriminate between one dictator and another. Has possession of wealth, of easily acquired and irresponsible wealth, had something to do with this queer transformation?' (Mackenzie, Diary, 354).*

My dear Nancy

Charlotte is flourishing extremely in this hellish heat. I am a mere spectre of myself. My clothes are dropping off my attenuated body. The frightful cold I caught in the freezing Mediterranean has been nearly baked out of me at last; but I am the wretchedest of men, working furiously to distract my attention from myself.

I am finishing – practically rewriting – my play called The Millionairess. People will say you are the millionairess. An awful, impossible woman.

Meanwhile Russia is going from success to success and justifying our trips to the tip top. The Foreign Office is licking Stalin's boots; and Communist China, which we have been desperately trying to ignore, is sweeping away the wretched Kuomintang and bringing up a solid bit of the real China against Japan. You can say 'I told you so' twice a week to our own Kuomintang.

I can no more. They are making up the mail for Aden, which we expect to reach tomorrow morning. Not the dim and distant Aidenn where a rare and radiant maiden whom the angels name Lenore [sic] – no such luck, but at least a place where one can post a letter to you.

G.B.S.

The **Kuomintang** ('national people's party') was founded in 1912 with the original objective of establishing parliamentary democracy and socialism in China. Civil war between the Kuomintang and the Communists (formerly joined in a two-party coalition) had begun in 1926, and by the end of 1935 the Communists had been forced to retreat and establish strongholds in northwest China. **Japan** entertained long-standing interests in China (for example, Manchuria) and finally invaded China in September 1937. The final paragraph alludes to a stanza from 'The Raven' (1845) by Edgar Allan Poe (1809–49): "'Prophet!' said I, "thing of evil! – prophet still, if bird or devil! / By that Heaven that bends above us – by that God we both adore – / Tell this soul with sorrow laden if, within the **distant Aidenn**, / It shall clasp a sainted maiden whom the angels name Leonore – / Clasp a rare and radiant maiden whom the angels name Leonore." / Quoth the Raven "Nevermore."'

59 / To G. Bernard Shaw   [*no address*]
                                                      9th May 1935

[TLU (c): Reading]

Dearest G.B.S.

I was so glad to get a line from you, but sorry to hear that you are getting so thin. I can't understand it, unless it is because you will write disloyal praise about your rich friends.

[Nancy Astor]

60 / To Nancy Astor   Malvern Hotel, Malvern
                                             25th August 1935

[ALS: Reading]
The Shaws' sixth visit to the Malvern Festival took place 21 July–31 August 1935. They had been in South Africa when T.E. Lawrence was killed in May 1935.

Dearest Nancy

... We have been having a busy time here. The Festival very bright & the play a success. At least it filled the House, & the people said they liked it. It was a bit over their heads. It has been a joy driving about this lovely country – & the weather has been just right for us. We stay here for the Three Choirs Festival at Worcester next week: after that we may go back to Ayot & London anytime. G.B.S. sends his best of love. He is well & busy & rather enjoying himself. His second new play, The Millionairess, will probably be done soon in London. Let us go to see that together ...

26th

I had a nice little correspondence with Mrs Arnold Lawrence. I think I like her & she will turn out well & help. They told me there is no hurry about sorting out the letters which was a relief, & they sent me a bundle of mine – very decent of them. I cannot face the idea of that grave in Dorsetshire – so horribly *wrong*. He should have been cremated. And it's really dreadful to me to see The Seven Pillars knocking about all over the place at every house I go into – after keeping my own copy so jealousy *apart* all these years. I think this horrible exploitation of T.E. the instant he was down is about the most revolting thing I have encountered in life. I'd like to talk to you about it all sometime. You understand.

I dont agree at all about the Abyssinian business: but G.B.S. says the same as you do. 'Why run into danger just for the Abyssinians,' you say, & he says. *I* think that the selfishness & supineness of the 'Great Powers,' first over China & now over Abyssinia is going to be the world's undoing. You are a Christian. Well: do you remember: 'Sirs: ye are brothers: why do ye wrong to one another' & 'which think ye was brother to *him that fell among thieves*?' 'He that shewed mercy on him.' 'Go: & do thou likewise.'

ever

Love

Charlotte

Shaw's latest **play** at the Malvern Festival, *The Simpleton of the Unexpected Isles*, was produced on 29 July 1935 (its first production was at the Guild Theatre, New York, 18 February 1935). The annual **Three Choirs Festival** dates from 1724 and rotates among the cathedrals of Gloucester, Worcester, and Hereford. The Shaws attended the festival regularly. *The Millionairess*, which Barry Jackson had hoped to produce at the 1935 festival, received its first performance on 4 January 1936 in Vienna (see Conolly, 75–9). The play was first performed in England at Bexhill-on-Sea (17 November 1936), but a professional **London** production did not occur until 27 June 1952 at the New Theatre. **Mrs Arnold Lawrence** [née Barbara Thompson] (d. 1986) was the wife of T.E. Lawrence's youngest brother, Arnold W. Lawrence (1900–91), sometime Reader and later Professor of Archaeology at Cambridge University (1944–51). Presumably Mrs Lawrence was in the process of returning Charlotte's **letters** to T.E. Lawrence. After Charlotte's death, Shaw presented these letters to the British Museum, later the British Library (see Letters 158 and 159). Lawrence was discharged from the Royal Air Force on 26 February 1935 and, on 13 May, crashed near his cottage, Clouds Hill, in **Dorsetshire** while riding the motorcycle given to him by the Shaws. He did not regain consciousness and died on 19 May. Nancy Astor attended his funeral on 21 May at St Nicholas, Moreton, Dorset, where he was buried. In a note to his *Seven Pillars of Wisdom*, published in various forms (beginning with a private edition in 1922), Lawrence wrote that the book '[p]articularly ... owes its thanks to Mr and Mrs Bernard Shaw for countless suggestions of great value and diversity: and for all the present semi-colons' (Harmondsworth: Penguin, [1962], 10). A border incident in December 1934 between **Abyssinia** (Ethiopia) and Italian Somaliland gave Mussolini the opportunity to intervene; he then rejected offers of arbitration by the League of Nations, and invaded Abyssinia on 3 October 1935. **Sirs: ye are brothers ... another** is taken from Acts 7:26 while **which think ye ... thieves** is from Luke 10:36 (part of the parable of the Good Samaritan).

61 / To Nancy Astor   Ayot St Lawrence, Welwyn, Herts.
11th December 1935

[TLS: Reading]

Since Shaw's last letter to Nancy Astor, Stanley Baldwin had succeeded Ramsay MacDonald as Prime Minister in June 1935. A general election took place on 14 November 1935, which, Nancy told Edith Lyttelton, she 'never felt less like fighting' (letter, 18 October 1935 [Reading]). The National Government retained control of Parliament with 429 seats, although Labour gained more than 100 additional seats for a total of 154. Nancy was returned again in Plymouth with a 6097 vote majority (Craig, 216). She invited the Shaws to spend Christmas at Cliveden, and Charlotte replied (9 December 1935 [Reading]) that she had spoken to Shaw about the possibility, but did not think he could be persuaded. Shaw maintained he was too busy before he and Charlotte departed for their Pacific (and final) cruise in January 1936.

Beloved Nancy

I'm afraid it's quite impossible. I have all my year-end business to get through, and a heap of jobs to settle before our departure on the 22nd; and to do this out of reach of my papers amid the distractions of Cliveden is beyond my aged powers.

Why can you not, as other Americans do, take up that big lumping house and move it nearer to us? Then we could run in and out? But you are just too far off.

You have made me face all I have to do; and I am appalled. Charlotte has set her heart on one book that I have to get through the press. I foresee that it will have to wait until we return; but I darent say so.

Why dont you come with us? You could keep off the Honolulu maidens of forty who insist on hanging flower garlands on me.

The village post is going.

Bless you!
G.B.S.

The **one book** was possibly the Standard Edition of *The Simpleton of the Unexpected Isles*, *The Six of Calais*, and *The Millionairess*, published by Constable on 24 March 1936.

62 / To Nancy Astor   Ayot St Lawrence, Welwyn, Herts.
6th July 1936

[APCS: Reading]

The Shaws took a cruise to the Pacific via the Panama Canal, leaving on 22 January 1936. En route they visited Miami, Honolulu, San Francisco, the Grand Canyon, and several cities in Mexico, with Charlotte sending Nancy Astor several picture postcards marking their progress (Reading). Shaw worked on various pieces during the trip, but one book he completed was Geneva, *two days before their arrival back in England on 6 April 1936. Although very little of whatever correspondence took place in 1936 has survived, the Shaws and Nancy Astor saw each other regularly, often for lunch. Although Shaw here rejects Nancy's invitation, Charlotte lunched with the Astors on 8 July. Thomas Jones was also present and recorded: 'I had written the day before to ask Charlotte if she would build the new Library for us at [Coleg] Harlech. She refused at lunch to do so on the ground that she hated England and was going to leave all her possessions to Ireland'* (Diary, 229). *On 12 July Shaw travelled to the Birmingham Repertory Theatre for rehearsals for the Malvern Festival, which he then attended (25 July–22 August). The festival included a production of* Saint Joan *starring Wendy Hiller (1912–2003), who also played Liza Doolittle in* Pygmalion. *Shaw was unhappy with her performances (see Laurence, Letters, 436–8) and with the hoopla surrounding his eightieth birthday on 26 July. After the festival the Shaws embarked on a holiday in North Wales. The Astors spent September until early December 1936 in the United States and Bermuda. Their visit included an October reunion at Mirador*

(Nancy's ancestral home in Greenwood near Charlottesville, Virginia) of the surviving Langhorne sisters (Irene, Nancy, Phyllis [1880–1937], and Nora [1889–1955]). 'It was also the last time the remaining four would all be together' (Fox, 407). The Astors' visit was marred in November when Nancy's nephew, David 'Winkie' Brooks (1910–36), committed suicide by falling from a New York City hotel window (Fox, 410–13).

It is impossible for me to go up to London this week: I am overwhelmed with jobs to do before I leave for Malvern on Sunday. I can only send my portrait, which is not the *very* latest, with my love.

G. Bernard Shaw

Shaw's **portrait** is on the reverse of the postcard.

63 / To Nancy Astor

4 Whitehall Court SW1
25th March 1937

[ALS: Reading]

Shaw, Nancy Astor, and numerous luminaries appeared in the film The King's People, *written by the actor-dramatist John Drinkwater (1882–1937) to celebrate the coronation on 12 May 1937 of King George VI (1894–1952). Although shown all over the British Empire, it was not successful (letter from Michael Mindlin to Shaw, 27 October 1944, BL 50524, f. 206). Nancy was apparently dissatisfied with the film and wanted it withdrawn. However, Shaw himself made his mark: 'Of all the people, actors or otherwise, asked to [be themselves] in* The King's People, *the only two who seemed to be without nerves or difficulty were Sir Austen Chamberlain, who, after all, is accustomed to being on view, and Bernard Shaw – well-known to newsreel camera men as one of the most unself-conscious actors in the world' (*Film Weekly, *6 March 1937, 29).*

Dearest Nancy

You have slain J.D.; and you may ruin the redhaired one [Shaw] if you cancel the film. The thing is so entirely ephemeral and so harmless and goodnatured that it will not hurt any of our dignities. So let it stand.

As far as I know, he was not in the least a loose liver. A man should be allowed one change if he justifies it by becoming thereafter a model family man.

By the way, we must be careful. The film is not yet a month old; and already two of its actors – Austen and John – have dropped in their tracks quite unexpectedly. If we follow I shall really begin to agree with you that God is displeased.

Your thought was 'God shall smite *thee*, thou whited wall.'

And He has, but very mercifully.

G.B.S.

John Drinkwater (**J.D.**) died on 25 March 1937. Nancy Astor, despite her own divorce, must have raised objections to Drinkwater's divorce from Cathleen Orford. Subsequently he married Daisy Kennedy. Sir **Austen** Chamberlain (1863–1937), Conservative MP and variously Chancellor of the Exchequer, Conservative leader, and Foreign Secretary, had died on 16 March. Sir Orpheus in *Geneva* is 'Shaw's portrait to the life of Sir Austen Chamberlain' (Holroyd, 402). '**God shall smite *thee***' is taken from Acts 23:3.

64 / To Nancy Astor   Ayot St Lawrence, Welwyn, Herts.

11th December 1937

[ALCS: Reading]

In the interim since the previous letter, the Shaws spent two holidays at Sidmouth, paid their annual pilgrimage to the Malvern Festival, which featured a production of The Millionairess *(Conolly, 93–7), and declined Nancy Astor's invitations in September and November to spend time with her in Plymouth. Shaw received a letter from Gene Tunney (11 October 1937, BL 63186, f. 90) inviting him to spend a winter vacation with him in Florida. Nancy Astor extended a similar invitation to Charlotte in her 10 December 1937 letter (Reading): 'We are sailing for Florida on Friday, the 17th. I don't suppose there is any chance of you and G.B.S. coming, but if we got there and found it very nice and quiet, do you think you might consider coming out in January?' The Astors' holiday was primarily for Waldorf's health: 'Uncle W. hasn't been well ... It's something called inflamed bronchial tubes I think. Anyway he craves the sun and what is the good of being that rich if you can't do those sort of things occasionally? Aunt N. didn't want to go a bit, at first; now she is resigned to it and anyway she knows it's the right thing for her to do' (Grenfell, Darling, 28).*

Gene Tunney wants us to come to Florida and spend the winter on his island.

How do you get there? Do you go to New York and fly down south or sail straight to Miami?

Not that there seems the ghost of a chance of moving these two old wrecks; but there is something infectious in Waldorf's impulse. It will do *you* a lot of good. We therefore rejoice in it.

Tell Attlee and Ellen to stick to it that his *official* position forbad him to visit Franco until he became a recognized belligerent. Nothing like correctness.

G.B.S.

Gene Tunney had a home on an island (Hobe Sound) some 25 miles north of Palm Beach. Shaw's twenty-year friendship with Tunney is recounted in Gene Tunney, 'G.B. Shaw's Letters to Gene Tunney,' *Collier's*, 23 June 1951, 16–17, 51–3. Clement **Attlee** (1883–1967), who had been a Labour MP since 1922, became leader of the Labour Party in 1935 and later (1945–51) Prime Minister. His visit with **Ellen** Wilkinson in early December 1937 to one of the International Brigades fighting on the Republican side in the Spanish Civil War caused a furore: 'Various British newspapers ... criticized him for having given the clenched fist sign in reply to the Spanish forces' salute; they alleged that by doing so he was signifying approval of Communism' (Harris, 139). General Francisco **Franco** (1892–1975), leader of the Nationalist forces in Spain, remained the country's dictator from his victory against the Republicans until his death.

65 / To G. Bernard Shaw [3 Elliott Terrace, The Hoe, Plymouth]
10th October 1938

[TLU (c): Reading]

During the period between the previous letter and this one Shaw, as usual, was busy with his own work. On 4 June 1938 he collapsed, suffering from pernicious anemia, from which he took six weeks to recover (see Chappelow, 43, and Laurence, Letters, 501–2). Meanwhile Nancy Astor was supporting enthusiastically Neville Chamberlain's appeasement policy with Germany: 'We are rejoicing in the miracle of peace and know that it is the answer to prayer. I am glad you are not in the House of Commons for I am afraid you would become very disgusted with your fellow human beings. They are really beyond human comprehension' (5 October 1938 letter to Lady [Anne] Cecil Kerr (1883–1941) [Reading]).

I always knew you would get on the films before you grew up. I do wish you could put St Joan on – it would be such a help to civilization at the present moment. Can't you do it here, and leave Hollywood out?

I am hoping to see you both next Saturday.

I suppose that Charlotte, being a Pacifist, wanted to go to war, but I know you are pleased with Neville Chamberlain's performance.

I wish you would come down here.

[Nancy Astor]

Shaw spoke the preface to the **film** of *Pygmalion*, which premiered in London on 6 October 1938 (on Shaw and the various attempts to film *Saint Joan*, see Dukore, passim). Neville **Chamberlain** (1869–1940) had been a Conservative MP since 1918 and succeeded Baldwin as prime minister in May 1937. On 15 September 1938 he flew to Berchtesgaden to see Adolf Hitler (1889–1945) in an attempt to defuse the increasingly tense situation created by Hitler's *anschluss* (reunification) policy. A further visit by Chamberlain on 29 September resulted in the 'Munich Agreement,' which recognized Germany's right to annex the Sudetenland in western Czechoslovakia. 'In the debates on 5 and 6 October that followed the Munich crisis Lady Astor had cried "nonsense" when Churchill declared, "We have sustained a total and unmitigated defeat"' (Brookes, 121).

66 / To Nancy Astor   Ayot St Lawrence, Welwyn, Herts.

1st January 1939

[ALS: Reading, Holroyd (e), Sykes (e)]

Towards the end of 1937 the Astors and their circle of friends and politicians became known as the 'Cliveden Set' (the term was coined first in Reynolds News, *28 November 1937). It was widely believed they wielded considerable political power, most notably with regard to foreign policy (see Rose, passim, and Sykes, 364–410); in 1938 Nancy's fellow Conservative MP Henry Channon (1897–1958) noted in his diary that 'there is already talk of a so-called "Cliveden" set which is alleged to be pro-Hitler, but which, in reality, is only pro-Chamberlain and pro-sense' (Channon, 154). However, it is probably more accurate to describe the 'Cliveden Set' as a think-tank comprising varying and often shifting opinions, with even Nancy and Waldorf Astor sometimes at odds with each other (see Ellis, 413–16, 424–5). One of several articles that played upon contemporary phobias about the Set was a sensationalistic, conspiracy-theory-ridden piece in* Liberty *written by Frederick L. Collins. He suggested that a visit to Germany by American aviator Charles A. Lindbergh (1902–74) was suspicious; he further asserted that Lindbergh was 'in the employ of Lady Astor and her friends.' Collins also called the Set 'Britain's second Foreign Office ... [I]t is obvious that this ascendant group in British public life is hell-set for Hitlerism.' Shaw's rebuttal to Collins came at Nancy's suggestion: 'I sent [the article] to G.B.S. and said, half jokingly – "I feel you will have to tackle this and not me" ... [I]t was really a most gallant thing for the old boy to do' (6 January 1939 letter to Thomas Jones [Reading]). Charlotte wrote to Nancy (1 January 1939, Reading) approving Shaw's article and expressing her belief that it would answer Collins very effectively. Three months later Shaw and Nancy characterized rumours about the Set as a 'senseless fable' and a 'fantastic invention' (*Sunday Graphic, *5 March 1939).*

My dear Nancy

I agree that the Liberty article should be contradicted; and since you authorise me to blab about Cliveden I am by this post sending to Liberty a full dress article (gratuitous) about you and Waldorf and Garvin and Geoffrey [Dawson] which will, I hope, explode the Collins story. Possibly it may infuriate you; but I think it will do the trick. And you will like the bits about the two editors.

I am remarkably well considering my recent adventures. Once a month they squirt 'Pernemon Forte' (I believe it is the gastric juice of a hog) into my muscles. Usually it does not interfere with my movements; but last time I went out to lunch with the Londonderries too soon after the operation, I felt queer in the cab; and when I had given up my hat and things in the hall in Park Lane I flopped bang on the flags, and upset the whole luncheon party, to say nothing of apparently dropping dead under Charlotte's eyes. The Ls were very nice about it; and after a good sleep I was unusually well.

We were snowed up for Xmas (first time since Cliveden), but got up to town on Thursday. Yesterday we returned, and started for a walk on the assumption that the thaw had made the ground safe. We had hardly taken five steps when Charlotte slipped and crashed like an upset motor bus. As I turned to pick her up my feet flew from under me and I did a back fall of the most picturesque [sic].

But neither of us is a jot the worse; so do not be disturbed by the rumors which spread from these disasters. I take it that you are all right, though with the usual allowance of malingering relatives. Why dont you let them die? I never attend the bedsides of *my* sick relatives. They never die, unfortunately.

G.B.S.

'Why Did Hitler Give Lindbergh a Medal' by Frederick L. Collins (1882–1950) was published in *Liberty* (New York), 17 December 1938, 6–8. Shaw's **full dress** response was 'Bernard Shaw Answers Frederick L. Collins about Lady Astor,' *Liberty*, 11 March 1939, 7–8 (Shaw's typescript of the article, entitled 'The Cliveden Legend,' is BL 50698, ff. 96–100). Shaw pointed out that numerous people from many spheres were entertained at Cliveden and that Nancy was 'essentially an eclectic hostess.' Shaw's article provoked a response ('An Open Letter,' *Liberty*, 22 April 1939, 11–12) from the American novelist Upton Sinclair (1878–1968), who challenged Shaw's defence of Nancy. Sinclair thought Nancy was disingenuous when she claimed she was not all that influential. James Louis **Garvin** (1868–1947) was editor (1908–42) of *The Observer*, which was owned by Waldorf Astor. Shaw's **recent adventure** was a fainting spell on 16 December 1938 at the home of Charles and Edith (1879–1959) **Londonderry** (see Laurence, *Letters*, 520–1).

67 / To Nancy Astor
4 Whitehall Court SW1
2nd April 1939

[ALCS: Reading, Holroyd (e)]

After attempting to dissuade Hesketh Pearson from writing a biography of him (Laurence, Letters, 512, 519–20), Shaw agreed to assist Pearson and subsequently vetted his work. He wrote a similar letter of introduction to Beatrice Webb (Michalos, 234), who was unimpressed by Pearson but whom she helped because she thought Shaw was trying to do him a good turn (Mackenzie, Diary, 429). Pearson interviewed Nancy Astor on 26 April 1939. Nancy also provided Pearson with various letters that he quoted in the biography, and he was eager to see any future correspondence between Shaw and Nancy in case there might be a revised edition (Pearson letter to Nancy, 17 November 1942 [Reading]).

Hesketh Pearson, a littérateur who specializes in biography and has been commissioned by the publishing firm of Collins to operate on me, is very anxious to get from you some account of our Russian elopement. I have no power to prevent these 'lives' of me, and therefore do what I can to substitute information for invention, as a well told lie can never be overtaken.

This is only to let you know that H.P. is a genuine biographer and a presentable person, should he attempt to interview you.

G.B.S.

Hesketh Pearson (1887–1964), a writer and a former actor who had performed Metellus in the original English production of *Androcles and the Lion* (1913), published his biography of Shaw in 1942. Its English title was *Bernard Shaw: His Life and Personality*, and its American *G.B.S.: A Full Length Portrait*.

68 / To Nancy Astor
4 Whitehall Court SW1
27th July 1939

[TLS: Reading, Holroyd (e)]

Nancy Astor had evidently invited the Shaws to spend a holiday at her home in

77

Plymouth. Shaw declined because of Charlotte's poor health (the apparent lumbago), which was still recurring when they finally went on vacation (Letter 71).

My dear Nancy

Charlotte is in a state because she thinks she agreed to go to Plymouth at the end of a fortnight. It is possible that she may have done so. We are both slightly dotty with age, and easily get muddled especially as to our movements.

There is no serious likelihood of our being able to go to Plymouth. The housekeeping is a simple matter for you; but Charlotte would make a terrible responsibility of it, and worry her life out. Also she is afraid in her present condition of being out of immediate call of me at night; and her recollection of Elliott Terrace is of a dozen steep flights of stairs with only one room on each landing. In short, she dare not face it and must go to a hotel, if we can find one, as there only can she feel completely irresponsible.

It is very good of you to offer us the house, and quite idiotic of us not to jump at it; but the only way I can keep Charlotte up at present is by deciding that we are NOT going to do something; so you must leave us out of account and have those stairs mounted by younger people.

I was sorry to miss you yesterday; but I had a committee that reached from 5 to 7.30. At 7 Charlotte concluded that I was run over.

G.B.S.

Shaw's **committee** on 26 July 1939 was the Executive of the National Theatre Committee.

69 / To G. Bernard Shaw   [*no address*]
                                                         28th July 1939

[TLU (c): Reading]

Dearest G.B.S.

I can understand about Plymouth, and it does not make a scrap of difference, I shall always be able to get it ready for you if you want it.

In the meantime I write you my plans. I go to Cliveden to-day and remain until next Friday, when I go to Sandwich to stay until the 25th, unless I have to go to Scotland. Would you like me to find out if there are any rooms at the Hotel at Sandwich? I believe the sea air would do Charlotte good.

[Nancy Astor]

Waldorf Astor was planning a holiday beginning 4 August at his lodge on Jura, **Scotland**, which Nancy wanted to avoid.

70 / To Nancy Astor   Ayot St Lawrence, Welwyn, Herts.
15th August 1939

[ALCS: Reading]

Charlotte is just well enough to pack and move; and we must clear out of Ayot to give the staff their holiday; but we havnt found anywhere to go to as good as Rest Harrow. If only we could play golf – either of us!

And we should spoil *your* holiday.

I expect we shall end by rusticating at Whitehall Court. London is quite pleasant in August. Malvern (where my play has been a success) implores us; but I can bear no more of it.

Both our dearest loves.

G.B.S.

One of Nancy Astor's several athletic skills was **golf**. Shaw's **play** was *In Good King Charles's Golden Days*, which was performed at the Malvern Festival on 12 August 1939.

71 / To Nancy Astor   [4 Whitehall Court SW1]
[*c.* 28th August 1939]

[ALCS: Reading, Sykes (e)]

The Shaws decided finally to spend their holiday at Frinton-on-Sea and travelled there on 29 August in Astorian splendour, as their chauffeur, Fred Day (1883–1959) recalled: 'The last real tour I did with [the Shaws] was to Frinton-on-Sea during the summer of 1939. We had just taken over a new 25–30 h.p. Rolls, a "Wraith" with coachwork by Freestone & Webb' (Chappelow, 43). They remained at Frinton until 28 September despite Britain's declaration of war on Germany on 3 September.

Henceforth until the end of September we shall (D.V.) be at the Hotel
Esplanade, Frinton-on-Sea, Essex. I feel it to be my duty to be in the
front line when the German fleet opens fire; but I rejoice in your safety
behind the Goodwin Sands.

I wrote to The Times about the absurd jitter when Stalin took the
Führer by the scruff of the neck; but the letter was meant to give
Geoffrey [Dawson] a jolt: I did not expect it to be inserted. We should
have celebrated the news with illuminations.

Stalin's grin was immense.

Charlotte's recovery from her breakdown (that was what the lumbago
was) is not yet consummated; but I have hopes that a month of specially
good sea air will complete her recovery. We go down on Tuesday.

G.B.S.

Shaw's letter to *The Times*, 'Can Anyone Explain?' was published on 28 August 1939. He
alluded favourably to **Stalin** gaining possession of White Russia, the Ukraine, and part of
Poland as part of his non-aggression pact with Germany, signed in the summer of 1939.

72 / To Nancy Astor   [Hotel Esplanade, Frinton-on-Sea]
28th September 1939

[TLS: Reading, Holroyd (e), Letters, Pearson, Sykes (e)]

*A period of relative calm (known as the 'phoney war' or 'bore war') followed the
initial declaration of war, although a British Expeditionary Force was sent to
assist France and Belgium. It was eventually attacked and was evacuated from
Dunkirk at the end of May 1940. Shaw's instant analysis 'that the war is over' is
typically provocative (and see Letter 74).*

My dearest Nancy

I think it is time for you, as a sensible woman trying to keep your political
household of dunderheads and lunatics out of mischief, to get up in the
House and point out the cruelty of keeping up the pretence of a three
years war when everyone who can see three moves in front of his or her
nose knows that the war is over. The pretence is ruining people in all
directions at home and slaughtering them abroad.

The thoughtlessness of our guarantee to Poland has left us without a
leg to stand on. Most unfortunately we pledged ourselves to go to her aid

WITH ALL OUR RESOURCES; and when it came to the point we dared not use the only resource that could help her (our air bombers); for we had not a soldier within hundreds of miles of her frontiers nor a sailor in the Baltic; and a single bomb from us on the Rhine cities or Berlin would have started a retaliation match which would have left all the cities of the west in the same condition as Madrid and Warsaw. We should have warned the Poles that we could do nothing to stop the German steamroller, and that they must take it lying down as Chekoslovakia had to, until we had brought Hitler to his senses.

Fortunately our old pal Stalin stepped in at the right moment and took Hitler by the scruff of the neck: a masterstroke of foreign policy with six million red soldiers at its back.

What we have to do now is at once to give the order Cease firing, and light up the streets: in short, call off the war and urge on Hitler that Poland will be a greater trouble to him than half a dozen Irelands if he oppresses it unbearably. But we must remember that as far as Poland's business is anybody's business but Poland's, it is more Russia's business and Germany's than ours. Also that we cannot fight Germany *à l'outrance* without ruining both ourselves and Germany, and that we cannot fight Russia at all (neither can Hitler). The diehards who are still dreaming of a restoration of the Romanoffs and Bourbons and even the Stuarts, to say nothing of the Habsburgs, must be booted out of politics.

We should, I think, at once announce our intention of lodging a complaint with the International court against Hitler as being unfitted for State control, as he is obsessed by a Jewish complex: that of the Chosen Race, which has led him into wholesale persecution and robbery. Nothing should be said about concentration camps, because it was we who invented them.

I write this at Frinton in Essex; but we return to Ayot to-morrow and shall perhaps see you soon. Charlotte has had a terrible time here, but is much better this last week.

Waldorf might wave the red flag a bit in the House of Lords. Chamberlainism is no use on earth to him; and he might incidentally give America a lead. Geoffrey [Dawson] has heroically inserted two letters of mine in The Times, and has a third in his locker. I am deeply obliged to him.

Proletarians of all lands, unite!

The Labor Party is making the damndest fool of itself.
Our best love to you both.

In haste – packing

G.B.S.

During the second Boer War in South Africa (1899–1902), as a response to Boer guerilla
tactics, Lord Kitchener (1850–1916) conducted a scorched-earth policy and removed Boer
women and children to **concentration camps**, where many of them died. Shaw wrote this
letter at **Frinton** but on Whitehall Court stationery. Shaw's letters to *The Times* were
'Theatres in Time of War' (5 September 1939) and 'Poland and Russia' (20 September
1939).

73 / To G. Bernard Shaw   [*no address*]

3rd October 1939

[TLU: Reading]

While at Frinton, Charlotte Shaw had been confined to her bed for two weeks with
what was still believed to be lumbago (Gibbs, 312).

Dearest G.B.S.

I am miserable about Charlotte, I had no idea she was so ill.

I don't agree with you about Stalin. He and Hitler are blood brothers
and very bloody brothers at that. I wish I could do as you want me to but
I can't. I feel this evil thing must stop and who is to stop it but the
Germans themselves or us? Perhaps we may be able to do it together. I
am here all this week and may be next. Are you moving to London for
good[?] Would you send Charlotte here and let me take care of her for a
while? You are too young? [*sic*] Let me have her please. But I know she's
hopeless and won't leave you nor would I if I could help it. Please read
this letter ??????? [*sic*]

[Nancy Astor]

74 / To Nancy Astor   Ayot St Lawrence, Welwyn, Herts.

5th October 1939

[TLS: Reading, Pearson, Sykes (e)]

Shaw's notions about the war, touched on in earlier 1939 letters, were given fuller
expression in 'Uncommon Sense about the War,' which was published in the New

Statesman *(7 October 1939 and a day earlier in the* New York Journal-American*).*
His article repeated some of the same phrases he used in Letter 72. Nancy Astor
wrote to Philip Kerr (7 October 1939 [Reading]): 'I have some priceless letters from
Bernard Shaw. He feels that Russia is right, and we must give in to her, and that
Stalin is still the cleverest man in Europe.'

My dear Nancy

Send out instantly for this week's New Statesman. There you will find full
instructions as to your line about the war. Everybody wants to have these
instructions issued; but nobody but myself can afford to – or dare – issue
them.

The worst is over with Charlotte. She bore the journey here last Friday
without turning a hair; and though she still will not venture beyond the
gate on foot for fear of bringing back the lumbago she is quite herself
again.

Waldorf has been letting the Government have it for taking a month
to do a day's work. I have seen Governments take thirty years to do a
week's work, and then have it settled over their heads by fire and sword,
including the burning of several of Charlotte's birthplaces. That is how
people who want things done prefer even Hitler and Musso and Ataturk
to Westminster. It is a pity you did not spend a few years on a municipal
corporation to learn the difference between real government and the
party game. You should write up in your study my old warning IF YOU
TAKE THIRTY YEARS TO DO HALF AN HOURS WORK YOU WILL
PRESENTLY HAVE TO DO THIRTY YEARS WORK IN HALF AN
HOUR, WHICH WILL BE A VERY BLOODY BUSINESS.

As you are the only living person known to have bullied Stalin with
complete success; and as he is by countless chalks the greatest statesman
you ever met, and the pleasantest man except myself, you must stop
blackguarding him like an Evening Standard article writer. To our shame
we have betrayed and ruined Poland out of sheer thoughtlessness; but it
is to our credit, and to that of France and Germany, that when it came to
the point of starting a European bombing match we funked it and left
Poland to her fate.

Stalin rescued her. Do you remember that journey through Poland
with the harvest still standing and the long wheel spokes of golden strip

cultivation turning round us. It looked lovely; but did you know, as I knew, that strip cultivation means poverty and ignorance, savagery, dirt, and vermin? Not to mention landlordism. Well, Stalin will turn that into collective farming; and the Pole will no longer be a savage. The Pole will keep his language, his laws, his character as a citizen of a Federation of Republics like the United States, only much more highly civilized. And with such an object lesson staring his part of the booty in the face, Hitler will have to make his National Socialism emulate Russian Communism or else find Poland worse for him than ten Irelands. So be comforted; and join me in three cheers for the Red Flag (*young* Glory) the Hammer and the Sickle.

We two are both absentee landlords; yet Stalin was civil to us.

Forgive these politics; but you cannot get away from them, and I may as well give you some with hope and comfort in them to enable you to bear all the murderous cant and folly with which you are deluged.

So Proletarians of All Lands, Unite; and to hell with the Pope by all means; and may whisky be ever thirteen and ninepence a bottle!

Take care of yourself, dear Nancy: we love you.

G.B.S.

Kemal **Atatürk** (1881–1938) was founder of the Republic of Turkey and its first president (1923–38). **Pope** Pius XII (Eugenio Maria Giuseppe Giovanni Pacelli, 1876–1958) was elected pope earlier in 1939 and reigned until 1958. His neutral stance towards the Nazis during the Second World War has proved to be controversial.

75 / **To Nancy Astor**   4 Whitehall Court SW1
                                               8th November 1939

[ALCS: Reading]

Interspersed with miscellaneous news, Shaw inserts a touch of mischievous teasing when he reminds Nancy Astor of the 1936 abdication crisis. Even though divorced herself, Nancy had little sympathy for Mrs Wallis Simpson and believed that, before the crisis, Edward VIII was 'playing fast & very loose' (October [1936] postcard to Thomas Jones [NLW, Class Q, vol. 2, f.34]). After Stanley Baldwin informed the House of Commons of Edward's decision to abdicate, Henry Channon encountered Nancy in the emptying House: '... Lady Astor sang out to me "people who have been licking Mrs Simpson's boots ought to be shot"' (Channon, 99).

Charlotte has braved the journey to town at last, and seems none the worse for it. We shall go down again on Saturday as usual.

That is all the news.

Of course your niece has been ill: when has there ever been a time when your relatives were not ill?

Damn your relatives! Let them perish.

I wonder whether this move of Albert and Wilhelmina will upset the Imperialist apple cart. If it fails, our only consolation will be that the P.M. or Halifax have put us so completely in the wrong that we shall fight like a pirate crew with the rope round our necks, knowing that if we are beaten we have no mercy to expect. We shall therefore be unanimous and ruthless.

If public opinion in Europe forces us to produce a war aim, what would you say to a constitutional monarchy in Poland, with the Duke of Windsor as monarch and Queen Wally as his consort? Unemployed kings are a bit dangerous.

Charlotte sends messages for which I have left no room.

G.B.S.

Nancy's ill **niece** is unidentified; she had numerous nieces. *The Times* (8 November 1939) reported that King Leopold III of Belgium (1901–83), one of whose names was **Albert**, and Queen **Wilhelmina** of the Netherlands (1880–1962) had sent a telegram to the 'belligerent parties ... As Sovereigns of two neutral States, having good relations with all their neighbours, we are ready to offer them our good offices' to obtain an 'equitable peace.' Edward Frederick Wood, 1st Earl of **Halifax** (1881–1959) was Foreign Secretary (1938–40) and had supported **P.M.** Neville Chamberlain's earlier appeasement policy. Halifax was a possible successor when Chamberlain resigned as Prime Minister in May 1940; however, Churchill commanded wider public support. Nancy favoured Lloyd George for the office (Jones, *Diary*, 457). Edward VIII (1894–1972) abdicated on 11 December 1936 so that he could marry Mrs Wallis Simpson (1896–1986); he took the title of **Duke of Windsor**. From September 1939 until May 1940 he was given what was essentially a make-work position with the British military mission in France. From 1940–5 he was Governor of the Bahamas.

76 / To G. Bernard Shaw   [*no address*]
                                          8th January 1940

[TLU (c): Reading]

In November 1939 Waldorf Astor had been elected Lord Mayor of Plymouth; he served for five years. His and Nancy's fearless support of the people of Plymouth during extremely heavy bombing by the Germans (beginning in March 1941) became almost legendary (see Sykes, 436–41). Noel Coward recalled: 'I remember in 1942 walking with her through the devastated streets of the town one morning after a bad blitz, and her effect on the weary people was electrifying. She indulged in no facile sentimentality; she was cheerful, friendly, aggressive, and at moments even a little governessy. She dashed here and there and everywhere, encouraging, scolding, making little jokes' (Coward, 441). Privately, Nancy was more disdainful: 'The Air Raid sirens are becoming a perfect pest at Plymouth. Every night we are being dragged out of bed to the dug-outs, but never again for me. I have made up my mind to be bombed in my bed!! It is so tiresome working all day, and spending your nights in uncomfortable dugouts with most uncongenial company' (2 July 1940 letter to Philip Kerr [Reading]).

Dearest G.B.S.

We are here until the 12th – then London. I hope I shall be seeing you on the 18th.

Please send me a line how Charlotte is. I have neglected her and everybody else because the work of a Lady Mayoress combined with all there is to do at home is perfectly appalling.

I have a young friend who is with the Ministry of Information at Aden. He wrote me this and asked me to pass it on to you, which I do gladly.

I am perfectly delighted at the Secretary for War's resignation – or would you call it a 'get-out' – and hope to Heavens he won't come back again. I wish him no evil but I don't like careerists.

[Nancy Astor]

Nancy's **young friend** and his letter are unidentified. Leslie Hore-Belisha (1893–1957) was **Secretary** of **War** and President of the Army Council (1937–40). In 1939 his brusque manner, coupled with a reforming zeal to render the military more efficient, incurred the ire of the top brass, which led ultimately to his resignation on 5 January 1940 (see Minney, *Belisha*, 250–86 and Channon, 227–31).

77 / To Nancy Astor   Ayot St Lawrence, Welwyn, Herts.
                                          21st September 1940

[TLS: Reading, Holroyd (e), Sykes (e)]

The Battle of Britain, the air war between Britain and Germany, began on 10 July 1940 and concluded on 1 October 1940. When actually close to success, the Germans on 7 September switched from attacking air bases to bombing London, the 'Blitz.' That event and a fall Charlotte Shaw suffered on 6 September resulted in the Shaws retreating to Ayot. Although Shaw here claims Charlotte was infuriated by the bombs, she reassured Beatrice Webb (10 October 1940) that she was safe and that being killed outright by a bomb would be an easy death (see Dunbar, 285). Blanche Patch was frightened by the bombing in London and moved to Ayot on 11 September.

Nancy asthore

I have just received the enclosed letter (you can burn it) with an astonishing paragraph which I have underlined in red ink. I have informed the lady that it is founded on the Russian imagination, not on fact.

Charlotte has had another accident. She stumbled and came down plump on the gravel on both her knees, one of which took most of her weight and has since been disabled for walking. For a week she had to go upstairs backward, with me at the helm. Now she goes forward between her stick and the bannisters, and will soon, I hope, be completely mobilized.

This happened the day before the Blitz-krieg began in earnest, and gave us an excuse for skulking down here instead of coming up to town for half the week in our regular routine. We can see the flashes over London and hear the distant thunder of the guns. Casual raiders occasionally drop a bomb near enough to shake the house and alarm the shelterless village; there is a dump about a mile off where they make me jump by banging off all the delayed action bombs that fall into the county; and we have a little pip-squeak of a siren that gives us all the London alarms quite unnecessarily; but we sleep in our beds regardless. Happily Charlotte, who hates the distant sounds, is infuriated by the big bangs, which she takes as personal insults.

One day lately I was walking along Castelnau – of all places – at the far side of Hammersmith Bridge, when a very smart little car pulled up suddenly beside me with a shout of 'Mister Shaw! Jake!' He [Jake Astor] looked extraordinarily well: ever so much better than he did at the polo match, and was in the highest spirits. We forgot the difference in our ages and chatted as man to man.

This may take weeks getting to you; but if it ever arrives drop us a card to say that you and Waldorf and the infants are alive and well.

sempre a te
G. Bernard Shaw

The **astonishing paragraph** occurs in a disjointed and distraught letter from Virginia Soermus, wife of Julius Eduard Soermus (1878–1940), a violinist and communist who led workers through the streets during the failed Russian revolution of 1905. He was an inspiration for the painting 'The Fiddler' (1912), by Marc Chagall (1887–1985). The paragraph reads: 'Do you remember Sir Charles Trevelyn telling you about me in connection with Lady Astor kissing Stalin.' In 1931 Mrs Soermus had sounded out the Labour MP James Maxton (1885–1946) on whether Shaw might assist her financially (BL 50520, f. 55; see also Elliot, 53). **Castelnau** is the southern road leading to Hammersmith Bridge, London.

78 / To Charlotte F. Shaw   [Cliveden, Taplow, Bucks.]
                                                      7th October 1940

[TLU (c): Reading]

Nancy Astor had offered the Shaws a home at Cliveden for the duration of the war, a notion Charlotte declined as being but a 'lovely dream' (Holroyd, 442).

Dearest Charlotte

I am sorry you won't come to see Cliveden as I really think it would be better.

I only deserted Plymouth when I had to look after the Lord Mayor [Waldorf]. I have been down here a week and must now return to London for Tuesday and Wednesday.

Of course I will look after Jimmy Deacon. She is absolutely cracked. There is no chance of her getting it done so you need not worry about that!

I've had such an amusing letter from Jakie saying that it is raining, the food's beastly and an air raid's on and the noise too terrific, and that he has only had one pleasant day in a month when he went to Epsom to ride a horse, but that he is very lucky to be where he is – which amused me.

Our last letter from Bill was written August 29th. He is on leave at Mount Carmel for two weeks. I'll save his letter to read to you because it is very interesting – but when are we going to meet?

David's at Deal.

Plymouth is perfectly beautiful and very quiet and if you and G.B.S. won't come to Cliveden will you come there?

[Nancy Astor]

Jimmy Deacon is unidentified; and see Letter 79. **Jakie** Astor, who had once wanted to be a jockey, had joined the Life Guards. **Epsom** in Surrey is noted for its race track where the

Derby is run every June. **Bill** Astor, an intelligence officer, had been posted to Ismailia. Julius Caesar reputedly landed in 55 BC at **Deal** in Kent, where David Astor was with the marines building defences. Nancy's three Astor sons' exploits contrast with those of her other son, Bobbie Shaw, mentioned in the following letter.

79 / To Charlotte F. Shaw

Chalk Farm, Wrotham, Kent
19th October 1940

[TLU (c): Reading]

Robert 'Bobbie' Shaw had tried unsuccessfully to enlist in the Scots Greys regiment. Instead, he served in a barrage balloon squadron in Kent, where he had lived since 1931. He was wounded in less than heroic circumstances (which were revised when related to his mother): rather than being with his barrage squadron, Bobbie was in a pub when a bomb fell, killing all but himself and a few others. Nancy sent Charlotte further reports of Bobbie's progress on 2 and 7 November 1940 (Reading). Charlotte told Nancy that Shaw was 'like a lion ... He is working as hard as ever, & he has taken to lopping & pruning trees' (27 October 1940 letter quoted in Holroyd, 441–2).

Dearest Charlotte

I am down here with Bobbie who was wounded when a bomb fell killing all but one of the men who were with him. He had a baddish time, but is now infinitely better and out of danger, and I am much relieved.

On the very same night 4 St James' Square was bombed and partly burned out. We lost four or five rooms entirely but nothing important was seriously damaged except my bedroom. We are told that the structure is sound and the house can be restored. The terrible problem at the moment is that it is still pouring with water and the ceilings dropping, and we shall not be able to live in it for some time. Still, no one was hurt and we have much to be grateful for that the house stands at all. There were numerous fires right beside us that night and ours was best taken care of.

Yes, I did get the letter you sent to Jura. It was the message about Miss Deacon in Plymouth you wanted me to see. There is nothing to worry about. She is crazy and really 'cuts no ice' at all.

Cliveden is all ready for you – bombed or no. My advice to you is not to wait to be bombed out!!!

[Nancy Astor]

80 / To Nancy Astor   Ayot St Lawrence, Welwyn, Herts.
                                                    30th January 1941

[TLS: Reading, Holroyd (e), Letters]

*When Mrs Patrick Campbell was writing her autobiography (My Life and Some
Letters [1922]), Shaw wrote to Edith Lyttelton that she was 'bent on making a
sensational public appearance as my mistress ... No actress, it seems, can resist the
role of a grande amoureuse' (25 January 1922 letter, Churchill College, Cambridge). The publication of Mrs Campbell's will on 18 January 1941 raised a
similar spectre by including the provision 'It is my desire, should the copyright be
free or permission obtained, that the Bernard Shaw letters ... be published in their
proper sequence and not cut or altered in any way ... in an independent volume to
be entitled "The Love Letters of Bernard Shaw to Mrs Patrick Campbell" so that all
who read them will realise that the friendship was l'amité amoureuse' (Rattray,
267). In this letter Shaw is clearly apprehensive lest Charlotte see newspaper reports
of Mrs Campbell's wishes. Several people supported Mrs Campbell financially,
including Bridget Guinness. Nancy Astor and Edith Lyttelton both contributed to
her insurance premiums (Dent, 313–14), although Nancy decided in 1938 to
cease doing so because 'it would be throwing good money after bad' (31 May 1938
letter, Edith Lyttelton to Nancy [Reading]; 10 June letter, Nancy to Edith Lyttelton
[Reading]). The Shaw–Campbell correspondence was published eventually by
Alan Dent in 1952 as Bernard Shaw and Mrs Patrick Campbell: Their Correspondence.*

My dear Nancy

I put you off on Tuesday partly for your own sake. Calling here on your
way to Plymouth is much the same as calling at the North Pole on your
way to Monte Carlo. I enclose an itinerary to keep by you for future
excursions.

 Charlotte had better be left alone just now. She has had a bad return
of her lumbago and has been bedridden for weeks, well enough except
for the dread of bringing on the pain by moving about, and raging
because of the confinement and helplessness. Her nerves are all in rags;
but she is just beginning to venture on a little movement; and until she
has lost her dread of a return of the pains I dare not let her face the
excitement, however joyful, of a sudden visit from you. She will tell you
herself when she feels well enough to entertain you. At present the mere

suggestion of your coming sets her worrying. As Miss Patch is staying with us we have no spare room now. The village pub would not be good enough for you. You would be caught in the black-out and certainly killed. We cannot get the things you ought to have to eat. All nonsense, of course: but terrible to her in her present condition. A few days ago a friend of ours drove into an unlighted refuge at 35 miles an hour and smashed his car to pieces in the dark. Charlotte is convinced that if you could not get back by daylight the same would happen to you.

As to those letters, my press cuttings are carefully handpicked before they go upstairs, so nobody here except Miss Patch and myself is worried by them. The huge success of my correspondence with Ellen Terry was a tremendous temptation to Stella, who would have had to beg her bread but for the £500 a year left her by Bridget Guinness; but I was adamant as to their publication, though I reminded her that she could always sell the originals to private collectors. But she would neither do that nor divorce George, who offered her an alimony of £800 a year. When we are all dead the letters will help to pay for the education of her great grandchildren. She must have left plenty of others, the copyright of which will expire 50 years after the death of the writers. They will be available for publication on certain terms 25 years after.

A letter written by her to me just before her death began 'Dear dear Joey' and on the last day on which she was intelligible she said something about me; so there was no malice between us. Her doctor said he could cure her of her pneumonia – had cured her, in fact, but, said he, 'I cannot keep alive a woman who has no intention of living.'

Is it worth while to have been an enchantress when the charm no longer works? She had many gifts but no *savoir vivre*.

We have had no bombs here since the middle of November, when we had eight within a stone's throw. We are without any shelter or fire brigade or protection of any sort; but so far we are more frightened than hurt. We have not been in town for months. Miss Patch had to go up on Tuesday and walked into four alerts. At Whitehall Court we have had a window or two broken. We heard that No 4 had been hit, and we are now a bit anxious about Elliott Terrace, but hope that God will take care of his own.

G.B.S.

Christopher St John (Christabel Marshall, d. 1960) edited Shaw's **correspondence** with the actress Dame **Ellen Terry** (1847–1928) as *Ellen Terry and Bernard Shaw: A Correspondence* (1931). Mrs Patrick Campbell (née Beatrice **Stella** Tanner, 1865–1940) made her mark in *The Second Mrs Tanqueray* (1893) by Sir Arthur Wing Pinero (1855–1934), and later created Liza Doolittle in *Pygmalion* (1914). Her friend and benefactor had been **Bridget Guinness** (1871–1931). She had married **George** Cornwallis-West (1874–1951) in 1914. **No 4** was the Astors' home in St James's Square; **Elliott Terrace** was their home in Plymouth.

81 / To G. Bernard Shaw   [3 Elliott Terrace, The Hoe, Plymouth]
3rd February 1941

[TLU (c): Reading]

Nancy Astor's newsy letter here also reveals her ability to ignore the antagonism her actions could cause sometimes. She refers almost incidentally to seven broadcasts on the tradition of German militarism given by Sir Robert Vansittart on the BBC Overseas Programme, which were published as Black Record: Germans Past and Present *(1941). Nancy's question in the House of Commons about the propriety of serving civil servants publishing such a book provoked considerable hostility; she also thought there would be a 'lamentable effect' on anti-Nazi Germans in America whose support would be needed in the future (see Sykes, 432). Churchill replied simply and neutrally that Vansittart had received permission for his book (*The Times, *29 January 1941). In September 1942 Shaw locked horns with H.G. Wells when the latter resurrected 'Vansittartitis' in the columns of the* Tribune *(see Laurence, Agitations, 329–32).*

Dearest G.B.S.

I warn you I must come soon to see you even if I can't see Charlotte. I know exactly how she feels and I would not worry her for anything – but next week if it is humanly possible I must get down one afternoon and back again. If the roads are good I think I could manage it.

Waldorf and I came here on Thursday. Two alerts but no raids. Elliott Terrace is all right except for no hot water. The last bad blitz took most of the gas away. It's as cold as Christmas here but there's a lot to do and you would be pleased if you saw what a good Lord Mayor Waldorf is.

I am reading a book which I shall send on to you. David [Astor] gave it to Philip who read it at Lisbon. You can't think what a Press Philip got. I have had the Editorials from all over the States sent me. There is no getting round it – he did a great job.

Please look after yourself well. I could not bear the departure of another friend.

I am amused at what you say about the letters. Dear —— [Mrs Campbell] I am not surprised – did not want to live. With all of her gifts she had made a sad muddle of her life. Most enchantresses do. Poor D.D. Lyttelton will never get her Thousand Pounds back. I can afford to lose mine but for D.D. it is really a sad loss. She was so good to her.

Thank goodness you've got Miss Patch with you. I am keeping your instructions and if the worst comes to the worst I could spend the night at Hatfield House. If Michael [Astor] and his Unit of 5 Officers and 36 Men and about a dozen armoured cars arrive at Cliveden next Sunday for a week, I shan't be able to get down but if they don't I will be with you sometime next week. We are staying here until Thursday or Friday.

Did you read Vansittart's broadcast? It really was a disgrace, particularly from the point of view of infuriating the many Germans in America who are anti-Nazi. It seems a waste of money that we should pay him £3,000 a year for such stuff.

Please tell me what you are doing besides looking after Charlotte and yourself. Do you see anyone and are you writing anything?

I truly long to see you.

[Nancy Astor]

Refusing conventional medical attention, **Philip** Kerr died from uremia on 12 December 1940 in Washington, DC, while British Ambassador to the United States. **Hatfield House** in Hertfordshire was owned by James Gascoyne-Cecil, 4th Marquess of Salisbury (1861–1947) and, like Cliveden, was home to a military hospital during the war. Sir Robert Gilbert **Vansittart** (1881–1957), a Germanophobe, had been Under-secretary of State for Foreign Affairs (1930–8) and worked in foreign affairs until 1941, when he was created Baron Vansittart.

82 / To Nancy Astor   Ayot St Lawrence, Welwyn, Herts.
                                            14th February 1941
[ALCS: Reading]
The day before the date of this note Nancy Astor, accompanied by Thomas Jones, visited Shaw and the ailing Charlotte.

Great success. Patient much the better for it. Bless you.
                                            G.B.S.

83 / To G. Bernard Shaw   [*no address*]
                                          24th February 1941

[TLU (c): Reading]

Nancy Astor's comment here on the imminence of a blitz is a remarkable under-
statement. 'By the 20th March 1941 Plymouth had had 37 raids and hundreds of
alerts' (Sykes, 432). March and May 1941 saw official visits to Plymouth by King
George VI and Queen Elizabeth (1900–2002) and by Winston Churchill in efforts
to boost public morale (Sykes, 433–9).

Dear G.B.S.

It was such a pleasure seeing you and Charlotte and I am glad the visit
was a success. Tom Jones and I are determined to come another time.

I was relieved to see how much better Charlotte was but I expect she
has her ups and downs.

I long to get you to Plymouth. Never have you seen such glorious
weather as we are having, but I dare not ask you here as they seem to
expect a blitz any minute.

                                          [Nancy Astor]

84 / To Charlotte F. Shaw   [*no address*]
                                          12th July 1941

[TLU (c): Reading]

As a result of visiting the Shaws, Nancy Astor was troubled by their feebleness: 'I
went to see G.B.S. and Charlotte and found them so feeble and Miss Patch says
they must get away for a fortnight, so I am having them here on the 14th. It is not
easy, but I don't see anything else for them – hotels are impossible' (25 July 1941
letter to D.D. Lyttelton [Reading]; see also Letter 89). So Nancy invited them to
Cliveden, where they stayed 12–30 August 1941. However, Nancy was not to be
there to take care of them; instead, she entrusted them to her niece, the actress Joyce
Grenfell (1910–79): 'I was told by Aunt Nancy to keep an eye on them, take him
for walks and see that she was kept happy. Aunt Nancy herself was having a short
break up on the Island of Jura' (Grenfell, Joyce, 160, and see Letter 90).

Dearest Charlotte

Would you and G.B.S. come to Cliveden August 12th? I will take you as paying guests and make you pay through the nose! I do hope you will do this and I think you would if you realised how impossible it is stopping in hotels.

You will have complete quiet and do exactly as you like, within limitations. I cannot promise that to G.B.S. as he might turn it into a Summer School for Bolshies!

Yours

[Nancy Astor]

85 / To Charlotte F. Shaw   [Cliveden, Taplow, Bucks.]

16th July 1941

[TLU (c): Reading]

Nancy Astor's concern for a wounded soldier in the wartime hospital set up at Cliveden illustrates her compassionate trait.

Dear Charlotte

I am delighted you are coming. We may have to make it 14th instead of 12th August, but I will let you know definite dates later on.

You may have to arrange to have eggs sent over, as we find them a little difficult and I know G.B.S. eats a lot of eggs.

I am sure all will be well, and I am engaging a man to wait on you, and you will be no trouble, but a great source of pleasure and 'income' to me!!

Will you ask G.B.S. if he could possibly send a copy of 'St Joan' to Sapper Duncan who is in Ward 10, No. 5 Canadian General Hospital Taplow. I was talking to him today, and he would so appreciate it.

[Nancy Astor]

Sapper Duncan is unidentified.

86 / To Nancy Astor   Ayot St Lawrence, Welwyn, Herts.

19th July 1941

[TLT: Reading, Halperin (e), Holroyd (e), Sykes (e)]

Shaw's protestations over not supplying an autographed copy of Saint Joan *to one of the Canadian soldiers (Sapper Duncan) were spurious: in her undated letter to*

Nancy Astor (Reading), Charlotte Shaw reassured Nancy that the soldier would get his copy. However, Shaw's concerns about his teeth were genuine: while at Cliveden Shaw declined to do a radio program, according to Joyce Grenfell, 'because he says he's too old; which being translated means his teeth don't fit and make rude noises that would be particularly exaggerated on the air and his vanity wouldn't stand for such a thing. And I think he's right.' She also noted: 'Both the Shaws take trouble over their appearances and are well-rewarded by looking pretty and soignée. She is very bent now and a bit deaf and loses interest quite easily. He is less combative but still as anxious to be naughty and contrary as ever.' Both still provided 'stimulating' company (Grenfell, Darling, 227–8). Writing on 17 August, Thomas Jones (Diary, 490–1) was more judgmental: '[Shaw] no longer shocks with surprise except perhaps by his extravagant faith in the might and wisdom of Stalin ... It is amusing to hear him quite seriously concern himself about the financial future of the Shaws and the Astors ... and he is also writing a book on modern politics. But I'm sure he has nothing new to say.'

Dearest Nancy

Dont bother about eggs: I loathe eggs and never eat them when I can get anything else. People are always trying to stuff me with them in the belief that I must die if I dont eat something that is not vegetarian.

As to your Canadian soldier I dare not give him a book or an autograph. I should have the whole lot of them down on me clamoring for autographs. As it is, they stop me in the streets. What I will do is to inscribe a copy of St Joan to you. You can then inscribe it to the Canadian, who will have the autograph of a Viscountess to shew as well as mine. But tell him that it is a unique treasure, as I am absolutely unapproachable by autograph hunters.

We are not stuck on the 12th: the 14th or 15th would suit us better if we might stay until the 30th (Saturday) so as to give our people a couple of days to travel in. We should clear out in time to let in a weekender.

We shall be a horrid imposition. Ten years ago I could still earn my keep by entertaining your guests by my celebrated performances as G.B.S. Now if I attempt to talk my teeth fall out. I am a decrepit old bore; and you must hide me in a corner of your house as best you can or your friends will begin to shun Cliveden. You have not the faintest notion of what it is to be 85 and three quarters dead. Charlotte is still a bit of an

96

invalid, and cannot walk. She cannot even ride one of Waldorf's horses, though she could perhaps manage an elephant (if you have such a thing) with a very comfortable howdah.

This is the explanation of my hesitation to accept invitations which I should once have jumped at. By the end of August you may be saying Never Again.

your quondam
G.B.S.

87 / To G. Bernard Shaw   [*no address*]
22nd July 1941

[TLU (c): Reading]

Dear G.B.S.

All right, you can certainly come on 14th August. That will suit me just as well.

I don't care how many times your teeth fall into the soup! I will make out I don't see, and when you have put them in again, you can resume the conversation!!

[Nancy Astor]

88 / To Nancy Astor   Ayot St Lawrence, Welwyn, Herts.
25th July 1941

[ALCS: Reading, Holroyd (e)]
It would seem that, while her house at St James's Square was out of commission, Nancy Astor had asked Shaw if she might use his Whitehall Court apartment, or at least store some belongings there.

I havnt the least objection to your moving your few sticks in; but I protest strenuously against your moving me out. It shews a deficient sense of values.

However, we can manage it exactly to suit you by putting in a day or two at Whitehall, where I am paying £800 a year for nothing but the ground landlord's drinks & taxes. I am living on my capital and will end in the workhouse if the war lasts.

They have sent me the wrong book for your soldier. I am ordering another.

G.B.S.

Dont sleep on the Hoe. I shall be 85 tomorrow.

We are on the most cordial terms with the Maiskys; so that is all right.

Ivan M. **Maisky** (1884–1975) was the Soviet ambassador in London (1932–43).

89 / To Nancy Astor   Ayot St Lawrence, Welwyn, Herts.

2nd August 1941

[TLS: Reading]

Blanche Patch clearly had an active role in arranging the Shaws' visit to Cliveden, although there was also a measure of self-interest.

Dear Lady Astor

The plot worked splendidly. I could see that they were both rather frightened when they heard of that raid last Sunday night, and then your letter came on Tuesday morning and there was a feeling of relief in the air.

I am sure it will be good for *him* to have to see more people and not be able to write these interminable letters in shorthand which I have to transcribe. I always think it is a sign that a holiday is needed when people refuse to stop working. And in his case he *had* to stop when they used to go on those three months cruises.

Yours sincerely
Blanche Patch

90 / To Charlotte F. Shaw   [*no address*]

13th September 1941

[TLU (c): Reading]

Nancy Astor's inconsequential reference to Waldorf's health belies the fact that she may have played a role, albeit minor, in bringing on the heart attack Waldorf suffered during the summer of 1941. Nancy had wanted some chocolates that had been sent from the United States for the people of Plymouth. When Waldorf refused to allow this, Nancy flew into a rage, was publicly rude to Waldorf, and declared

she would not accompany him on a vacation to Rock, Cornwall. Shortly after-
wards Waldorf had a heart attack; so Nancy relented and accompanied him to
Rock, but only for a day. Later they went on holiday to Jura (Sykes, 444–5).

Dearest Charlotte

We returned after a rather terrifying journey for at one moment we
thought the fog would hold us permanently on the Island of Islay.

The holiday did Waldorf a great deal of good and I enjoyed being away
from the telephone but otherwise as you know, it's not my idea of a
holiday.

I hear from everyone that you both looked better when you left us and
what I hope it means is that you will come back again soon. I am trying to
keep your rooms for you but it may be difficult.

I had three busy days in London, mostly about Nursery Schools and
women's work, and we came here Wednesday. Please let me know how
you both are.

I haven't seen G.B.S.'s article about the Webbs but will try to get it.

I saw Maisky last week and he is blooming: gives a party every day.

I also saw H.G. Wells at the Authors' Luncheon and he asked affectionately after you. He's a strong-looking old sinner if ever there lived
one.

[Nancy Astor]

The Isle of **Islay** lies southwest of Jura, where the Astors had again vacationed at Tarbert
Lodge. A local ferry sails between Jura and Islay from where the mainland ferry departs.
Shaw's **article** on Beatrice and Sydney Webb was 'Two Friends of the Soviet Union,' *Picture
Post* 12 (1941), 20–3.

91 / To Charlotte F. Shaw   Cliveden, Taplow, Bucks.
                                                    3rd January 1942

[TLT: BL 56494, f. 146]
Nancy Astor repeats her apparent indifference to Waldorf's health (see Letters 90,
92).

Dearest Charlotte

Waldorf has had to go to Jura as he has not really recovered from that attack he had; that has made it impossible for me to get to you, and I am off to Plymouth to do both our jobs, today.

I wont be back altogether until about [the] 20th, and I vow I will get to you after that.

Mr Brockington told me he spent a happy day with you, which I am delighted to hear, and he gave such a good account of you both.

Please ask G.B.S. to write me a line to Plymouth, giving me full details about yourselves. I will be there until next Thursday.

I return here for that weekend, as it is the boys' last few days here with their Unit. Then I go back to Plymouth on the following Tuesday and stop there for about a week, and I think that brings me to [the] 20th.

I am just off, so forgive my not signing this.

with love,

p.p. NANCY

Leonard W. **Brockington** (1888–1966) was a Canadian lawyer, chairman of the Canadian Broadcasting Corporation in 1936, and adviser to the Canadian government (1939–42). Later he was to upset Shaw, at least temporarily (see Letter 198).

92 / To Charlotte F. Shaw   Cliveden, Taplow, Bucks.
                                         2nd February 1942

[TLS: BL 56494, f. 157]

Once more, in her typically forceful fashion, Nancy Astor was attempting to arrange a holiday for the Shaws, this time at Mullion in southern Cornwall. Charlotte replied on 6 February 1942 (Reading) that they would think about her proposal.

Dearest Charlotte

Waldorf is really better for the first time for two years, and now he will be able to do his part at Plymouth, and I cannot tell you what a relief that is to me.

I still insist on Mullion in April! You could take a night train – I will go with you – and get out at Truro, and it is then about 3/4 hour's drive to the hotel.

Once you get there I think you may want to stop many many months, as it is really a unique place, and the only one in England that I know of. So I shall arrange rooms provisionally for Easter, or around there.

I hoped to get to you this week, but my chauffeur has got the 'flu, and the roads are absolutely unbearable, and I may have to go to Plymouth on Monday next.

I hate writing this, as I truly long to see you both, but I am sure you will understand.

Tell G.B.S. to write to me for a change – the lazy fellow! What about his new Book? The snow is like it was when you were both here years ago. I wish you were both snowed up here now – with much love my dearest Charlotte & GBS

Nancy

Shaw's **new book** was *Everybody's Political What's What?* which he did not complete until 23 November 1943. Nancy thought the title 'is appalling, is too long. Couldn't it be "Saucy Sue" or something short and snappy, or "Dumb Girls' Guide [to] Politics"' (7 November 1941 letter to Charlotte Shaw [Reading]).

93 / **To Nancy Astor**   Ayot St Lawrence, Welwyn, Herts.
4th March 1942

[TLS: Reading, Holroyd (e)]

On the afternoon of 19 February 1942 Nancy Astor and Thomas Jones visited the Shaws at Ayot. Blanche Patch 'had taken a day off ... much to Nancy's relief, who thinks she is a tyrant and probably is a very efficient caretaker. G.B.S. still retains great vitality, dresses perfectly, talks whenever he is given a chance, and often when he is not. Nancy and he both want to talk at once ... The two Shaws are enormously pleased with the Russian advance ... Of course all talks with G.B.S. lead sooner or later to money and taxation. He growled that the £29,000 which he made out of the Pygmalion *film had all been taken from him by our tax collectors' (Jones,* Diary, *496–7). Talk must also have turned to Nancy's proposed Cornwall holiday because on 25 February she wrote to Colonel Francis F. Oates, the proprietor of a hotel in St Just, Cornwall: 'I am very anxious to bring Mr & Mrs Bernard Shaw down sometime about the middle of April. Do you think it would be possible for them to have two adjoining bedrooms, a sitting room and bathroom. I would go with them, and I should just want one room' (Reading). As a result of this letter from Shaw, Nancy wrote again to Oates on 9 March (ibid.) cancelling the arrangements for April but hoping May might be a possibility.*

My dear Nancy

You are of course quite right about us two needing a change. We do; and if we were ten years younger we should be off like a shot. But at 152 years of age – a condition which you are happily unable to conceive – the exertion of a move has to be set against its benefit, and the balance is always changing in favor of keeping quiet. Charlotte has had a return of her lumbago: her back has been pretty tiresome this past week. I have moments in which I feel nearly – only nearly – equal to anything; but I know I should fall asleep after packing two pair of socks.

In short, I see no prospect of our being well enough to dream of travelling to Lands End as soon as the beginning of April. Charlotte never contemplated anything sooner than the beginning of May, even under your powerful immediate personal influence.

As to St Just, nothing on earth would keep you there for three days; and without you we should simply go mad or go home. We might as well go to St Albans, which is only half an hour off.

I write in haste to catch the village post; so this is not to count as a letter.

G.B.S.

94 / To Charlotte F. Shaw   3 Elliott Terrace, The Hoe, Plymouth
19th March 1942

[TLS: BL 56494, f. 158–9]
Although much of this letter is typed, there are lengthy holograph additions with concomitant illegibility. In response to Nancy's importuning invitations (which continued through April), Charlotte replied on 25 March 1942 (Reading) that she was unable to travel but would like to do so later.

Dearest Charlotte

I am still hoping about Cornwall in May but that is some time ahead.

I am not at all certain that a visit to London would not do you both good but I could easily look after you at Cliveden in April if you felt inclined to come just for a week-end. It is so easy, getting in your motor and getting out, and you know what good care we take of you. So please think over these things.

I am here until April 2nd but just go up for two days – Tuesday and Wednesday – for meetings and a wedding at Cliveden, & return here again.

It is quite true – there were two letters: one from St Just and one from Mullion. I want a lot of strings to my bow and above all I want to get you away.

April weather here, sun and showers.

Tell G.B.S. I think I like Major Barbara better even than Pygmalion and thought it brilliantly done. We saw it at the Hospital and the Canadians thoroughly enjoyed it.

The young King of Jugo Slavia comes down to take the salute on Saturday. I must tell you about him when I see you; an amusing lad but very young for his age and very revolutionary.

Yesterday I visited a modernist exhibition and I bought some photographs of the paintings. There is a Sickert and there is G.B.S. helping either you or me on to the ice. Tell him it is exactly his leg, whiskers and all!

You will be proud to see how Plymouth is carrying on. How I wish you could. The Harbour was so lovely today. I wish each day was 12 hours longer. I never seem to get through. Waldorf fairly well not [*illegible*] & I should like to get him away some where with you two. Much love dearest Charlotte. Consider coming to Cliveden – or go [as well?] to London. Get away you must. Much love & please take great care. You are very [precious?] to me – in fact I [*illegible*] to you and *GBS*. You may not think it but I do. I will try to ring you up from London.

[*illegible*]

Nancy

[*illegible*] GBS for me.

The film of ***Major Barbara***, directed by Gabriel Pascal (1894–1954) and starring (Sir) Rex Harrison (1908–90) and Wendy Hiller, had premiered in London on 7 April 1941. (On Pascal's films of Shaw's plays, see Dukore, passim.) Nancy Astor personally arranged the showing of films for the troops at the Canadian Hospital at Cliveden (see Thornton, 308–11). **Young King** Peter II of Yugoslavia (1923–70; reigned 1934–45) had fled to London when Hitler invaded his country in 1941. Born in Munich, Walter **Sickert** (1860–1942) was a naturalized British impressionist painter who liked to sketch London theatres and their audiences.

95 / To Nancy Astor   Ayot St Lawrence, Welwyn, Herts.
9th April 1942

[ALCS: Reading]

Charlotte's poor health recurs as a topic in Letters 95–102. Eventually a corset was prescribed as a means of providing support to her back.

Charlotte has ricked herself again and had two days in which any movement gives her horrid pain. She is now in bed. She is not worse 'in herself'; but she is quite unfit to travel. This is what makes it so impossible for us to make any plans that would take us away from home or even to London. A change would be good for her one way, and in another possibly kill her.

However, we ought both to be killed. Our age is ridiculous.

The Pope has paired Japan by receiving China as well. Otherwise the Church would cease to be Catholic.

You and Waldorf must need a holiday far more than we do. I certainly dont need one until my book is finished.

G.B.S.

After the Japanese attack on Pearl Harbor on 7 December 1941, **Pope** Pius XII established diplomatic relations with both Japan and China in an effort to gain support for peace. In March and April 1942 Chinese and Japanese ambassadors were appointed to the Holy See. Shaw was continuing to work slowly on his **book**, *Everybody's Political What's What?*

96 / To Nancy Astor   Ayot St Lawrence, Welwyn, Herts.
16th April 1942

[ALCS: Reading, Holroyd (e)]

Charlotte is decidedly better. She is still in bed; but she is no longer crazy with pain and despair, and can be talked to reasonably. Tomorrow – or next day at latest – she will, I hope, be up and about.

It has been a diabolical attack; but the acute stage is over.

Pardon a war economy postcard.

Patch has been away since Monday. She returns tomorrow. Except the maids she is the only one of us who isnt deaf: a great point in her favor at the telephone.

G.B.S.

97 / To Nancy Astor   Ayot St Lawrence, Welwyn, Herts.
22nd April 1942

[ALCS: Reading]

Your letters please Charlotte greatly; but your plans are impossible. Her case is graver than you think. Her spine has collapsed to such an extent that she cannot stand without hurting herself unbearably by a one-sided stoop that brings her left ribs down on her haunch bone. We are ordering a corset that will hold up her shoulders; and if this fails she will be permanently bedridden, and I shall have to find – God knows where! – a resident nurse; for Mrs Higgs who is 75, will collapse too if she has to nurse Charlotte and our ration books as well.

Our osteopath was here this morning. He says nothing can be done except try the corset. He understands what has happened, and that she is beyond manipulation.

Do you know of a C.S. [Christian Scientist] practitioner who can renew old bones?

Forgive my bothering you with all this; but you had better know.

G.B.S.

The **osteopath** is unidentified.

98 / To Nancy Astor   Ayot St Lawrence, Welwyn, Herts.
24th April 1942

[ALCS: Reading]

Charlotte's amazing powers of recuperation are now asserting themselves. She is well enough today to be terrified by the suggestion of a nurse. Our little staff in our little house is willing to work 48 hours a day to stave off such a calamity. I have had to assure them all, Charlotte included, on my honor, that there is no immediate danger of a new arrival. So let it be between ourselves for the moment that if the worst comes to the worst, and the strait waistcoat proves a failure (she is to be measured for it on Monday) I shall turn to you for your dearly kind help.

I am sending you a book about my immoral youth. The first few pages will be enough for you.

G.B.S.

The book about Shaw's **immoral youth** might have been *Shaw Gives Himself Away: An Autobiographical Miscellany*, published in a limited edition by the Gregynog Press in 1939. It included a revised and abridged preface to *Immaturity*. Shaw revised the miscellany as *Sixteen Self Sketches*, which was published in 1949 (see Laurence, *Shaw*, 1: 235–7, 258, and Jones, *Diary*, 371–2).

99 / To Nancy Astor   Ayot St Lawrence, Welwyn, Herts.

30th April 1942

[ALS: Reading, Sykes]

An anonymous person sent Lord Berners (Gerald Hugh Tyrwhitt-Wilson, 1883– 1950), composer, novelist, and painter, an unidentified book about Christian Science that he assumed came from Nancy Astor, to whom he wrote and com- plained. After telling Shaw, Nancy received an apology from Berners, who asked her in return how she might have felt had she received a Roman Catholic tract (Nancy's antipathy towards Roman Catholicism was notorious). She replied to Berners on 8 May 1942 (Reading): 'Certainly the hatchets will disappear. Your reference to Margot [Countess of Oxford and Asquith, 1894–1945] sending me an R.C. pamphlet did the trick! / That book could never have been by anybody who knew anything about Christian Science. In fact it must have been written by its bitterest enemies.'

We have known B[erners] for years and years. He is no ordinary peer: he writes, paints, and composes music quite outstandingly, and is enough of a good fellow to be friends with us.

It would be a misfortune to have him feud with you merely because some C.S. zealot has sent him a book which he supposed came from you. I am (rashly) sending him a line to say that this must not be, as you two are to my knowledge deserving persons in spite of your unfortunate rank.

Charlotte is much better, and horrified at the notion of your trying to keep her alive superfluously, when Waldorf needs all your care with half his career still before him.

You exaggerate the value of the Christlike. There are lots of them about, mostly even more futile than I. You yourself have quite as much Christ in you as is good for you.

In great haste –

G.B.S.

100 / To Nancy Astor   Ayot St Lawrence, Welwyn, Herts.

9th May 1942

[ALCS: Reading]

Shaw was always concerned about financial matters and here presumably refers to
some tax-avoidance scheme with regard to his American royalties.

Dillon's proposal would land me in prison for conspiracy to defraud the
British Treasury. My plays earned £20,000 in America last year. Of this
America took £13,500 in tax; Kingsley Wood took £6340 on the balance;
and I was left to starve on £160.

If I had, for the sake of a [ge]sture, given the whole £20,000 to
America, I should have defrauded the British Treasury of £6340, and got
credit for a £20,000 gesture which had cost me only £160.

I have explained this to Katharine, and told Clarence, who had no
right to drag you into the affair (what a chance for the Labor Left to ask
questions!) to – in effect – go to hell.

Charlotte, still mending but very infirm pending the arrival of the
corset, proposes, if it proves a success, to test herself by a change to
London before venturing on Cliveden. Dont for your life mention the
hospital to her: she would see herself in a ward with 50 soldiers and
would die on the spot. She does not want to let you burden yourself with
an invalid.

G.B.S.

Clarence **Dillon** (1882–1979), an American investment banker with reputedly one of the
keenest minds on Wall Street, had been introduced to the Astors by Nancy's sister Irene
Gibson (see Perez, 126). Sir **Kingsley Wood** (1891–1943) was a Conservative MP who held
several ministerial posts, including Chancellor of the Exchequer (1940–3). He died
suddenly on the day his 'pay as you earn' (PAYE) tax scheme was announced (it was
implemented in 1944). **Katharine** is unidentified.

101 / To Nancy Astor   Ayot St Lawrence, Welwyn, Herts.

25th May 1942

[TLS: Reading, Masters (e), Sykes (e)]

The corset for Charlotte's as yet undiagnosed back ailment helped to relieve her
discomfort somewhat, although it required adjustments (see Letter 102). When
Shaw declined to speak about Stalin, Sir Malcolm Darling (1880–1969), with the

BBC's Hindustani service, wrote promptly to Nancy Astor asking her to write some 1500 words on Stalin, which would then be translated into Hindustani for broadcasting. Nancy replied to Sir Malcolm on 1 June 1942 (Reading): 'I am so sorry I could not possibly write about Stalin. G.B.S. knows that he could, and he wont. / We only saw Stalin [in 1931] for about two hours, and he asked us as many questions as we asked him.'

My dear Nancy

The corset has been so far a success that Charlotte wears it and has actually taken some turns in the garden with it. This is only a try-on: possibly when it is finally fitted she will be quite reconciled to it.

She is desperately tired of being ill and not in the least resigned to it. She must have fits of feeling that something ought to be done about it, and that nobody is doing anything. But what can we do? She has no faith in any doctor within reach; and I know too well that there is no doctor anywhere who can cure lumbago and old age. The less her pain, the greater her impatience. However, her worst bodily pains have ceased; and her mental rebellion against being immobilized and unable to go to London is congenital and can't be cured.

By the way she always asks how Waldorf is; and I encourage this anxiety, as it takes her mind off herself.

The times are changing with a vengeance. Cripps, the Leader of the House, makes speeches which might be made by Stalin; and The Times leaders on them next day approve of every word of them. The Archbishop of Canterbury comes out with a Penguin volume advocating a full Socialist program. Nobody expresses the least surprise.

I am asked to speak over the world wireless on Stalin. I refused, but suggested that they should ask you; but this was only to get rid of them: I dont advise you to. Hesketh Pearson, in his biography of me which I have just read in proof, reports you as saying that Stalin never smiled and was grim. This is rubbish: Stalin may not have smiled; but he laughed repeatedly with the greatest goodhumor [*sic*]; and this was evidently his habit. However, Pearson quotes my account of how completely you bowled Stalin over when you attacked him about the children. I was very favorably impressed by the way – after the first shock of incredulous amazement with which he received your assertion that he didnt know how to treat children (the Bolsheviks are specially proud of their putting the children before everything) – he saw that you had really something to say; listened like a lamb; and not only took your address, which seemed mere politeness, but did exactly what you told him.

But what will happen when he licks the Germans for us? Victory will at once end the truce between the Bolsheviks and Vansittart, Winston, Laval, the old Tories, the plutocratic Liberals, and our suburban snobs. If the defeat and extinction of Hitler is followed, as it well may be, by the relapse of Germany into plutocracy, our whole blessed reaction will try to combine with Germany and Italy against the U.S.S.R.; and they will have their way unless our Labor people make it clear that they will face a civil war rather than fight Russia. This situation will be the same in the U.S.A., France and Italy. The promised new order about which we are all prating may be a new world war. However, I shall be dead then. *Après moi le déluge!* Which side will you take?

I have a lot more to say – about nothing. I really must confine myself to postcards.

G.B.S.

Sir Stafford **Cripps** (1889–1952), Beatrice Webb's nephew, was elected a Labour MP in 1931 and served in several government posts including Leader of the House, minister of aircraft production, and Chancellor of the Exchequer (1947–50) in the post-war Labour government. William Temple (1881–1944) became **Archbishop of Canterbury** in 1942 and wrote the Penguin Books Special no. 104, *Christianity and Social Order* (1942). **Hesketh Pearson** reported that Nancy told him: 'Stalin is a quiet, dark-eyed person, well-behaved and very grim. He did not smile once while we were with him.' He continued: 'It was Lady Astor, and she alone, who got the better of Stalin. She told him that the Soviet did not know how to treat children ... [Stalin] soon guessed that this feminine tornado had perhaps something to teach him' (Pearson, 329–30). Pierre **Laval** (1883–1945) was Premier of France (1931–2, 1935–6) and head of the Vichy government (1942–4). He collaborated with the Germans in order to stem what otherwise, he believed, would be the spread of Bolshevism; his collaboration resulted in his execution in October 1945.

102 / To Nancy Astor   Ayot St Lawrence, Welwyn, Herts.
                                                      7th June 1942

[ALCS: Reading]

The corset has gone back for further adjustment under the direction of the osteopath; and Charlotte, deprived of it, is a collapsed wreck. When it comes back, it will, I hope, be more effective than before. She misses it so much that it was evidently useful as far as it went. But Charlotte is still far from being movable; Cliveden is out of the question for the moment; and she insists on my telling you so lest you should reserve rooms for us and miss some less troublesome guests. We are both only fit for the infirmary at present. The day before yesterday I got a touch of the sun and was drunkenly giddy for 24 hours. All right now. You too, I hope, after Cornwall.

G.B.S.

103 / To Nancy Astor   Ayot St Lawrence, Welwyn, Herts.
11th July 1942

[ALS: Reading, Holroyd (e)]

The Shaws paid what was to be their final visit to Cliveden from 21 July to 14 August 1942. (Interestingly, after Charlotte's death and despite repeated invitations from Nancy Astor, Shaw never stayed again at Cliveden. Indeed, he only ever stayed there in Charlotte's company.) During their visit both were examined thoroughly by doctors at the Canadian military hospital at Cliveden, who diagnosed Charlotte's ailment as osteitis deformans *(Paget's disease), rather than the earlier diagnoses of lumbago, rheumatism, or fibrositis: 'We were both vetted in a thoroughly businesslike manner ... Charlotte, much bowed by her* osteitis deformans, *and crawling about with difficulty and sometimes in pain, was pronounced incurable at her age. I was passed sound in wind and limb; so when I go I shall probably go all at once' (letter to Beatrice Webb quoted in Henderson, 870; see also Laurence, Letters, 634).*

Dearest Nancy

We are arranging to come to Cliveden on the 21st and leave for London on the 14th of August. If we hear nothing to the contrary we shall take this as settled.

Should we die on your hands, which may happen at any moment now, ask [Edwin] Lee to have us cremated. I think I had better deposit a sum with him in case.

Our ashes can be scattered on your favorite flower bed, or put into on[e] of the great urns on the lawn.

always your devoted
G. Bernard Shaw

After their respective deaths, Charlotte and Shaw were cremated at Golders Green crematorium. Ultimately their **ashes** were mixed together on 23 November 1950 and scattered in the grounds at Ayot (see also Letters 165, 167).

104 / To Nancy Astor   Ayot St Lawrence, Welwyn, Herts.
16th July 1942

[ALS: Reading, Sykes]

This is apparently the last letter Charlotte Shaw wrote to Nancy Astor; no subsequent letters have been located.

Nancy – dear darling I do love you. No one but you could possibly have done all this so beautifully & *happily* – I am so looking forward to getting to Cliveden and you!

The nurse will give me courage as I am rather anxious – it will be in London I shall really want her – after Cliveden – to trot about with me & it will be good to get to know her first at Cliveden.

Remember Whitehall Court is there all the time if you want to get rid of us.

Ever
Charlotte

105 / To Nancy Astor   Ayot St Lawrence, Welwyn, Herts.
17th July 1942

[ALS: Reading]

Shaw wrote this pro forma letter for Nancy Astor to hand to her butler, Edwin Lee, to eliminate any difficulties over his dietary requirements during his stay at Cliveden.

Dear Lady Astor

Just a line to say that the usual vegetarian supply of maccaroni, rice, haricots, eggs, is no longer necessary, and will be wasted if laid in.

I now live on bannock bread (sent to me daily by the Army & Navy Stores) and marmite, which I carry about with me. The rest of my meal is ordinary vegetables as for everyone else. I dont even need oatmeal, as I carry a special breakfast food which requires no cooking as well as the marmite.

In short, the chef need make absolutely no special provision for me. He will sleep all the better. I bring my own iron ration.

faithfully

G. Bernard Shaw

Bannock bread is a round flat unleavened loaf made from oats or barley. '100% vegetarian' **marmite** is a salty-tasting yeast extract used, among other things, as a spread on bread.

106 / To Nancy Astor   Cliveden, Taplow, Bucks.
                                                                 22nd July 1942

[ALS: Reading]

Joyce Grenfell was again on hand to entertain the Shaws at Cliveden: '[Charlotte] is very frail this year and bent. He is younger and very much on the spot, I thought. His teeth fit less well than they might and he rattles them ferociously at meals and in excited conversation ... She is gentle and sweet and has the only really green eyes I've ever seen. Must have been a great charmer in the old days. Still has it now' (Grenfell, Darling, *261–2). Shaw's last natural tooth was extracted on 27 October 1945 (Laurence,* Letters, *757). Nancy also tried to bully Thomas Jones into seeing the Shaws at Cliveden and was truculent when he failed to comply: 'I was horrified at your not coming down to see G.B.S. and Charlotte. It has done them good, but somehow I don't expect her back again. You knew they were coming, and you failed me completely, and not for the first time!' (12 August 1942 letter, NLW, Class Q, vol. 2, f. 65).*

Dearest Nancy

Here we are, settled in, and both of us much the better for the change. The drive from Ayot took only 66 minutes; and Charlotte did not turn a hair. I slept here tremendously. Your people received us with enthusiasm; and Miss Crowley (is that her name?) is a success.

Altogether it looks as if you may have some difficulty in getting us out of Cliveden.

Waldorf seems at the top of his form. Joyce assisted last night at dinner.

So all is well.

G.B.S.

Miss Crowley is unidentified; she may have been the nurse mentioned in Letter 104.

107 / To Nancy Astor   Ayot St Lawrence, Welwyn, Herts.

17th August 1942

[ALCS: Reading, Holroyd (e)]

We are safe back in our house, which we find surprisingly small after Cliveden. For half Saturday I felt almost as tired as I did when I landed at Harwich from the Moscow trip; but it passed off. The place is strangely still and dull: we miss your tempestuous presence. Somehow this time I got hold of Cliveden – or did Cliveden get hold of me? – more completely than ever before.

I stole a book from your study, but will return it when I have finished it.

Charlotte is none the worse, and looks better. My mother's half sister's daughter, Judy Musters, has just arrived in high spirits, her ailing mother and husband having just died and set her free. She is a darling, and has no children. Miss P[atch] is holidaying in her hotel in London as her numerous friends all over England are servantless, and Blanche has no taste for housekeeping or maiding.

That is all my news.

G.B.S.

Georgina 'Judy' Musters (née Gillmore, 1885–1974) was Shaw's cousin and his secretary (1907–12) and later substituted occasionally for Blanche Patch. She married Harold Chaworth Musters (1871?-1942) in 1912. After Shaw's death she conducted a lengthy and very interesting correspondence (Reading) with Nancy Astor that contains extensive references to Shaw.

108 / To Nancy Astor   Ayot St Lawrence, Welwyn, Herts.

28th August 1942

[ALS: Reading]

James J. 'Judy' Judge (c. 1868–c. 1953), a Plymouth journalist, was a frequent visitor at Cliveden. He often wrote Nancy poems and took photographs of the various events at Cliveden. Shaw here acknowledges some photographs Judge had sent him. 'Jake' Astor, now a major, had been involved in August in the badly planned Dieppe raid in which many Canadians were killed attempting to storm the beach (see Jones, Diary, 503).

Nancy asthore   .

Fill in J. Judge's address on the enclosed envelope and post it for me after looking at the contents.

Judy [Musters] leaves on Monday: everyone brokenhearted. B.P. [Blanche Patch] returns Tuesday: Charlotte fractious. No other news.

Now that Jake is safe back it is as well that he was there. We brought him better luck than the Kent lad [Bobbie Shaw].

G.B.S.

109 / To Nancy Astor   [Ayot St Lawrence, Welwyn, Herts.]

[c. September 1942]

[ALS: Reading]

Dearest Nancy

I took the enclosed to remind me of Cliveden. You can use them as postcards to people when you must write and have nothing to say. That is my own situation at present. I am slaving away at my book; and one day is like the one before, only shorter. Breakfast to lunch, work. Lunch to tea, sleep and deal with the morning's letters. Tea to dinner, saw logs in the garden. Dinner to bed, read and listen to the war news. Germans proceeding according to plan: Russians fighting stubbornly. Always stubbornly. None of our aircraft missing until the figures for the month contradict the figures for the day. German hawhaw propaganda voiced by Irishmen and so stupidly provocative that it is probably paid for by the M. of I. [Ministry of Information] as well as by Goebbels. Irish 'traitors' are first rate double-crossers. Stalin's brain the only one in Europe in office: impresses Beaverbrook as it impressed me. Raid on a town in the south west: little damage and few casualties. Yes; but the S.W. means Plymouth; and Nancy is in Plymouth. Hope she doesnt sleep in Elliott Terrace: the easiest target in England.

Charlotte no worse than at Cliveden. Dreadfully bored by the village: longs for London: husband doesnt care if he never saw London again: finds Ayot and Cliveden much better to work in. Patient Patch does my business, types my shorthand for the printer, fills up all chinks in the housekeeping, knits for the soldiers and makes soft dolls for the Red

Cross, and knows more about everybody in the village than I learned in 35 years.

Second title for the book MACCHIAVELLI MODERNIZED. Ha! ha! ha!

Joyce [Grenfell] as your understudy did her level best. Everybody made much of us.

G.B.S.

The Anglo-American William Joyce (1906–46), known as Lord **Haw Haw**, broadcast propaganda on behalf of the Germans for which he was hanged as a British traitor, although he tried to claim American citizenship (he had been born in Brooklyn, New York, to an English mother and an Irish father). Joseph **Goebbels** (1897–1945) was Hitler's minister of propaganda. William Maxwell Aitken, 1st Baron **Beaverbrook** (1879–1964), was the Canadian-born proprietor of the *Daily Express, Sunday Express*, and *Evening Standard* (London). He was minister of aircraft production (1940–1). Shaw's jesting **second title** was originally a subtitle (later dropped) for *Everybody's Political What's What?* (Laurence, *Shaw*, 1: 245).

110 / To Nancy Astor

Ayot St Lawrence, Welwyn, Herts.
22nd October 1942

[TLS: Reading, Holroyd (e), Letters, Halperin (e), Sykes (e)]

Shaw's litany of his domestic and financial woes was occasioned when Violet Elsie May Pond, later Mrs Fred Liddle (b. 1922), the Shaws' housemaid, was called up for wartime national service. Shaw's notion that he might appeal personally to the Minister of Labour and National Service, Ernest Bevin, naively underestimates Bevin's class consciousness. Moreover, Bevin had helped found and then lead the Transport and General Workers' Union. Such a powerful adversary notwithstanding, Nancy Astor seized on the opportunity to work on Shaw's behalf with missionary zeal. Violet Pond's possible exemption from national service recurs as a topic in many of the letters, 110–26.

My dear Nancy

Double double toil and trouble: they are taking away our housemaid on the 28th of November; and our one remaining maid will probably give us notice rather than stay singlehanded: she certainly would if she were a sensible Englishwoman. Charlotte is distracted; but I have not fired all my guns yet, and may intimidate the local people by a battery of figures. My income tax for the duration so far amounts to over £90,000. My copyrights, which cost the country nothing, have brought in over $100,000 paid to myself direct; and this is only ten per cent of all the dollars imported on the job. From the Barbara film I have had nothing; but it has brought in at least half as much. I can satisfy an accountant that I have brought over a million and a half dollars to London for nothing but my signature to an agreement. But I have lost money by the transaction, and have had to work seven days a week all the time with only Blanche Patch to help me, managing the business and making fresh copyrights to make more dollars to pay our debt to America.

I hope this will make the local people sit up. If it doesnt I must appeal to Bevin personally and ask him to tell them that my work is of national importance, and that I am not to be interrupted or molested.

I tell you all this stuff so that you may tell him that if he breaks up my home I shall dump myself and Charlotte and Blanche on your doorstep at Cliveden and spend the rest of my life there.

I have not enough skill in Christian Science to cure Charlotte's worrying. I hardly like to ask her what on earth it matters what happens to us in the few months that are left to us of 86 years. Even if we freeze or starve to death we have had our day, and should scorn to lag superfluous. I find this a cheerful way of looking at it: she doesnt: I only seem to be making light of her sufferings – which, by the way, are pretty bad. I dont believe that corset fits scientifically.

I have been reading Hitler's Mein Kampf really attentively instead of dipping into it. He is the greatest living Tory, and a wonderful preacher of everything that is right and best in Toryism. Your Party should capture him and keep him as a teacher and leader whilst checkmating his phobias. On the need for religion, on the sham democracy of votes for everybody, on unemployment and casual labor, he is superb. The book is really one of the world's bibles, like Calvin's Institutes (written when Calvin was 23), Adam Smith's Wealth of Nations, Marx's Capital; it has changed the mind of the reading world. We must lick his rabble of Rosenberg's and ruffians; but we really mustnt hang him. But there is not much danger of that: when his army cracks, he will turn up in Ireland, renting the Vice Regal Lodge like Louis Napoleon at Chislehurst or the Kaiser at Doorn; and who can touch him?

Where he has failed is in not making the occupied countries the better for his coming, as Julius Caesar managed to do in Spain. To put it another way, he has failed as Messiah. His army service suited him and made him a Terrorist and a tough. His smattering of cheap science (which is not a Tory subject) filled his head with a crude notion of 'the survival of the fittest' which would justify the ruling of the U.S.A. by a Congress of grizzly bears. And so he will be a failure. But then most of the Messiahs have been failures, though they had their points all the same.

I see we shall hear your voice from the Brains Trust next week. They have just been discussing why America has got along with fewer wars than Europe. None of them pointed out that the Americans were so busy killing one another with revolvers and bowie knives, to say nothing of lynchings, that they had no time for killing anyone else except redskins. Murder is sporadic in Europe and endemic in America. How far is this still true?

I must stop. You must be pretty busy just now; but we cannot resist giving you a hullo occasionally.

Always your

G. Bernard Shaw

We listened-in to Smuts. A very proper well spoken piece; but he probably delivered it in 1899 with 'British' changed to 'Boer' and 'Hitler' to Rhodes.

Do tell Churchill and Ll. G. [Lloyd George] that the House of Commons way of speechifying is pitiably ridiculous through the mike. Stopping for ten seconds between every word to wonder what the devil you can say next ('thinking on one's legs') is not made good by uttering the word when it comes as if it were an oracle, especially when it is only a preposition or conjunction.

Ernest **Bevin** (1881–1951) had been appointed by Churchill in 1940 and served in his war cabinet until 1945; he then became Foreign Secretary (1945–51) in the post-war Labour government. John **Calvin's** (1509–64) *Institutes of Christian Religion* (*Institutio Christianae Religionis*) was first published in 1536. **Adam Smith**'s (1723–90) *An Inquiry into the Nature and Causes of the Wealth of Nations* appeared in 1776. Alfred **Rosenberg** (1893–1946) was the German Reich Minister for the eastern occupied territories. The **Brains Trust** was a BBC radio program that began in 1941 as 'Any Questions?' Nancy recorded her program, for which she received a fifteen guinea fee, on 22 October 1942; it was broadcast on 27 October at 8.15 p.m. **Smuts**'s recorded address to Parliament urged help for Russia and was broadcast on 21 October 1942. English-born Cecil **Rhodes** (1853–1902) developed grand imperial visions of expanding the British Empire when he moved to British South Africa.

He was Prime Minister of Cape Colony (1890–6) until he was forced to resign after the 1895 Jameson raid, which aimed at overthrowing the Boer government of Paul Kruger (1825–1904). The incident led to the second Boer War.

111 / To Nancy Astor

Ayot St Lawrence, Welwyn, Herts.
28th [October] 1942

[ALS: Reading, Lash (e)]

Shaw's letter survives as a transcript made by Bruce Gould (1898–1989), editor of the Ladies' Home Journal *(1935–60), in a letter from Gould to Nancy Astor dated 16 November 1942 (Reading). Gould misdated Shaw's letter 28 February 1942. Eleanor Roosevelt (1884–1962) visited England from 23 October to 15 November 1942, inspecting war damage and reviewing women's war efforts, as well as visiting American servicemen in hospitals and camps. Gould remarked in his letter to Nancy that Mrs Roosevelt regretted she had been unable to visit Shaw but felt she could not give time to indulging her own pleasures.*

The B.T. [Brains Trust] was quite a success for you. I expect they'll ask you again. Joad was the brightest of the others.

Your only slip was about loving one's neighbours. Nobody who loves the human race in its present temper is fit to manage a whelk stall.

Jesus did not love the Pharisees, nor the evil and adulterous generation that asked him for a conjuring trick.

Bring the First Lady [Eleanor Roosevelt] to tea when you come. When she returns home the first question they will ask her is 'Have you seen Shaw?' If she has to say No it will cost Franklin at least half-a-dozen votes at the next presidential election.

G.B.S.

C.E.M. **Joad** (1891–1953) became head of the philosophy department at Birkbeck College, London, and was a successful and notable contributor to the 'Brains Trust.' He coined the popular catchphrase 'It depends what you mean by ...' (see also Letter 220).

112 / To Nancy Astor

4 Whitehall Court SW1
27th December 1942

[TLS: Reading]

In the second and third paragraphs of this letter Shaw has muddled (perhaps deliberately in order to tease Nancy Astor over her life-long crusade against alcohol) some recent news about Nancy's family members (which she corrects in Letter 113). The Shaws had spent Christmas 1942 with Judy Musters, who remembered it as a distinctly unfestive occasion, brightened only by a few slices of turkey she and Charlotte ate together (21 December 1958 letter to Nancy Astor [Reading]).

My dear Nancy

Our telephone conversation was a failure the other day either because I am deaf and dotty or because the instrument went wrong. You sounded an infinite distance away; and I gathered nothing except that there was half a chance of our seeing you again. Blanche Patch, whose hearing is intact, is really a safer go-between. She is away at present until next Wednesday. Meanwhile Judy holds the fort.

We got a shock when somebody reading the newspaper announced that Jakins [Astor] had had his appendix removed; but it was only his uncle, in whom it wont make any difference.

More agreeable was the news about David [Astor]. I cannot get it out of Charlotte's head that the bride is connected with the Drink Trade! Is there any foundation for this fancy?

Bevin and McCorquodale have turned me down, saying quite frankly that the Labor Ministry darent do a good turn to the 'wealthy and influential.' This to me! living on an overdraft, and the most complete political and social outsider in England! If they consider me wealthy and influential what must they think of you?

However, we shall get through somehow: Charlotte can bear the worst better than the worry of uncertainty. And her worries obey the law of the Conservation of Energy: if it's not one thing it's another.

sempre a te

G.B.S.

Malcolm Stewart **McCorquodale**, later 1st Baron McCorquodale (1901–71), was elected a National Conservative MP in 1931 and was Parliamentary Secretary to the Minister of Labour and National Service (1942–5). He and Bevin **turned down** Shaw's request that Violet Pond be exempted from national service (see Letter 110).

113 / To G. Bernard Shaw   [*no address*]
                                                      28th December 1942

[TLU (c): Reading]

Michael (not David, as Shaw thought in the previous letter) Astor was married on 28 November 1942. Nancy was critical of this alliance with the 'Drink Trade'; on 10 November 1942 (Reading) she wrote to Edith Lyttelton in typically blunt, acerbic fashion: 'I hope to see you soon and tell you all about Michael. The girl is charming and it is, as you say, a bad stable but a good filly: better that than the other way round.'

Dear G.B.S.

I am horrified by Bevin and McCorquodale, and I cannot let it go at this. They have taken everyone they could from us, but I shall fight to the last kitchen-maid! so don't give in yet.

Michael has married a stepdaughter of John Dewar the distiller, so you were wrong!

Jakie [Astor] did have his appendix out, and is thoroughly enjoying it, he is here with us now. It was a military affair! he had a pain in his stomach and the Army said it was an appendicitis. I protested, but the Surgeon said he would be so much more vital without his appendix, so Bill [Astor] said 'In that case have the cage made.' His Colonel on hearing of his increased vitality offered £5 to the surgeon to put it back! – so you see what he is like.

We had a very quiet Christmas, all five sons were here, but they have lost so many friends in Libya, so they could not be very gay, but had very good appetites!

I did hope to get you this week, but things turned up, but I am going to get on to Niece Judy [Musters] tomorrow to ask her all about you.

I must wish you both the very best of wishes for 1943, and may it bring us peace.

[Nancy Astor]

Barbara Mary Colonsay McNeal (d. 1980) was the **stepdaughter of John Dewar** (1856–1929), the famous distiller of Scottish whisky. Her marriage to Michael Astor ended in divorce in 1961; a year later she married Viscount Ward of Witley (1907–88).

114 / To Nancy Astor   Ayot St Lawrence, Welwyn, Herts.
                                            31st December 1942

[TLS: Reading]

*In her campaign to help the Shaws with their domestic problems, Nancy Astor
enlisted the assistance and collusion of Blanche Patch, who wrote Letter 115
(detailing the Shaws' situation) for official consumption. Regardless of overt or
covert motives, the two letters combined give a fair assessment of the Shaws at the
end of 1942.*

Dear Lady Astor

I hope the enclosed is what you wanted me to write. I have tried to put it
as if I didnt know that GBS had already appealed to you.

What is so unfortunate is that Mrs Shaw has always discouraged any
acquaintance with the few 'gentry' that live near by and no one is
allowed to come across the doorstep. There are some nice kindly people
(one family having a nice old trained nurse living with them), but
although I have tea with them once a week – I should have died from
loneliness without this relaxation!! – I mustnt talk about them in this
house. A pity because their 3 sons have done extraordinarily well and are
devoted to their home, in spite of GBS saying that parents and children
dislike each other. All the same it puzzles him that I, being one of eleven,
am good friends with all my surviving brothers and sisters, and am also
the daughter of a Conservative parson.

I do hope you will be able to think of some way of circumventing these
tiresome Ministry people.

Yours sincerely
Blanche Patch

Although Judy Musters can manage well enough when I am away, Mrs S.
would soon get irritated if she had to have her in *her* rooms. I know how
to make myself scarce and more like a fly on the wall.

The **enclosed** was Letter 115. Details of Blanche Patch's extensive family, including her
Conservative father, the Rev. Henry Patch, can be found in Patch, passim.

115 / To Nancy Astor   Ayot St Lawrence, Welwyn, Herts.
                                                    31st December 1942

[TLS: Reading]

Dear Lady Astor

I promised to let you know about our domestic affairs and know how
concerned you will be to hear that the Ministry of Labour refuses to
allow our appeal to keep Violet Pond, our housemaid; she may be called
up at any time. This decision comes from the London Office to whom St
Albans referred the matter.

I really believe it will kill Mrs Shaw. As you know she is now 86 (GBS is
6 months older), suffers from Paget's Disease, and is getting more and
[more] feeble. She is now very dependent on our cook-housekeeper
[Mrs Higgs] who is nearly 70 and has been with her for over 30 years.
This unfortunate cook in addition to looking after Mrs Shaw has to do all
the cooking (GBS being a vegetarian needs special dishes), does all the
ordering of food supplies from Welwyn Garden City, 5 miles off, and
manages the ration books. She can't possibly find time to clean the
kitchen and passages, wash vegetables and the many other duties that
Violet has to undertake. In addition her old husband, our gardener, who
lives in the house, is crippled with rheumatism and the poor woman is
often up at nights trying to relieve *his* pains.

We have another maid but she already has as much housework as she
can manage in addition to looking after the Shaws' clothes, and now that
we have closed the London Flat (our maid there is now a bus conduc-
tress) I have to live here which means another bedroom in use and a
study for me to work in. Most people think I should be able to help in
the house, but though willing I am over 60 – have twice been ill with a
strained heart – and have all GBS's theatre work (play licences and
receipts as well as his writing and Income Tax business to attend to) have
no typist to help me and honestly don't feel equal to anything more.

There isn't a soul in this isolated village who could come in daily and if
we could *find* a nurse she wouldnt come when she heard there is nothing
in the way of a bus to get her anywhere in her time off. And if she came
she would only add to the housework.

Considering the fame that GBS has brought to this country (to say nothing of the thousands of dollars) I do think the authorities might give his case a little more consideration and allow him this measure of comfort in his last years with us. He is gradually getting thinner and thinner and weighs about nine stone – not much for a man over 6 feet tall!

Forgive this mournful letter, but I am very worried and, as you know, the Shaws have absolutely no relatives to rally round them. Well, there are 1 or 2 impecunious cousins that he has to support.

Yours sincerely
Blanche Patch

Mrs Higgs's **old husband** was Harry Higgs (1874–1961), Shaw's gardener. As late as 1944, Shaw provided financial assistance to his **impecunious** second cousin, Mary Ethel Davis (1880–1962): 'When she was married to the late Sebastian Davis, I always had to make both ends meet for her in her housekeeping accounts' (Laurence, *Letters*, 725).

116 / To Blanche Patch
Cliveden, Taplow, Bucks.
1st January 1943

[TLS: Cornell]

On the same day Nancy Astor wrote to Ernest Bevin: 'I am sorry to bother you personally but I am really horrified at the lack of consideration that the authorities are showing about Bernard Shaw. / I feel quite certain you would not like this to happen, nor would the country. I want to first consult you, but if you feel you cannot do anything, I shall have no hesitation in taking it to a higher authority. I am perfectly willing to take it to the Prime Minister, but I am writing to you as I don't believe you can know about it' (Reading; the letter is misdated 1 January 1942). Nancy received a pro forma acknowledgment dated 4 January 1943 (Cornell). This letter contains holographic additions.

Dear Miss Patch !! She [the typist] left out the Miss.

Thank you so much for your letter, I have sent it on to Bevin, and I have told him I will have no hesitation in sending it to the Prime Minister, if he cannot do anything.

It really is staggering! and the way these two live all alone now seems a tragedy. Poor poor souls. Thank God I have got you.

Your note interested me enormously, and I hope to be able to discuss it with you. I am hoping to get down next Wednesday or Thursday, so please warn them. & I am so glad you realize that I *do* want to help you *all* I can. Am always *ready*. Never forget that it's a [illegible].

N[ancy Astor]

117 / To G. Bernard Shaw   [*no address*]
                                             5th January 1943

[TLU (c): Reading]

Dearest G.B.S.

The enclosed letter is from the friend of Philip Lothian's. I cannot remember all the conversation, but I know he was delighted to meet you. Please let me have the letter back some time.

If the weather holds I may see you on Thursday. I have got to go to Plymouth that night, but I rather hope to get down in the afternoon to vet you both before going.

I sent a personal letter to Bevin about your maid being called up, and I told him if he could do nothing I would write to the Prime Minister!

I do hope Charlotte is better, and that I may get to see you. You are a very provocative person, and your letters in 'The Times' always start something going.

[Nancy Astor]

The **enclosed letter** has not been located. Shaw's most recent letter to **The Times** (28 December 1942; reprinted in Laurence, *Agitations*, 332–3), about 'English usage,' iterated his inveterate stance against standard grammar and spelling. The latter 'costs us the price of a fleet of battleships every year in writing and printing superfluous letters.'

118 / To Nancy Astor   Ayot St Lawrence, Welwyn, Herts.
                                             9th January 1943

[ALCS: Reading]
Nancy Astor's concern for Shaw is revealed in this letter by the pair of stockings she knitted for him, a mundane yet notable task for a busy person.

124

The stockings are a success; but Charlotte complains that they make my everyday suit shabby, which is absurd, as it is hardly more than ten years old.

Violet [Pond] is summoned to appear before the Umpire for his final verdict next Saturday, the 16th. Whether this is a result of your powerful intervention or a mere coincidence I know not; but Charlotte has hopes.

I used to take a bath every morning; but now I cut down that allowance considerably and am not noticeably dirtier. If Violet goes Maggie can do a lot of her daily routine every second or third day, and nobody the worse. Old people are not so particular.

My apologies to Major [Jakie] Astor. The years fly past me now like weeks; and I can hardly realize that my young friends are now dignified seniors. He will be a brigadier before I can wink.

It was disappointing not to see you; but a glance at the weather that morning convinced me that a visit was impossible.

G.B.S.

Maggie was Margaret Caskie, the Shaws' parlourmaid.

119 / To G. Bernard Shaw   [*no address*]
                                                11th January 1943

[TLU (c): Reading]

Dearest G.B.S.

The car arrived to take me to you but the driver said it was very foggy outside of London and he advised me not to go. It was a bitter disappointment as I much wanted to see you both and felt unhappy at coming West without having done so.

I am delighted the stockings fit. Do you want me to start another pair? If so, let me know at once.

I feel pretty certain that they won't take your Violet [Pond], so tell Charlotte not to worry. I shall take the case through the House of Commons to the House of Lords and even a Petition to their Majesties (though I could not expect them to do you a kindness!).

I have just heard to-day that the Halifaxs' youngest son has lost both of his legs in Egypt. Their second boy was killed. This third was such a handsome creature. The war gets worse every day in spite of your friends the Russians knowing exactly how many prisoners and tanks they take ten minutes after the battle: what good story-tellers they are: it is a pity we have not got some of their talents – it would cheer some of our people up a good deal!

The Major – J.J. Astor – enjoyed his week after the operation but now is getting impatient for the battle.

It is so nice at Plymouth and I shall bring you down in the summer whether you want to come or not. We may have to carry Charlotte squealing but I'd be even willing to do that to get you here.

You will be pleased to hear that I have made my will and I hope you will not forget to mention me in yours, though you are certain to outlive me!

The American who is running their 'Soldiers' Sheet' told us the other day that when the American Troops got over here, for the first two or three months all of their letters were full of disappointment at England and the English, but they have entirely changed now and can't make out why they were so misled about the English, and are amazed at their kindness and hospitality. How I wish you were able to speak to them! – and me. Much love to you both – and *Violet* will Remain.

[Nancy Astor]

Lord Halifax's **youngest son** was Richard Frederick Wood, later Baron Holderness of Bishop Wilton (1920–2002), who was elected Conservative MP for Bridlington (1950–79) and served in several ministerial capacities. He was an advocate for the war-disabled. Their **second boy** was Francis, who was killed in battle in 1942.

120 / To G. Bernard Shaw　　　　　　　　　　　　　　[Plymouth]
18th January 1943

[Holograph draft for TEL: Reading]

Is Violet [Pond] still with you? Please answer Plymouth not returning Cliveden until Saturday.

Nancy Astor

126

121 / To Nancy Astor   Ayot St Lawrence, Welwyn, Herts.
19th January 1943

[TEL: Reading]

VIOLETS ATTENDANCE AT THE COMMITTEE IS DEFERRED TO THE
TWENTYEIGHTH.

[G. Bernard Shaw]

122 / To G. Bernard Shaw   [*no address*]
19th January 1943

[TLU (c): Reading]

Dearest G.B.S.

I am delighted to hear it. I won't send you my letter to Bevin but it was
pretty hot! This is what he has replied.
  I've not answered it yet but I'd like you to see it.

Yours
[Nancy Astor]

Bevin's reply to Nancy Astor has not been located but may be inferred from the next letter.

123 / To Nancy Astor   Ayot St Lawrence, Welwyn, Herts.
23rd January 1943

[ALCS: Reading]

Do not take any further trouble about Violet [Pond]. I made it quite
clear to McC[orquodale] and through him to B[evin] that I have no case
for the local committees and am dependent on the special knowledge of
the Minister for exceptional decision at H.Q. B's letter referring you to
the ordinary routine (which of course we know as well as he does) means
that he does not attach any importance to me or my work and will not
interfere. To this there is nothing to be said: he is within his rights and
powers; and it would be a mistake to quarrel with him about it. You must
wait for some future occasion to get a bit of your own back. For the
moment he is safe in his attitude of being incorruptible by wealth,

beauty, and influence, or even by a sense of what he and his Labor colleagues owe to the old Fabians.

But probably he never read a word of my political stuff, and knows me only as the author of Not Bl—dy Likely.

I am sorry our affairs have exposed you to a rebuff, but feel pretty sure that you will get even with him someday. We hope to see you next week.

G.B.S.

Liza Doolittle's retort, **'not bloody likely'** in *Pygmalion* (Act 3), created a sensation in 1914.

124 / To Nancy Astor Ayot St Lawrence, Welwyn, Herts.
29th January 1943

[ALCS: Reading]

Mrs Higgs & Violet [Pond] have been before the Umpire tribunal.

Result: they will consider the matter and let Violet know. It will take some little time.

They questioned Mrs Higgs closely about Charlotte's illness and the house service.

It looks hopeful.

Any chance of seeing you?

G.B.S.

125 / To G. Bernard Shaw [Plymouth ?]
12th February 1943

[Unsigned typescript for TEL: Reading]

DID YOU GET THE SWEETS DELIGHTED ABOUT VIOLET PLEASE WRITE PLYMOUTH LOVE

NANCY ASTOR

126 / To Nancy Astor Ayot St Lawrence, Welwyn, Herts.
13th February 1943

[ALCS: Reading, Letters, Sykes (e)]

Nancy Astor's campaign over Violet Pond succeeded in gaining her a deferral from

*national service; however, by the beginning of June, Violet had decided she wished
to serve (see Letter 134). She was not called up for service until January 1944
(Letter 146).*

Violet is respited until the 27th May.

The sweets arrived happily just when my ration gave out. I gobble
them with much gusto.

Tell Winston [Churchill] to stop talking alarming nonsense about
unconditional surrender. Make him explain that the surrender cannot
be unconditional, but that we shall dictate the conditions. As to whether
'we' includes Uncle Jo[e Stalin], the less said just now the better.

G.B.S.

Beginning in January 1940, **sweets**, many foods, and other commodities were rationed,
although bread, potatoes, vegetables, and fish and chips were not. Sugar ceased to be
rationed in 1949, and all rationing ended in 1954. In addition to discussing military strategy
at the Casablanca Conference (12–23 January 1943), Churchill and Roosevelt established
the policy of the **unconditional surrender** of Germany, Italy, and Japan.

127 / To Nancy Astor   Ayot St Lawrence, Welwyn, Herts.

27th February 1943

[ALS: Reading]

*William Henry Beveridge (1879–1963), a former director of the London School of
Economics, had been appointed to review social-insurance schemes, which resulted
in the Beveridge report, published in 1942. The report proposed a comprehensive
social-security system using national insurance to fund it. The result was the
National Insurance Act of 1946 and the National Health Service in 1948. The
report 'was exactly what Waldorf had always been advocating. Not so Nancy. She
now turned against everything Waldorf and David stood for ... Nancy declared
"They call it the Welfare State. I call it the Farewell State"' (Fox, 456). The
deterioration of Charlotte's health recurs in most of Letters 127–38.*

My dear Nancy

Yesterday Charlotte fell and damaged her right arm.

Violet [Pond] being respited, Maggie [Caskie], the other maid, went
off to Ireland to see her mother, reported to be gravely ill there.

The household is consequently excited.

No bones are broken; and the local doctor is bandaging Charlotte with lead lotion. She is a bit more disabled, but otherwise rather the better for the change, as small real evils are more bearable than the ones she invents when all goes well.

I wish they would not announce raids on S.W. towns when you are under fire there.

Though you are anti-Beverage, be pro-Beveridge. The report is a cheap ransom, well within the country's means, especially as the workers will have to produce the £2 a week themselves, in addition to the interest on their present savings.

Gandhi is not in the slightest danger (he is probably doing a cure) but the King should release him at once as a gesture to undo a gross Hitleritish blunder.

I will return McC[orquodale]'s letter when I can find it if it matters. I am deeply grateful to YOU.

G.B.S.

During the summer of 1942 **Gandhi** and the leadership of the Indian Congress were imprisoned for demanding, through civil disobedience, the immediate withdrawal of Britain from India.

128 / To Nancy Astor   Ayot St Lawrence, Welwyn, Herts.
                                             6th March 1943

[ALCS: Reading, Holroyd (e)]

Your letter took four days to reach me, crossing mine.

I possess 18 pairs of stockings in various stages of shrinkage and darning (except your two new ones) but all wearable and fairly presentable; so I cannot plead urgent necessity.

You have a knitting rival (Dolly Walker) who knits gloves for me, and now wants to try her hand on stockings.

Mahatma G[andhi] is not a crook; he is a saint, and as such under the covenant of grace, of which the King is the minister. Just like Mrs Eddy, or Mahatma G.B.S.

Charlotte has recovered from her fall, and is none the worse for it.

I send this to London, as you will presumably be coming up to elect the new Speaker.

G.B.S.

Dorothy **'Dolly' Walker** (1878–1963) was the daughter of the socialist and publisher Sir
Emery Walker (1851–1933), whom Shaw had known since 1885. The **new Speaker** of the
House of Commons, installed on 9 March 1943, was Douglas Clifton Brown, later 1st
Viscount Ruffside (1879–1958). He served as Speaker until 1951.

129 / To Nancy Astor

Ayot St Lawrence, Welwyn, Herts.
14th March 1943

[ALCS: Reading]

Charlotte has had a very bad turn for a couple of days, but is better now.

On Friday we shall have a specialist here who will leave by the 3 o'clock
train; so the later afternoon will be free for you. Come if you can.

Dolly [Walker] promises four pairs of new stockings and undertakes to
turn two old shrunk pairs into one full size.

Perhaps I had better mention that I made Dolly's acquaintance when
she was six and I was twentysix.

G.B.S.

130 / To Nancy Astor

Ayot St Lawrence, Welwyn, Herts.
11th April 1943

[ALCS: Reading, Holroyd (e)]

*Nancy Astor was again pressing the Shaws to stay with her at Cliveden, which
Shaw resisted, citing Charlotte's weakened condition.*

It is now nearly half through April; and the weeks are flying past like
Hurricanes and Spitfires.

As far as I can see, and barring miracles, there is not the faintest ghost
of a chance of our joining you at Cliveden in May; so let our rooms go.

Charlotte is recovering slowly from her late very bad turn, and is trying
a new treatment (unregistered). She can get upstairs without being
helped; but this is the most that [can] be said for her mobility.

I am using a war economy postcard. If you are surcharged on Edward
VII, let me know.

G.B.S.

Edward VII refers to a postage stamp.

131 / To Nancy Astor   Ayot St Lawrence, Welwyn, Herts.
                                        21st May 1943

[ALS: Reading]

Nancy asthore

Charlotte is immovable: she cannot sit down or stand up comfortably
without help: I have to lift her and let her down and follow her up and
down stairs as she pulls herself up by the bannisters, without which she
could not face stairs at all. We can manage this sort of thing at home; but
at Cliveden it would mean making scenes several times a day, including
meals; and this she could not bear. [Edwin] Lee and Arthur [Bushell]
would probably give notice.

How far she will improve no one can say; but there is no chance of her
being available in June, nor much of August being possible.

Our contemporaries are considerately dying in all directions: Olivier,
Burns, Beatrice, and others unknown to you, all reminding us that our
time is up. I am waiting only to finish my book.

Why are the young Astors shedding their appendices so prodigally?
Does it make any noticeable difference in them?

I must break off to attend to my invalid ——

                                        G.B.S.

Sydney **Olivier**, 1st Baron Olivier (1859–1943), was a Fabian and friend of Shaw and the
Webbs; he died on 15 February 1943. John **Burns** (1858–1943), leader of the 1889 London
Dock Strike, was one of the first three Labour MPs to be elected to Parliament in 1892. The
model for Boanerges in *The Apple Cart*, he died on 24 January 1943. Shaw had kept **Beatrice**
Webb's death on 30 April 1943 from Charlotte. Shaw's **book** was *Everybody's Political What's
What?*

132 / To Nancy Astor   Ayot St Lawrence, Welwyn, Herts.
                                        23rd May 1943

[ALS: Reading]

*During Shaw's later years Blanche Patch became more and more Nancy Astor's
confederate in the latter's various attempts to assist Shaw. Blanche provided
Nancy with sundry information or her own viewpoint, as here.*

Dear Lady Astor

I am sure you will not tell the Shaws that I have written; but I thought I'd let you know that if you still want them to come to Cliveden, I do not think you will get Mrs S. there unless it can be arranged for her to have her meals in their sitting room. Her back is now so very bowed that eating before other people is no pleasure to her (GBS & I don't matter as we are used to it) & apart from this she is now not equal to eating & talking to others at the same time. The poor old lady is certainly very difficult & what we are going to do I can't think, though I am trying to see if we can get a maid-nurse for her. Looking after her is getting too much for our elderly cook-housekeeper, & I don't mind saying that she has always terrified *me*, & I am useless except for the *very* slight secretarial jobs she asks me to do.

If only she had been a bit more friendly with other rather younger women who might now rally round them, but she has always treated with contempt the ordinary women who make life comfortable for her, but are not mentioned in Who's Who. Is this very disloyal on my part? Anyhow it's true.

Yours sincerely
Blanche Patch

133 / To Blanche Patch   [Clovelly? (Devon)]
Monday [24th] May [1943]

[ALS: Cornell]

This letter is dated 'Monday 25 May' and assigned to 1947 by Cornell. It clearly belongs to 1943 as the response to Blanche Patch's previous letter. However, 25 May 1943 fell on a Tuesday. Nancy's handwriting is again responsible for indecipherable words.

Dear Miss Patch

GBS wrote me he felt Cliveden impossible but you make it seem probable – If she [Charlotte] can get a nurse, I can arrange about meals. She can have them all in her room or sitting room. I feel for her sake she should try to come. I can see he needs it. Saying nothing of you. – I do see what you mean & understand. To have gone through life with so few [wanted ?] friends is tragic – but she never wanted them poor poor soul. Please tell GBS that you must have a nurse. I wrote him I felt it was absolutely necessary for all of you.

I must be in Plymouth until June 8th but will be back then & ring you up & come down if I can. If they come it must [be] before August when our staff get their holidays so look out for a nurse & I will get an old [tray carrier ?] & the rooms ready. – I have had [nearly ?] 10 days rest here & wish you could see this glorious country here. Write me to Plymouth please. & cheer up you have done & are doing a grand job.

[Sincerely ?]
Nancy Astor

134 / To Nancy Astor   Ayot St Lawrence, Welwyn, Herts.
1st June 1943

[ALS: Reading, Holroyd (e)]

My dear Nancy

Just a line to say that Cliveden is quite impossible for us this summer. You may dispose of the rooms confidently on that assumption. Charlotte is much more disabled than you think, and her general condition more serious. She knows that Cliveden is out of the question. What she needs is a nurse who would not go mad in this dull village and would not be above doing her own housework and feeding with the domestic staff.

Violet [Pond] now wants to be called up, and will not appeal again for reservation. There is a possibility of another recruit from Eire.

Dont bother any more about us: there is nothing to be done.

If Charlotte were a Christian, C.S. [Christian Science] might help her; for the state of her mind, if not of her body, is a psychological problem; but I know of no psycho-therapist within reach heathen enough to interest her.

However, I must not worry you with our troubles: they will all be finished presently at Golder's Green.

The Cliveden set is really a Fascist set, originating with Milner in South Africa, and picking up Virginia on the way hither. Fascism is an attempt to moralize Capitalism and enrich it at the same time through Fabian

State organization: Comte up to date, in fact. Stalin's way is the alternative.

The enclosed review may amuse. Or may not.

G.B.S.

Both Charlotte and Shaw were cremated at **Golders Green** crematorium in London. Viscount Alfred **Milner** (1854–1925) was a colonial administrator who was High Commissioner to South Africa (1897–1905). There he surrounded himself with his 'kindergarten' of Oxford graduates (including Philip Kerr) to help him run the country and train for similar assignments for themselves. An ardent, if idealistic, imperialist, Milner's inflexibility helped to cause the second Boer War (see Rose, 46–9). Auguste **Comte** (1798–1857), the French philosopher, wrote on social and political systems applicable to the industrial age. Shaw's **enclosed review** of *Fabian Socialism* by G.D.H. Cole appeared in *Tribune*, no. 335 (28 May 1943), 11–12. Shaw probably saw Cole's book in manuscript in early February 1942. In a 7 February 1942 letter to Beatrice Webb he commented: 'I have read Cole's book, and think the opening chapters very good: he is really a Socialist ... In the later chapter on Democracy he lapses into nineteenth century drivel about Love' (Michalos, 263).

135 / To Nancy Astor   Ayot St Lawrence, Welwyn, Herts.
17th June 1943

[ALS: Reading, Holroyd (e)]

My dear Nancy

The maid nurse problem remains unsolved; and the patient, in fending for herself, hurts herself so much that she declares that bits of her bones break off. She now comes down to meals; but the difficulty with which she crawls about is heartbreaking, and seems to be getting worse, though in other respects she is better.

The war will end when the interest on gilt edged rises again to five per cent, just as it began in 1898 and 1914 when the rate fell to two and a half. All the rest is hot air, guff, and bugaboo.

I doubt whether it is wise at this moment to lie as the B.B.C. does about the raids. Every day we hear about a tip & run trifle with little damage, a few casualties, and two raiders shot down in a southwest town, when the truth is that Plymouth has been heavily blitzed. The effect is to make us take it easy just when we need a touch of the whip to make us buckle-to.

I know what it is possible to know here about Russia because I get it from the horse's mouth, and never had any illusions about it. Nothing that you are told is true, because your informants understand neither their own position nor the Russian one. As you know, I never try to convert anybody: my business is to teach the natural laws which govern all political action without regard to parliamentary labels. I'm a philosopher, not an election agent. And I must not start a second sheet, paper being so scarce.

G.B.S.

The **horse's mouth** may have been the Russian ambassador, Ivan M. Maisky. Although writing in 1940, Thomas Jones remarked: 'I fancy [the Shaws] see Maisky fairly often' (*Diary*, 456) after hearing a favourable discourse on Russia from Shaw.

136 / To Nancy Astor   Ayot St Lawrence, Welwyn, Herts.
17th June 1943

[TLS: Reading]

Blanche Patch's detailed account of the domestic situation at Ayot provides an interesting contrast to Shaw's own brief mention of it in the previous letter. Patch provided Beatrice Webb with a similar earlier account on 29 April 1941 (Michalos, 256–8).

Dear Lady Astor

I dont know how much of our affairs GBS may have told you, nor do I know if he has ever realized how the house is run. And this I say because he solemnly told us that if he was entirely on his own he would live on preserved foods that required no cooking and so the necessity for a cook and washing-up would not occur. I ventured to say that the actual dwelling would need some attention as well as the care of his raiment – but this was, of course, dismissed in his usual casual way. I'm not sure that he doesnt think we could easily live as the Russians do – and how he would hate that.

However, what I meant to tell you is that the position here as regards help has somewhat altered. Our maid Violet [Pond], having said she no longer wishes to be exempted from military, or rather war service, has been medically passed for the A.T.S. and may be called up at any time. Mrs Higgs, our cook-housekeeper says it will be quite impossible for her to do the rough work such as cleaning the kitchen and its pots and pans etc. in addition to the dressing and undressing of Mme Charlotte, as

Gabriel Pascal calls her. And I quite agree that she can't do any more, but daily help here for the kitchen is unobtainable, we shall never get an oldish servant to come to this isolation even if we could hear of one, and anyone engaged for maid-attendant wouldnt do the rough work.

Every now and again Charlotte sends Mrs Higgs to have 'a little talk' with me because she is sure I must know of Registry Offices in London that can supply maids. The 'little talk' is always a pouring-out of Mrs Higgs's troubles and how her husband wont allow her to do the rough work (and quite right at her age) and various other grievances and I am left in a state of nervous prostration feeling utterly powerless to cope with the situation.

I am arranging for Mrs Judy Musters to come here about the beginning of July and am hoping that if a crisis occurs here it will occur in my absence. The local doctor (4 miles away) is a very capable fellow and would never take offence although Char[lotte] has bouts of turning against him, but GBS likes him, and I know he can be relied on in any emergency to do the right thing.

Certainly the aged are one of the major problems of this hateful war. Some people I have got to know across the road have an old mother landed on them and she is positively senile and can never be left alone for 5 minutes. Their house is larger than this one and domestic problems worse than ours.

All this is as usual quite unofficial, and just to let you know how we are getting on. I should say that Mrs S. is rather more helpless though she comes downstairs. Memory very bad some days.

Yours sincerely
Blanche Patch

The **A.T.S.** was the Auxiliary Territorial Service. **Judy Musters** acted as Shaw's secretary from 6–20 July 1943.

137 / To Nancy Astor   4 Whitehall Court SW1
31st July 1943

[ALS: Reading, Sykes (e)]

On 26 July 1943, Shaw's 87th birthday, the Shaws travelled to Whitehall Court. They expected to return to Ayot on 23 August (Chappelow, 76), but their stay in London was lengthened by Mrs Higgs's illness (see Letter 138). During the summer Nancy Astor had written to a Mr Yandell, a friend working for the American Red Cross, to ask him to bring various items of clothing for her from America, which was prohibited by current rationing laws. Her letter was intercepted by the wartime censor and Nancy was ordered to appear at Bow Street Magistrates' Court in London on 30 July. There she was fined £50 with £10 costs (see 'Lady Astor Fined for Clothes Offence: Attempt to Get Rationed Goods from U.S.,' The Times, 31 July 1943, and Sykes, 463–4). The Daily Mirror (31 July) took the opportunity to note the irony that, minutes before her court appearance, Nancy had spoken in a House of Commons debate on education and had said: 'When I hear people speaking in the House of Commons about education, I sometimes marvel that the country trusts us as much as it does.' It also noted the magistrate's ('the beak') censure of Nancy: 'It is astonishing that a lady in her position should be so completely ignorant as to do a thing of this kind.'

My dear Nancy

The beak was most friendly: the penalty was the very least he could choose on a plea of Guilty, which was quite wrong. Your counsel should have pleaded Not Guilty, but the facts are all fully admitted, and greatly regretted by Lady A., who acted in complete ignorance of the law, quite innocently. She does not defend or excuse her ignorance; but it was genuine and widely shared even in parliament.

However, as the magistrate put that view for you, and did his kindest – a tribute to your popularity – it doesnt matter now.

That afternoon after seeing Waldorf I met your youngest [Jakie] in civvies in Bond St and asked him anxiously what had happened. He knew nothing of the case. I explained the gravity of the situation. His view was that you are working much too hard and that a year in the clink would do you a world of good. He may be right; so go slow for a bit.

Be very careful not to use the Red Cross car for private visits. By an odd accident I have just learned that Y's use of it was being watched. And that is in fact why I indite this note; for you must not put your head in the lion's mouth again.

And speak well of Russia. Ask the new ambassador to tea; and convince him that you are Stalin's first and dearest friend in England. That will not cost you a single vote; but a word to the contrary may cost you your seat.

sagely your
G.B.S.

Y was probably Mr Yandell (unidentified). The new Russian **ambassador** in London (1943–6) was Feodor Tarasovich Gusev (1905–87), who earlier had been Soviet minister to Canada.

138 / To Nancy Astor   4 Whitehall Court SW1
                                            21st August 1943

[ALCS: Reading, Holroyd (e)]

We shall be in London for another month perhaps. Mrs Higgs has crocked up with a cyst, and must go to St Albans and be operated on in Bartholomews there. And until she recovers we may not be able to get food cooked at Ayot. This *contretemps*, instead of upsetting Charlotte, has given her something serious to think about, which is very good for her.

Your letter in The Times was badly needed. William Morris used to say that it is very difficult to judge who are the best people to take charge of children, but it is certain that the parents are the very worst.

This afternoon I was robbed by a variety of confidence trick of which I had never heard. I fell for it like the greenest of yokels. But the poor devil got the wrong wallet and missed £20. The other he took may have had a fiver or two; but the documents are worth nothing to him.

G.B.S.

Nancy's **letter** on 'Nursery Schools' (one of her favourite causes) was published in *The Times*, 19 August 1943. She believed them to be 'the modern Sunday-schools – places where children learn without tears how to share, how to serve, and how to stand on their own tiny feet without pushing their little neighbours down.' Shaw shared the view of socialist poet **William Morris** (1834–96) that parents were not the best people to bring up children. A full account of the **confidence trick** played on Shaw can be found in Chappelow, 133. Essentially, a stranger persuaded Shaw to clean up the back of his coat in a lavatory and there robbed Shaw of his wallet. Shaw professed to being more concerned over the loss of his 'British Museum Reading Room ticket of 1880' than of the money. His engagement diary records a visit on 23 August 1943 from Sergeant Ottersly of Scotland Yard, presumably to investigate the incident.

139 / To Nancy Astor   4 Whitehall Court SW1
                                            22nd August 1943

[ALCS: Reading]

I forgot to say that the Baltimore Archangel can write to me for an appointment. He need not bother Waldorf: I shall not forget his seraphic name.

The ownership of urban land is fundamental in the Class War. The landlords will all sign the Atlantic Charter; but they will not give up a single slum until they are either bought out with money raised by taxation of their own incomes (the Fabian plan) or shot out (the plan of the old Irish Ribbon Lodges and the Bolsheviks).

This war of Schrecklichkeit [overwhelming intimidation] is horrible; but it will frighten all the belligerents into peace, victors and vanquished alike, let us hope. Now the B.B.C. lies about Plymouth!!!

G.B.S.

The **Baltimore Archangel** is unidentified. The **Atlantic Charter** was issued on 14 August 1941 by Churchill and Roosevelt; its eight points included prohibitions on aggrandizement and territorial changes without the consent of the people concerned. The **Irish Ribbon Lodges** refers to the opposing Protestant and Catholic lodges in Ireland, which were represented by orange and green ribbons.

140 / To Nancy Astor   4 Whitehall Court SW1
                                                 28th September 1943

[ALCS: Reading, Sykes (e)]

Charlotte Shaw had begun to decline some five weeks earlier; she died on 12 September 1943. (Shaw's own account [Laurence, Letters, 679–81] provides full details of her final days, as does his letter to Clara Higgs [Chappelow, 78]). She was cremated at Golders Green on 15 September, with only Shaw, Nancy Astor, and Blanche Patch in attendance. Shaw was apparently rather irritated by Nancy's presence ('[She] could not stay away,' Letters, 680.) In her solicitous concern for the Shaws Nancy probably felt a proprietary right to be present and she was a difficult woman to be gainsaid. Joyce Grenfell reports visiting Nancy around this time: 'and then I went to see Aunt N., who had fully recovered [from her court case] and was full of G.B.S., whose hand she's been holding this week since Charlotte died. She says he is wonderful and very spry' (Darling, 326–7).

I had an engagement this evening that I could not defer, as I had already put it off once. I heard the part of the concert that was broadcast.

Except for next Friday afternoon (Lady Rhondda) I have so far nothing fixed up this week, though there is heaps to do; so dont worry about me.

Last Friday I had a long talk with D.D [Lyttelton].

The letters have stopped at last; and correspondence, though copious, is normal and Patchable.

G.B.S.

141 / To Nancy Astor   4 Whitehall Court SW1
                                                          12th October 1943

[ALCS: Reading]

Yousuf Karsh (1908–2002), who was born in Armenia and moved to Canada in 1924, was renowned for his photographic portraits of famous people. Shaw's sitting for him on 14 October 1943 was supposed to take only five minutes but lasted much longer. Karsh's portrait was used as the frontispiece for Everybody's Political What's What? *(see Letter 142). In December 1942 the Astors had signed Cliveden over to the National Trust in order to avoid ruinous death duties; however, they continued to live there, opening the property to the public on terms negotiated with the Trust. Shaw eventually succeeded in doing likewise for his own house ('Shaw's Corner') at Ayot. He had also begun the business of winding up Charlotte's estate.*

The Canadian photographer, who turns out to be Armenian, and so clever that he has got round me and is fixing up an electric installation for a regular studio sitting, is coming on Thursday at 12. It is just as well that you will be in Plymouth, as we shall talk photography all the time.

No news, but endless business here: National Trust (Ayot will go the way of Cliveden), Public Trustee, valuations for probate, and two big films to negotiate, besides the book to finish.

G.B.S.

The **two big films** Shaw was negotiating were *Caesar and Cleopatra* and *The Doctor's Dilemma*. Filming of the former began on 12 June 1944 (see Letter 159). *The Doctor's Dilemma* was not filmed until after Shaw's death; it premiered in 1958, was directed by Anthony Asquith (1902–58) and starred (Sir) Dirk Bogarde (1921–99) and Leslie Caron (b. 1931) as the Dubedats. Shaw finally finished his **book**, *Everybody's Political What's What?* on 23 November 1943.

142 / To Nancy Astor   4 Whitehall Court SW1
                                               15th October 1943

[ALCS: Reading]

Letters 142–4 reflect to a small degree some of the effects of Charlotte's death upon Shaw.

I have to go down to Ayot next Thursday, the 21st, to shew the place to Hubert Smith of the National Trust, who says he met me at Cliveden. I shall stay over the week end, possibly longer if the food is possible, hunting for Charlotte's papers and my own; for there is the probate to be documented; and I have to make my will anew. I had a long interview with the Public Trustee about it on Wednesday.

The Armenian [Yousuf Karsh] took a prodigious number of photographs of me yesterday. I suffered them gladly on the chance of getting an up-to-date frontispiece for my book. Miss Patch also posed.

This tale has no moral.

                                               G.B.S.

Hubert Smith was appointed as the chief agent of the National Trust in 1943. The secretary of the Trust was James Lees-Milne (1908–97), who later discussed the transfer of Ayot with Shaw and described the meeting in his *Diaries: 1942–1945: Ancestral Voices & Prophesying Peace* (1995), 276–80.

143 / To Nancy Astor   4 Whitehall Court SW1
                                               25th October 1943

[ALCS: Reading, Sykes (e)]

Good! I will come on Wednesday the 3rd November at 1.30. If you prefer 1.15, phone Blanche (surname Patch).

The extra light at Ayot was very refreshing. Everything was in apple pie order, though the maids have been entirely self-acting since July. Pretty good thatt (Bridges spelt it that way for emphasis) I think.

When I come across some intimate thing of Charlotte's I still quite automatically say an affectionate word or two and am moved just for a moment.

                                               G.B.S.

Robert **Bridges** (1844–1930), who was appointed poet laureate in 1913, shared Shaw's interest in phonetics (see Laurence, *Letters*, 24).

144 / To Nancy Astor

Ayot St Lawrence, Welwyn, Herts.
27th December 1943

[ALCS: Reading, Holroyd (e)]

Nancy Astor may have complained to Shaw about the pressures of 'public work,' at both Plymouth and Westminster. In late November and early December 1943 she had agreed with the unpopular decision by Herbert Morrison to release imprisoned British fascists such as Sir Oswald Mosley and his wife, Diana : 'Anyhow, it's not the British way to keep dying people in prison, particularly if they are uncondemned.' However, she remained staunchly antifascist: 'Please don't class me as a Mosleyite, Stalinite, Hitlerite or Musso-ite; I am not among the "ites" and you shouldn't be either!' (30 December 1943 letter to Sean O'Casey [Reading] quoted in Krause, 155; see also Sykes, 465–6). In the same letter Nancy also invited O'Casey to visit her at Cliveden.

Never forget that public work will kill the strongest mortal; for there is no end to it. Unless you train yourself to say flatly NO when you have reached the safety limit you will perish miserably and I shall survive you, which would be intolerable.

I am full of unfinished jobs, some of them unbegun; and I must take my own advice and not attempt to combine them with visits to Cliveden or even to Whitehall. Have I not talked enough in these 87 years? My last social effort was a lunch with Morrison. Present: Ellen Wilkinson and [Lady] Rhondda.

Charlotte's wardrobe (a problem) is almost disposed of now. The two priceless evening dresses to be worn at Cliveden will henceforth dazzle society on the shoulders of B.P. [Blanche Patch].

G.B.S.

Herbert **Morrison** (1888–1965), a Labour MP, served in various ministerial appointments; he was currently Home Secretary (1940–5). Shaw discussed the disposal of Charlotte's two **evening dresses** and other clothing in earlier letters to Blanche Patch and Judy Musters (Laurence, *Letters*, 686).

145 / To Nancy Astor   Ayot St Lawrence, Welwyn, Herts.
2nd January 1944

[ALCS: Reading, Holroyd (e)]

With Charlotte now dead, Nancy Astor's concern for Shaw's welfare found new impetus (see the Introduction, xxiv, for reasons why Shaw became the focus of Nancy's solicitude). Nancy even suggested that Shaw move in with her and Waldorf, a proposal her husband rejected: 'Poor G.B.S. – I can well imagine his being lonely – I w[oul]d naturally love to do anything to help him in his old age but permanent guests do tend to impede family life' ('Thursday' letter to Nancy Astor [Reading]). Shaw, however, was quite content with his new solitary condition. He told Sidney Webb: 'I am living alone here in Ayot; but I like being alone. After being taken care of devotedly for 46 years I rather enjoy being free to take care of myself. I work longer and later than Charlotte would ever have allowed me to; and a marked improvement in my health and vigor since her death shews what a strain her four years illness was, though I was not conscious of it at the time' (Laurence, Letters, 705–6). Moreover, he still had adequate household staff to run his day-to-day affairs. Consequently he fended off many of Nancy's proposed visits, sometimes politely, sometimes brusquely.

Dont come down here yet. The weather is not comfortable; the days are much too short; and until Mrs Higgs is fully restored, and my own affairs settled, I cannot entertain anyone, not even you, for more than an hour at teatime without a quite considerable upset of my carefully planned routine. I am getting through with my work faster and better now that I havnt to talk to anybody, and have nobody to consider but myself; but for a month or two I must be let alone. The lawyers will soon want me in London for the probate for some days; and then we can say our say.

As to a night here, I should have to ask Ethel Snowden, Ellen [Wilkinson], [Lady] Rhondda and B.P. [Blanche Patch] (Judy [Musters] also) to chaperon us; and there would be only one bed for them. And the Plymouth correspondent of the Morning Advertiser would expatiate on the profligacy of the aristocracy.

Keep Miss Dowie's eye on the Daily Mail this week.

G.B.S.

Ethel Snowden (1881–1951) was a suffragist and the wife of Philip Snowden: she refused to stand against Nancy in the 1922 election, declaring: 'I would not in any circumstances stand against Lady Astor. I am a Labour woman, but the work which Lady Astor is doing for women and children both in Parliament and the country makes her services invaluable' (Brookes, 34). Miss J.A. **Dowie** was Nancy's secretary. In the **Daily Mail** (6 January 1944), Shaw contributed to a symposium entitled 'How They Would Deal with Germany.' His fellow contributors included H.G. Wells and Sir Robert Vansittart.

146 / To Nancy Astor   Ayot St Lawrence, Welwyn, Herts.
6th January 1944

[ALCS: Reading]

I must come up to town on Wednesday morning, the 12th, for probate business, and shall be at Whitehall Court until Saturday morning next week.

I am not clear as to whether your letter calls off Friday. Anyhow I shall be here.

Violet [Pond] is called up for Friday next week to Pontefract in Yorkshire.

G.B.S.

After attending a training camp at **Pontefract**, Violet was posted to an A.T.S. hospital in London, and she later worked for Winston Churchill at Chequers (the official prime-ministerial country residence) and at 10 Downing Street. She was a technical adviser for the film *Gosford Park* (2001), the collector's edition DVD of which contains an interview with her entitled 'The Authenticity of Gosford Park' (on her life and career, see *The Times*, 4 August 2001).

147 / To G. Bernard Shaw   9 Babmaes St, Jermyn St, SW1
7th January 1944

[TLU (c): Reading]

Dearest G.B.S.

You put me off this Friday, and next Friday I shall be in Plymouth. But I am returning Saturday morning (the 15th) and would like to see you that morning before you return to Ayot – so either you must come to Babmaes Street, or I must come to you.

Is Violet [Pond] going away for good? If so, can we do anything else about it?

[Nancy Astor]

Nancy's **Babmaes** Street flat had actually been fashioned out of part of the back of her bomb-damaged St James's Square house.

148 / To Nancy Astor   Ayot St Lawrence, Welwyn, Herts.

10th January 1944

[ALCS: Reading, Sykes (e)]

Saturday's impossible: I shall have just time to deal with the morning's letters and catch the train to Welwyn Garden City. Four days is my limit at Whitehall: if I stay longer I am rationed. However, the weeks fly by quickly: I shall soon be in London again.

There is nothing to be done about Violet [Pond]. Charlotte could not believe that a house could be run or human life exist without at least two maids: the calling up of one of them was the end of the world for her. But now that Charlotte has gone, and B.P. [Blanche Patch] gone, and I alone here to be waited on, what possible excuse have I for demanding four indoor domestics instead of three? The neighbors are all doing their own house work: there is not even a charwoman. I am on velvet; so dont worry about me.

G.B.S.

149 / To Nancy Astor   Ayot St Lawrence, Welwyn, Herts.

24th January 1944

[ALCS: Reading, Sykes (e)]

Financial matters continued to weigh heavily on Shaw's mind. He told Sidney Webb: 'Charlotte's death has been a financial disaster for me' and gave him a lengthy account of his current finances (Laurence, Letters, 705).

I am all right bodily. Financially I am all wrong, swearing by Almighty God to the truth of documents which I have not read, and pretending that Charlotte's property, valued at £150,000, on which she and I have lived for 47 years, is a new acquisition for which I must pay £40,000. But that is not what worries me: I am as safe really as Rank or MacGowan: it is the folly of the coming Budget and the muddle of our economic ignorance that calls for the Brazen Head of Bernard to speak. So I am writing

146

to The Times: a snorter that will astonish the Labor Party and delight the plutocrats.

The Polish business is old hat. It has been staring us in [the] face for four years (Stalin's first three war speeches defined it emphatically and repeatedly) and we are much surprised and dismayed as if it had never been mentioned or thought of before. We are governed by infant schools.

I'm too bust for anything.

G.B.S.

J. Arthur **Rank** (1888–1972), a film-industry magnate, was head of the Rank Organization. Kenneth **MacGowan** (1888–1963) worked for RKO Studios and in 1947 became head of the Theatre Arts Department at the University of California, Los Angeles. *The Times*, 1 February 1942, published Shaw's 'The Coming Budget: Taxes and the Vicar of Bray,' in which he argued the budget threatened financial ruin, his own in particular. His suggestion (that exempting incomes over £20,000 from income tax would encourage people and thus stimulate the economy) was an early version of 'Reaganomics' and its 'trickle down' theory of economic wealth. The typescript of his letter (BL 50699, ff. 7–11) is entitled 'The Dreaded Budget.' The **Polish business** concerned Poland's and Russia's claims to various territories (see, for example, 'Russia and Poland: History and Lessons of a Fatal Feud: Settlement Vital to Both Parties,' *The Times*, 14 January 1944).

150 / To Nancy Astor Ayot St Lawrence, Welwyn, Herts.

29th January 1944

[ALCS: Reading]

Shaw did not feel the need for a 'change of some sort' until 26 February 1944, when his meeting with Field Marshall Montgomery took place at Augustus John's London studio (Letter 152).

The Times is holding up my long letter until it can make space for it.

Augustus John, painting General Montgomery, wants me to meet him in the studio; but I cannot come up to town yet.

I shall stick fast here until I suddenly feel that I must have a change of some sort; and I'm not near that point yet. That five months of London will last me a long time: another year of it would have killed me.

I am not overworking.

Dont *you* overwork either.

G.B.S.

Augustus John (1878–1961) was the renowned Welsh portrait painter. His portrait of Field Marshall Bernard **Montgomery,** later 1st Viscount Montgomery of Alamein (1887–1979), famous for his victory at the battle of El Alamein in 1942, was eventually sold to the University of Glasgow because 'Monty' did not like it, an opinion Shaw shared (see headnote to Letter 152).

151 / To Nancy Astor   Ayot St Lawrence, Welwyn, Herts.
                                          23rd February 1944
[ALCS: Reading]

The weeks fly by like minutes: you are back before I realize that you are gone.

The I.C.I. having left Ayot, the searchlight has been re-established. Result: on last Friday nights raid a bomb rocked the house and shook Maggie [Caskie] out of bed. The last two raids have made magnificent firework displays for us; but they have also wrecked B.P.'s [Blanch Patch] nerves to the extent of her contemplating a return to Ayot even at the expense of having to housemaid herself, Violet [Pond] having being snatched away by the Forces. So goodbye to my blessed solitude.

General Montgomery's *aide de camp* has arrived to fix me up for a sitting at [Augustus] John's on Saturday afternoon. State cars provided.

Estate duties on Charlotte's property, which does not enrich me by a single penny = £50,000.

My new will is almost impossibly troublesome. And the newspapers on Charlotte's will!!!!

                                          G.B.S.

'[I]n the early days [of the war], Imperial Chemical Industries [**I.C.I.**] used Ayot House as a kind of week-end refuge. Latterly, it was handed over to the Women's Land Army' (Patch, 37). Shaw's final **will**, which did not mention Nancy at all, is printed in Michael Holroyd, *Bernard Shaw: Volume 4: 1950–1991: The Last Laugh* (1992), 101–15. The particularly controversial parts of **Charlotte's will** provided funds to teach the Irish self-control, elocution, oratory, and deportment and to endow a university chair or readership to provide instruction in the same (see Dunbar, 187–92, and Laurence, *Letters,* 681).

152 / To Nancy Astor   Ayot St Lawrence, Welwyn, Herts.
                                          5th March 1944
[TLS: Reading, Sykes (e)]
As Shaw arrived for his 26 February 1944 meeting with Field Marshall Montgom-

ery at Augustus John's studio, he was encountered by Henry Channon: 'I don't think [Shaw] recognised me, but we chatted for a second and he remarked that I had a nice dog, and he patted my famous Bundi, who I thought rather resembled him. G.B.S. looked aged and feeble and was dressed in very dark tweeds and a black overcoat. His white whiskers and pink face looked like an enamelled portrait and had that pink lifeless quality of the very old' (Channon, 388). Shaw recounted the meeting in his 26 February 1944 letter to John (Laurence, Letters, 700–1) and advised him that the 'present sketch [of Montgomery] isnt honestly worth more than the price of your keep while you were painting it.' As Letter 153 reveals, Shaw's account here of his insouciant disposal of Charlotte's jewellery provoked Nancy's displeasure and her acquisitive instinct. If Thomas Jones's account (headnote to Letter 161) is accurate, Shaw sold the small residue of jewellery for £6, thereby incurring more Astorian ire.

Nancy asthore

Monty is a live wire, or rather bundle of wires, with Irish flexibility of mind, decidedly the most interesting general I have met since I did a turn in Tokio with a Jap general whose name I recollect (probably inaccurately) as Araki. To tell you all about the meeting would take too long: it must wait until we have a meeting all to ourselves. John was greatly pleased and wrote to say that the interview was a success, and that I did not dodder noticeably.

As the black-out has now receded to seven o'clock, and the days, though pretty cold, are much brighter, by all means come to tea here some afternoon if you have nothing better to do and can wangle a car. But dont come on next Friday, the 10th, as I have another lady on hand then. I am still happily alone, as B.P. [Blanche Patch] is still 'taking it' heroically. Her latest proposal is that if Mrs Higgs gets overworked she (B.P.) and Judy [Musters] should settle in here, as Judy is a capable cook, having had to feed her late mother and husband for years.

My will is giving me no end of trouble. I want to leave all I possess to the country for the country's good, and find that the country places every possible obstacle to such a proceeding whilst offering me every facility for bequeathing my goods to relatives whose sole idea of the use of property is to mortgage it and pawn most of the things they buy with the money thus raised.

Here I am with only a few months left to live; and I have to waste them on business and on superfluous belongings. Among these, by the way, is a small store of jewellery which Charlotte possessed. It has been rifled by B.P. and Mrs Colthurst (Charlotte's niece) but there may remain something that you would care to have. B.P. now wears the pearls, which are all artificial. Yours, I presume, are natural. Everybody has been very decent in dividing the spoils. I told them to take what they liked, *carte blanche* (especially blanche patch), with the result that there has been no rapacity: Blanche chose as conscientiously for the others as for herself. So there may be something left.

The village post goes at 2-30 on Sundays: so I must finish or I shall miss it.

We had a parachute mine dropped here in one of the recent raids. It stuck in a tree, and not only blew the tree to bits but killed all the pheasants. The whole countryside rushed for them. Local feeling for Jerry is friendlier in consequence.

G.B.S.

Shaw met General Sado **Araki** (1877–1966) in March 1933 when Araki was Japanese Minister of War. Shaw's engagement diary does not reveal who **'another lady'** might have been.

153 / To G. Bernard Shaw   [*no address*]
                                                  7th March 1944
[TLU (c): Reading]

Dearest G.B.S.

Your letter caused me the greatest pleasure.

I am horrified you have only a few more months to live. It means that I will very likely turn up, bag and baggage, so as not to lose a moment of your company before you depart. You *are* getting doddering or you would not have written me that!

I can't understand how you dare tell B.P. [Blanche Patch] to take what she liked of Charlotte's things before me. I am sure Charlotte would have preferred my having the first chance after her niece. However, there may be something left and I don't even want real pearls.

You will laugh when I tell you that I am due in London on the Navy to-day, Infant Mortality to-morrow and the Education Bill on Thursday. Instead of that, I am taking a cross-country trip with my nephew (Phyllis Brand's boy, home on leave and quite alone) and will be with him at Eydon till probably Friday – everything thrown over because of the family. Both you and Philip [Kerr] have often warned me about the family, but on I go!

I wonder who the lady is on Friday? Is it Rhondda – or someone gayer?

I thought you would like 'Monty' and I feel now that I must have been accurate. We thought him far and away the best we had met.

I will be down next week some time. I may have to be driven down by an Australian lady who is a newspaper correspondent. If you don't want her I can leave her in the car or try someone else – but I have to be conveyed.

[Nancy Astor]

Phyllis Brand was Nancy's 'beloved' sister who, in 1917, had married the economist and banker Robert Henry Brand, 1st Lord Brand (1878–1963). Their only son was Jim Brand (1924–45), a tank commander who was killed in action in Germany. The Brands' country home was **Eydon** Hall, near Daventry, Northamptonshire.

154 / To Nancy Astor   Ayot St Lawrence, Welwyn, Herts.
12th March 1944

[ALS: Reading; Holroyd (e)]
Shaw's brief, teasing note is written on a letter to him (dated 10 March 1944) from an unidentified female writer who asked Shaw to marry her, promised him he would not regret it, and proposed calling on him at Easter.

The lady is a perfect stranger to me.
You see, I am still in demand.

G.B.S.

155 / To G. Bernard Shaw   [*no address*]
4th April 1944

[TLU (c): Reading]
Nancy Astor's letter is apparently a follow-up to an unsuccessful telephone call in which she was trying to tell Shaw her latest family news.

Dearest G.B.S.

What I was trying to tell you was that Jakie [Astor], not being contented with the Commandos has now joined the Paratroops, and so got a week's holiday.

I am stopping here with him this week and have given up public life for the time being, as you have so often suggested that I should do.

Last night Jakie held forth about bores and non-bores. He put you and Cyril Alington (the headmaster at Eton) as the two most interesting talkers he had ever listened to. You have gone one up in my estimation!!

Jakie returns to work on Sunday night. If we could get a lift to you we would grab it, but it doesn't look like it unless a benevolent compatriot passed this way.

I may have to go to Plymouth next Tuesday night for a week and I shall try to get to you before leaving. I was all dressed up to come last week and my friend let me down.

You speak about working. I wish to Heaven I could see what you looked like and whether it was agreeing with you!

If you decide to leave this world, let me know, because I might decide to go with you.

[Nancy Astor]

Dr Cyril Argentine **Alington** (1872–1955) was headmaster of Eton (1916–33); he then became Dean of Durham.

156 / To Nancy Astor   Ayot St Lawrence, Welwyn, Herts.
                                                      6th April 1944

[ALCS: Reading, Sykes (e)]

Having skipped an earlier committee meeting on 9 March 1944 on the Education Bill (which later became the 1944 Education Act associated with the Conservative R.A. Butler [1902–82]), Nancy Astor played a crucial role during the debate on the committee stage of the bill on 28 March. She supported an amendment to clause 82 of the bill to provide for equal remuneration for male and female teachers. She said: 'During the years I have been in this House I have heard much nonsense about equality; the time has come to treat women on equal terms. If this were the last vote I ever gave in my life I would give it in favour of this Amendment, because I have watched teachers pressing for equal pay for 24 years and I have seen the prejudice with which they have been met' (Hansard, vol. 398, col. 1364). The amendment was put to a vote: '[T]he result was announced of 117 against the Government and only 116 for it. The first defeat Mr Churchill has sustained. The House gasped, as it began to realise the implications ... The young Tory reformers ... and Lady Astor are to blame' (Channon, 390). The next day Winston Churchill told the Commons that the government would move to 'reinstate the original Clause without the Amendment ... and to treat its passage throughout as a matter of confidence' (Hansard, col. 1452).

Dont come on Saturday. I have film business to transact with Gabriel Pascal here on that afternoon.

To old hands like me Equal Pay is a masculine Trade Union dodge to keep women out of industry, the calculation being that if employers have to pay a woman as much as a man they will always choose a man. So the Unions admitted women on condition that they earned the Union wage: that is, on the same terms as men. Artful, wasnt it?

But there was no excuse for trying to slip E.P. into an Education Bill; and if Winston had stuck to that with polite regrets there need have been no unpleasantness. The Vote of Confidence was worthless and actually damaging.

G.B.S.

157 / To G. Bernard Shaw   9 Babmaes St, Jermyn St, SW1
                                            3rd May 1944

[TLU: Reading]

Sometime in April 1944, the drama critic John Mason Brown (1900–69) visited Shaw 'in the company of Lady Astor and McGeorge Bundy ... Bundy says that he went along at Lady Astor's suggestion, so that a staff car could be used and she could save her petrol ration. Lady Astor was particularly interested in seeing Shaw ... was being made comfortable and generally taken care of' (Stevens, 146). At the time Brown was serving as a lieutenant in the United States Navy; he later became a columnist for the Saturday Review. *His meeting with Shaw was published as 'Back to Methuselah: A Visit to an Elderly Gentleman in a World of Arms and the Man,'* Saturday Review of Literature, *22 July 1944, 6–9. As Letter 177 reveals, Brown's article caused Blanche Patch some annoyance. Shaw apparently did not remember having met Brown before – for lunch on 5 July 1932 (Stevens, 93, 147).*

153

Bundy (1919–96) later served as a dean at Harvard University and in the Kennedy administration as a special assistant for national security affairs.

Dearest G.B.S.

When are you coming to Cliveden? You really must hurry up! I am getting impatient!

Could you make it about May 25th? Would that be convenient? – Or would you rather wait until June? Anyhow, I can't wait too long.

My two Americans were delighted to see you. I wish you could see the rapturous letter the literary fellow wrote about you!

Waldorf and I returned from Plymouth Saturday morning and there was a raid that night. Four hundred more houses destroyed and 1000 more damaged–and 6 people killed!

The coloured troops were scared stiff and cried loudly to the Lord to save them. One of them crept into a drain for safety and was blown out the other end!

[Nancy Astor]

158 / To Nancy Astor   Ayot St Lawrence, Welwyn, Herts.
8th May 1944

[TLS: Reading, Holroyd (e), Masters (e), Sykes (e)]

In addition to declining Nancy Astor's recurring invitations to Cliveden, Shaw was still occupied with clearing up Charlotte's affairs. In particular he was arranging for her extensive correspondence with T.E. Lawrence to be transferred to the British Museum (now the British Library).

My dear Nancy

Why should I come to Cliveden? I am quite well and contented here, where the spring is delightful and I can bore nobody with my old stories and general obsolescence. At Cliveden I should see Waldorf occasionally for five minutes at breakfast and you precariously for a few words later in the day when you were not away in London or Plymouth. All the rest of the time I should be either trying to get through my work and business out of reach of my papers and books of reference, or trying to entertain the fearfully miscellaneous crowd of nobodies whom your reckless Virginian hospitality tolerates. Now that the old Round Table South African group of Curtis, [Geoffrey] Dawson, [Walter] Elliot and Phil [Kerr] is gone, I have to act as the Cliveden Set. Do you want to kill me?

But perhaps that would be the kindest thing.

I now have to housekeep as well as be a great author. Mrs Higgs has given me notice that Higgs cannot face another winter here, and that she is at the end of her tether. Mrs Laden, a very capable widow who was on duty for us at Whitehall when Charlotte passed, is willing to come here and carry on; but matters will be a little difficult without a man here to replace Higgs.

He, by the way, cannot bear to leave his garden until he sees it through the summer; but he is terribly lamed by sciatica and really past his work without a gardener's laborer to help him.

I shall probably have to marry Mrs Laden.

I have found among Charlotte's papers some very interesting letters of hers to [T.E.] Lawrence, to whom in 1927 she told all the things about herself that a woman never tells to her husband. She had treasures in the way of Lawrence MSS. I am sending them all to the British Museum. There is also a letter to Charlotte from Mrs Sydney Smith, the wife of his commanding officer at Mountbatten, in which she describes quite frankly and innocently how she adored him. He was aware of this fact, and rather terrified by it.

My letter in The Times moved Anderson to promise some sort of concession to authors in the budget. I am trying to prevent his making a mess of it; for what he suggested in his speech was an exemption which they already enjoy: a champion example of How Not To Do It.

This is enough for one letter.

G.B.S.

The **Round Table**, founded in 1909, comprised a group of men, influenced by Alfred Milner, who placed great emphasis on the role in world affairs of consequential men (rather than the masses) and whose ideal was the British Empire. Lionel **Curtis** (1872–1955), one of Nancy's close friends, was a founder member of the Round Table, and in 1919 founded the Royal Institute of International Affairs. The Scottish Alice **Laden** (1901–79) had nursed Charlotte at Whitehall in the weeks before her death; she became housekeeper at Ayot on 19 September 1944. After Shaw's death she was appointed curator of 'Shaw's Corner,' and published *The George Bernard Shaw Vegetarian Cookbook* (1972). **Mrs Sydney** (Clare) **Smith** was the wife of T.E. Lawrence's Wing Commander when Lawrence was stationed at R.A.F. Mountbatten, Plymouth. She wrote *The Golden Reign: The Story of My*

Friendship with 'Lawrence of Arabia' (1940). Charlotte Shaw wrote to her on 17 May 1927 (BL 45922, ff. 5–12) and Mrs Smith replied on 20 May (BL 45922, f. 54). As Shaw indicates, both letters are (for their period) rather frank about the writers' lives. Shaw refers to his **letter in** ***The Times*** mentioned in Letter 149. Sir John **Anderson**, later Viscount Waverley (1882–1958) was Chancellor of the Exchequer (1943–5). Earlier he had been Home Secretary (1939–40); the Second World War air-raid shelters were named after him.

159 / To Nancy Astor   Ayot St Lawrence, Welwyn, Herts.

                                            30th May 1944

[TLT: Reading]

Where are you spending Whitsun?

I have sent all the letters to the British Museum, including one from the lady you mention. I have typed copies.

Lawrence was so desperately frightened at first lest he should have to play Joseph to Potiphar's wife that he may have left letters that are very unfair to her. He certainly communicated his apprehensions to Charlotte. But the letter she wrote to Charlotte after his death was so entirely frank, decent, and innocent as to how she 'adored' him that I thought it better to include it in the B.M. collection.

I half expected a visit from you last week. This afternoon, [Gabriel] Pascal and Vivien Leigh, who demands to be photographed with me as Rains was. She is to be Cleopatra in the film and Rains the Caesar.

No news here. Very hot weather. I am sitting in the shelter with Mrs Winsten (a very remarkable lady and artist) sitting outside in the sun trying to make a portrait of me as I write. I have to use the typewriter, as my hand is giving way at last.

Endless business over the Pay As You Earn business with the domestic staff, and the disposition of my property and Charlotte's.

                                            G.B.S. to Nancy

The **letters** are those mentioned in the previous letter and the **lady** is Mrs Sydney Smith. **Potiphar's wife** 'cast her eyes upon Joseph; and she said, Lie with me' in Genesis 39:7. **Vivien Leigh** (1913–67), star of stage and screen and wife of Laurence Olivier (1907–89), performed in several of Shaw's works. Shaw was unimpressed with her during the shooting of the film of *Caesar and Cleopatra*: '... Vivien gabbling tonelessly ... Does she always go on like that or should I have had her here to drill her in the diction of the part?' (Dukore, 169–70). Claude **Rains** (1889–1967) had an extensive stage career before becoming a film star in 1933. Clare **Winsten** (1894–1989) and her husband Stephen (1893–1991) were

Shaw's neighbours at Ayot. She was a painter and he the author of three rather fanciful and unreliable books on Shaw, including *Days with Bernard Shaw* (1949), which Shaw criticized in the *Times Literary Supplement*, 15 January 1949. Not entirely impartially, Nancy called it 'that appalling book ... G.B.S.'s letter seemed to me to rip it in two. I have always thought those Winstens were a danger and now I know it!' (20 January 1949 letter to Sydney Cockerell, BL 52703, f. 219). On **Pay As You Earn**, see the endnote to Letter 100.

160 / To G. Bernard Shaw   [*no address*]
                                                          2nd June 1944

[TLU (c): Reading]

Here Nancy Astor manages to combine rapid shifts in subject matter and tone with her possessiveness and jealousy. However, her genuine desire to see Shaw's 'typed copies' of Charlotte's correspondence with T.E. Lawrence reflects the close friendship she enjoyed with him.

Dearest G.B.S.

I must see your beautiful handwriting sometime. I don't mind the typewriter, but so much beauty has gone out of my life I can't let this pass too without a protest!

When you talk about the endless business of 'Pay-as-you-earn' with your domestic staff and you have only two, one of which you hope to marry – why all this trouble?

As to the disposition of your property, I have implored you to make me your heiress and once more I put it in writing! It is my only chance!

I missed being Lawrence's 'Lady Hamilton' and I can't be your 'Helen' – but at least let me be your heiress. I shall need every penny that you save!

I was off to Plymouth last night but my niece has improved so much in the last three days (after nearly a year in a Nursing Home) that I may have to give it up entirely and stay here – in which case I can certainly come to you.

So you are having your portrait done by a very remarkable lady [Clare Winsten], and you have seen Vivien Leigh. It all makes me slightly fidgety!

I suppose I can't have a copy of your typed copies, that is asking too much – but I would love to see them sometime when I come to see you.

Waldorf went to Plymouth last night. I don't know where the family is.

                                                          [Nancy Astor]

Lady Emma **Hamilton** (1761?–1815) was the mistress of Horatio Lord Nelson (1758–1805). The **Helen** of Greek legend was the wife of Menelaus; her elopement with Paris led to the Trojan War. Nancy's ill **niece** in this and letter 161 is unidentified; Nancy had a considerable number of nieces.

161 / To G. Bernard Shaw [Cliveden]
19th June 1944

[TLU: Reading]

A little before 15 June 1944 Nancy Astor, accompanied by Thomas Jones, visited Shaw. They travelled in 'a car labelled "For Christian Science Workers," whatever that means ... We found G.B.S. in a garden hut making out cheques for domestic bills. Since Charlotte's death he won't have Miss Patch, the P.S. [private secretary], down. She is at Whitehall Court ... He is ever so much better since Charlotte died. I noticed that when talking he gripped the arm of the chair with both hands, steadying himself while sitting erect, and talking with his usual clarity and emphasis, mainly about money, taxes, property, and his will ... He talked most tenderly of the last thirty or forty hours of Charlotte's life when she grew so extraordinarily young and beautiful to look upon that he 'phoned to Nancy to hurry up from Plymouth to see her. He had never seen her so beautiful and told her so ... He sold Charlotte's personal jewelry in a heap for six pounds! Nancy was furious at this, and on the afternoon we were there G.B.S. gave her Charlotte's box with bottles, scissors etc., a case of Irish origin, which Nancy took away with her, but will return later. It appears that Shaw intends to leave his country house and contents, as Tolstoy did, as a place of pilgrimage, and Nancy will see that there is a Charlotte room in it and put the box there. There are orders for his new Everybody's Political What's What? *for 75,000 copies before publication' (Jones, Diary, 518–20).*

Dearest G.B.S.

I should have written you at once and thanked you for our visit and for giving me Charlotte's lovely Chest. I shall keep it with great care, and some day leave it to Charlotte's rooms at Ayot – for I know it will become a shrine (like Tolstoy's) and it should be there.

It is a real picture of her aristocratic past and will explode her Communistic present!

I have been here at Cliveden ever since, and my niece is much better. I return to Plymouth this week, but not for long.

I hope you will make some plans about coming here. It looks as though we shall be here all August.

My Bobbie [Shaw] has been ill in Kent with pleurisy and I had to go down and see him. He said every one of those pilot-less planes passes over his house and it's an immense feeling of relief when they don't stop!

Please send me a line to London to let me know how you are, whom you are seeing and to reassure me of your affection – the proof of which will be for you to come and see me!

[Nancy Astor]

From June 1944 to March 1945 the Germans used jet-propelled **pilotless** aircraft, the V-1, to bomb London.

162 / To Nancy Astor   Ayot St Lawrence, Welwyn, Herts.

29th June 1944

[TLS: Reading, Holroyd (e)]

Shaw's Whitehall flat had suffered bomb damage previously, in 1941 (see Letter 80). This time the damage was more extensive: 'A window in my study was shivered into smithereens, my front door blown in, the grandfather clock prostrated, one of Charlotte's Tang horses shattered, and – comble de malheur – Strobl's bust of Lady Astor done in' (Laurence, Letters, 716). Shaw avoided telling Nancy the truth (Letter 165), and the bust was later repaired and presented to the House of Commons (Letter 228). Shaw's vague suggestion that he might avail himself of Nancy's hospitality led immediately to a shower of pressuring invitations from her. Blanche Patch returned to Ayot because of the damage to the Whitehall flat.

Dear Nancy (I used a warmer adjective; but B.P. [Blanche Patch] has toned it down)

The Whitehall flat has been blasted again; and if it is not made habitable before the servants here need a holiday I may be homeless. So there is half a chance for Cliveden after all, though I still hope to escape.

The pilotless bombs have driven everyone out of London, including Blanche, who has returned to Ayot. The village is crowded with refugees.

But the bombs in their blindness stray this way: two came down near enough to shake the house last week. In the next war there will be no black-out; nothing but a lethal firework display directed from Knightsbridge Barracks and the foreign Casernes.

After more work on it than a dozen plays would have cost me I have at last drafted my will and put it out of my day's work. But I am still trying to make a present of my Irish property to the town of Carlow. Nobody knows how it can be done; so I shall have to find that out. There are still things that I must settle before I am ready to die; and, when I am, I shall try whether I have another play left in me. What with all this business I have written myself out for a day; so this letter doesnt count; it is just a Coo-ee to remind you that I am still alive.

sempre a te
G. Bernard Shaw

PS   Mrs Winsten has painted an amazing portrait of me to perpetuate my memory in Ayot as its oldest inhabitant. You must see it next time you come.

---

163 / To G. Bernard Shaw   [*no address*]
1st July 1944

[TLT (c): Reading]
Nancy Astor had originally written this note herself. However '[a]fter writing this card, Lady Astor was afraid you would not be able to read it – so she asked me [secretary] to type it out for you.'

Dearest G.B.S.

I am delighted! I return next Thurs to Cliveden. Please come soon. Please. Much much love. Thank goodness the will's over. Have you remembered Me! I must be remembered by you – else I will be forgot!! However it doesn't matter posterity or fame – But now matters so please come. Love to Miss P— [Patch]. If Ayots bad go at once to Cliveden. P— too.

Y.
N....

164 / To G. Bernard Shaw   [*no address*]
3rd July 1944

[TLU (c): Reading]

Dearest G.B.S.

I sent you a hurried note but this is to urge you to come to Cliveden.

Would you like to come down to Cornwall in August? We have got a small place, very near the sea. It is North Cornwall, bracing and quiet. I believe you would love it. We'd go down about the 3rd or 4th of August. I have a notion it would be good for you to get right away, but it may strike horror to your soul.

[Nancy Astor]

165 / To Nancy Astor   Ayot St Lawrence, Welwyn, Herts.
10th July 1944

[ALCS: Reading]

The best news from my blasted flat in London is that your bust was *not* broken.

My will, like Charlotte's, will confine itself strictly to business except for the direction that my ashes are to be inseparably mixed with hers, as we agreed at my suggestion. As all I possess is yours now for the asking what could I possibly bequeath that you want?

I think I had better stick to my routine here until my affairs are all settled; for if I am uprooted and transplanted I shall probably die immediately. This is how I feel about it. But at any moment I may feel that I shall die if I stay here another minute.

At least one doodle-bug drops near enough to shake us, out of the daily hundred with ten killed as stated by Churchill.

G.B.S.

On Shaw's **ashes**, see Letter 103. **Doodlebug** was the colloquialism for the V-1 rockets.

166 / To Nancy Astor   Ayot St Lawrence, Welwyn, Herts.
                                                        4th August 1944

[ALCS: Reading]

*The medical profession was one of Shaw's recurring interests and here he reverts to
the contemporary debate about a national health service, which had been proposed
in the Beveridge Report (see Letters 127, 198).*

Now is the moment for the Church of Christ Scientist to cut in with a
vigorous reminder that the need for keeping a health service and a
sickness service carefully separate exists as urgently for adults as for
children. If we put our health in charge of the doctors instead of the
anti-doctors we shall have forty compulsory inoculations for every citizen
(T.E. Lawrence suffered them as a common soldier) and all childbirths
will be effected by the Caesarian operation with the midwives restricted
to counting the sponges.

Has C.S. got a competent spokesman; and if so, can you set him on?
I can do no more, having shot my (our) bolt.

                                                        G.B.S.

167 / To Nancy Astor   Ayot St Lawrence, Welwyn, Herts.
                                                        11th August 1944

[ALCS: Reading, Holroyd (e)]

*Nancy Astor was on vacation at Trebetherick, near Wadebridge in North Cornwall,
and evidently, without his consent, had made arrangements for Shaw to join her
there.*

I had to countermand the sleeper. You think of me as a man with a valet
and a secretary making all arrangements for me and leaving me nothing
to do but step into the train and out again into the station car. But what
could I do with such factotums for the rest of the year? And so for me
three removes are as bad as a fire; and a remove to Cornwall for a
fortnight or three weeks would cost me three days packing and arranging and thinking about the most wearisome trifles.

And before the first week ended Eden would call you up to London to
hear him talking about some victory or defeat or new secret weapon or
what not.

Do not be nervous about the ladies. I still regard myself as Charlotte's property. I really could not ask her to mix our ashes with those of a third party.

G.B.S.

Anthony **Eden**, later 1st Earl of Avon (1897–1977), was currently Foreign Secretary (1940–5); he eventually succeeded Winston Churchill as Prime Minister (1955–7). On **ashes**, see Letter 103.

168 / To Nancy Astor   Ayot St Lawrence, Welwyn, Herts.
                                                          16th August 1944

[ALS: Reading]

Blanche Patch may well have colluded with Nancy Astor in arranging the now doomed Cornwall vacation, and her letter provides an additional perspective on Shaw's current domestic arrangements. It also appears Nancy had invited Blanche to spend a holiday at her home in Plymouth.

Dear Lady Astor

It seems very tiresome & ungrateful of us to have upset your arrangements so speedily; but now that our domestic affairs are settling themselves I rather think it will be best for GBS to join you at Cliveden &, for the moment, he is, I hope, considering this favourably. I think the night journey would have been too much for him. One has only to watch him walking in the garden to realize that he is now an old man & very shaky.

It is definitely settled for Mrs Laden to come here about the 1st Sept & take over the h[ouse] parlormaid work while Maggie [Caskie] is away. After that she will succeed Mrs Higgs & as she was so very capable at Whitehall I am full of hope that she will be a success here. For the moment I must carry on – much as I long to forget GBS & all his works – & for this reason I have cancelled your kind arrangement at Plymouth. The war news is so good that I may be able to get back to London sooner than I expected. Apart from the bombs it suits me much better than this isolation – & now we've been visited by a plague of wasps!

Yours sincerely
Blanche Patch

169 / To G. Bernard Shaw   Trebetherick, Wadebridge, Cornwall
16th August 1944

[TEL: BL 50528, f. 103]

Nancy Astor (as had Blanche Patch in the previous letter) had concluded that, while Shaw would not agree to going to Cornwall, he might be persuaded to stay at Cliveden. Her hope proved in vain, now and in the future.

IF YOU WILL COME TO CLIVEDEN ABOUT SEPTEMBER 16TH FOR ONE MONTH I WILL NOT FORCE YOU TO CORNWALL. PLEASE ANSWER OR I SHALL RETURN AND COOK FOR YOU. LOVE NANCY.

170 / To Nancy Astor   Ayot St Lawrence, Welwyn, Herts.
17th August 1944

[ALCS: Reading]

The situation has eased up a little. Mrs Laden will take the job and settle in on the 1st September. If I can get petrol enough for my Rolls Cliveden is only 70 minutes off; and packing is easier now that I can use Charlotte's two motor trunks as well as my own. In fact I could drop in to tea even if I couldnt stay. The other difficulties may settle themselves before the middle of September.

The Observer has put in my Budget article as a silly season feature; but I am used to these covert insults. They serve my turn, which is always that of a *faute de mieux* stopgap.

G.B.S.

Shaw's **budget** article was 'How Much Money Do We Need?' *Observer*, 13 August 1944. In it Shaw presented various ways to achieve equality of income: 'The struggle will be between the progressive Levellers-up and the catastrophic Levellers-down: and the Progressives will win if and when they learn their political business.'

171 / To Nancy Astor   Ayot St Lawrence, Welwyn, Herts.
27th August 1944

[ALCS: Reading, Holroyd (e)]

Arrangements change from day to day. Mrs Laden, free from the 31st,

must have a holiday to recuperate after Whitehall with her parents in
bonnie Scotland. She seems to have a shooting lodge there as well as a
country house in Isleworth. Blanche [Patch] urged me to settle the
question of her remuneration. I explained accordingly that as I could
not do without her and she could do without me her strong position
entitled her to a blank cheque. As I have not the faintest notion of what
one pays a goodlooking housekeeper in the prime of life (have you?) I
had to cover my ignorance with this stage effect.

Maggie [Caskie] has, she is now told, no chance of a permit for Eire
until the end of September, and not much even then.

I cannot budge until I get the house on its new footing after the Higgs
abdication.

No doubt the story will change completely before the end of the week.

G.B.S.

Instead of a **blank cheque**, Mrs Laden agreed to £143 a year (see headnote to Letter 173).

172 / To Nancy Astor   Ayot St Lawrence, Welwyn, Herts.
10th September 1944

[ALS: Reading]

*Blanche Patch, who hated the isolation of Ayot, finally succeeded in arranging a
holiday away from Shaw and the household. She also appeared to be losing interest
in her job; however, despite her dissatisfactions, she continued as Shaw's secretary
until his death. Judy Musters substituted for Blanche 13–27 September 1944.
While Blanche was at Tempsford Hall, Nancy wrote to her on 14 September
(Reading): 'Thank goodness you got away. / I am perfectly certain you will feel
better when you come back and then we can talk things over ... I hope very much
that ... GBS will be coming to me next week but I see I must go to him.'*

Dear Lady Astor

I have at last succeeded in arranging a holiday & next Wed. the 13th go
to Tempsford Hall, Sandy, Beds. for 2 weeks. It is a sort of Hydro-Hotel &
has every imaginable form of spa treatment in which I may indulge by
way of amusement, though I am only going there because it is easy to get
at from here. Judy Musters comes on the 14th – the Higgs go on the 21st,
Mrs Laden arrives on the 18th & I hope will be well installed by the time

I return. All being well I shall then go back to London, as I couldn't face the isolation of a winter here. Besides GBS really likes being alone & I'm sure finds it very boring to have a second person – not his intellectual equal – always at meals. Probably its high time I retired being now 64, but I don't know how to effect the change. Perhaps when I'm less tired after 'Sandy' & am managing to sleep better I may think of a solution.

I hope your stay in Cornwall has given you a good rest.

Yours sincerely
Blanche Patch

Sandy lies due east of Bedford in Bedfordshire, only twenty miles due north of Ayot.

173 / To Nancy Astor   Ayot St Lawrence, Welwyn, Herts.
11th September 1944

[ALCS: Reading]

Instead of signing this letter, Shaw has written 'from G.B.S.' next to the date. Apparently Shaw was finding events genuinely 'tempestuous' because his engagement diary for 1944 is devoid of entries except for the following days in September: '13th "Judy to arrive; B.P. off for her holiday"; 18th "Day due back from his holiday"; 19th "Mrs Laden arrives"; 20th "Mrs Laden agrees £143 (2-15-0 weekly)"; 22th "The Higges leave at 11"; 27th "B.P. due back from her holiday."'

Still the weeks fly by like hours; the year has skipped over September from August straight into chill October; and there is not the faintest chance of my stirring from this spot for months to come unless the advent of peace and petrol enables and obliges me to go to London for a spell. A revival of Saint Joan is in contemplation there with Ann Casson in the part created by her mother (Sybil Thorndike); and though I must leave the production entirely to her father, I may have to be on the spot for business. Next week here will be tempestuous: Mrs Laden coming, the Higgses leaving, Judy [Musters] arriving, Blanche [Patch] & Maggie [Caskie] off for their holiday, [Fred] Day back from his, wages and pensions to be settled &c. &c. &c!

Ann Casson (1915–90) toured the provinces in 1944 playing Ann in *Man and Superman* and Joan in *Saint Joan*; she repeated the latter role at the King's Theatre, Hammersmith, in February 1945 (*The Times*, 21 February 1945). Her **father** was (Sir) Lewis Casson (1875–

1969), the English actor and director, who had a long career that included Shavian roles during the famous Barker-Vedrenne Court Theatre season of 1904–7. He played Warwick during this touring production of *Saint Joan*.

174 / To G. Bernard Shaw [*no address*]
14th September 1944

[TLU (c): Reading]

Dearest G.B.S.

I hear Miss Judy [Musters] arrives to-day and the Higgs go on the 21st and the Ladens arrive on the 18th, and Patch won't return for a fortnight. This seems that there is no chance of your coming to Cliveden yet awhile? Is there?

I am returning on Saturday and hoped to fetch you on Monday. I will ring you or Miss Judy up as soon as I get back and am truly disappointed. I expect it means that I shall have to spend October with you, which of course I am willing and rather longing to do!

Yours

[Nancy Astor]

175 / To Nancy Astor Ayot St Lawrence, Welwyn, Herts.
6th October 1944

[TLS: Reading, Holroyd (e)]

Although Nancy Astor's letters are missing, she was clearly continuing to urge Shaw to stay with her, a tactic that served only to increase his scarcely disguised irritability with her. Shaw was more concerned with the dislocations caused by the departure of his long-serving servants, the Higgses, which he describes here. Waldorf Astor had decided reluctantly to retire as Lord Mayor of Plymouth, a decision encouraged by the local Conservative party officials, who wanted to revert to the practice of filling the office with an elected city council member.

Nancy Nancy

You think I need a change. Gracious Heavens, there has been nothing but change here for weeks. Changing from Blanche [Patch] to Judy [Musters] and from Judy to Blanche; from being parlor maided and

valeted by Maggie [Caskie] to doing it myself; above all, the departure of
the Higgses from their home of forty years to fend for themselves in a
world in which they are museum pieces, driven out before a terrible New
Woman, of a species unknown to them, from the house where they had
been supreme indoors and out. Mrs Higgs had talked of overlapping the
new comer by a fortnight 'to train her.' Poor dear! she fled from her new
nothingness in two devastated days.

They went away in a handsome car, beautifully dressed, with the dog
on its lead, greatly excited. I kissed her goodbye, and waved after them
until the car disappeared round the corner. Always acting, you will say. I
thought so myself; but I must have felt the part: for when I went to the
shelter to write, I found that my pen wobbled a little in my hand. Next
day, it was as if they had been gone for twenty years.

Blanche and I have been gorging ever since. After Mrs Higgs's two
or three dishes, over and over again, Mrs Laden's meals are the
masterpie[ces] of a beribboned chef. Her soups! her sweets! her savouries!
we have to wait on ourselves; but we eat too much and enjoy doing it. I
shall not live so long on this luscious fare as I should on Mrs Higgs's.

It is a first rate move of Waldorf's making the mayoralty a present to a
proletarian. Probably it will give him more complete command of the
situation. It is often better to be behind the throne than on it. But the
landlords will do their very damndest to wreck the Town Planning Bill
(blast them!); and this will bring you into sharp conflict with the Conservatives, to whom neither of you naturally belongs. You must frankly run
up the Red Flag or let the Plan go. Meanwhile, you must watch the
amendments as a cat watches a mouse.

Dont read the book except when you want a nap. Just skim the index
and look up any page that interests you. It is just in time to help the
Plymouth plan as far as it can help anything at all.

I shall expect you next week. Maggie is due on Tuesday, but after her
journey from Ireland will be no good until Thursday.

G.B.S.

During a 19 October 1944 debate on the Town and Country **Planning Bill** (currently under
consideration in the House of Commons and which proposed introducing various con-
trols), Sir Herbert Williams (1884–1954), a Conservative MP, commented: 'I have never
known anyone attract more publicity per minute during her presence in this House than
the Noble Lady [Nancy Astor]. I have sometimes seen her interrupt before she reaches her

168

seat. At any rate the Noble Lady is fortunate that the principles of the Town and Country Planning Act were not applied say, 40 or 50 years ago to the ground rents of New York City' (*Hansard*, vol. 403, col. 2619). The **book** was probably *Everybody's Political What's What?* published on 15 September 1944.

176 / To Nancy Astor Ayot St Lawrence, Welwyn, Herts.
10th November 1944

[ALCS: Reading]

In 1942 Nancy Astor had disapproved of her son Michael's bride. However, she objected in no uncertain terms to Jakie Astor's marriage on 23 October 1944 to a Roman Catholic, Ana Inez 'Chiquita' Carcano (d. 1992), the younger daughter of Miguel Angel Carcano (1889–1978), Argentinian ambassador to Britain (1942–6). On 2 November 1944 (Reading) Nancy wrote to her friend Lady Minna Butler-Thwing (1887–1963) that the marriage 'has been a great distress to us, not on account of the nationality but of their different faiths. You more than most people will appreciate that. She is a charming girl and I like the parents very much. They were as apprehensive as we were.' Waldorf and Nancy were not among just seventeen guests at the wedding: 'within four minutes of the bride's entry on her father's arm the ceremony was over' ('Lord Astor's Son Weds,' unidentified newspaper clipping, NLW, Class Q, vol. 1, f. 127). The marriage ended in divorce in 1972.

Nothing to write about. One day, one week, one year is like another. Schopenhauer said that when we are young we hope every day that something will happen: in old age we thank God that nothing has happened. Quite true.

Geoffrey [Dawson] dead and Phil [Kerr] dead! The Cliveden Set is passing.

The Leader (the new picture paper) wants me to write an article about the Silver Wedding of Plymouth and Westminster. It would like some gossip about you; but I shall stick to the Suffragist movement and gossip about myself as usual, keeping you out of it all I can.

There will be a devil of a time after the General Election. Will you stand again? If yes, will you stand as a Churchillian or a Beveridgian or a Communist or (which I recommend) as Nancy Astor?

G.B.S.

Which is worse? the shoulder wound or the capture of Jakie by the Argentine?

The German philosopher Arthur **Schopenhauer** (1788–1860) was the author of *Die Welt als Wille und Vorstellung* (*The World as Will and Representation*, 1819), which influenced Shaw's work (such as *Man and Superman*). 'To ... Shaw the essence of Schopenhauer was his contention that the Will is the main driving-force of human existence' (Bentley, 48; see also 'Wagner's Own Exploration' in Shaw's *The Perfect Wagnerite* [1898]). In 'Women in Politics,' **Leader** Magazine, 2 (25 November 1944), 5–6, Shaw was as good as his word and stuck largely to his theme of suffragism: only his final paragraph concerned Nancy and the challenge she faced when, twenty-five years earlier, she became the sole female in the House of Commons and thereby 'raised the siege that had lasted for seven centuries.' A **general election** was not called until 5 July 1945, when Nancy did not stand (see Letters 178, 180–1, 183–5). In 1944 David Astor was assigned to liaise with the French Resistance and was subsequently wounded in the **shoulder** during an ambush. He was awarded the Croix de Guerre ('David Astor' [obituary], *Daily Telegraph*, 8 December 2001).

177 / To Nancy Astor Ayot St Lawrence, Welwyn, Herts.
10th November 1944

[ALS: Reading]

Blanche Patch again reveals her occasional exasperation with Shaw, which here stems from the visit in April 1944 by John Mason Brown and his subsequent article in the Saturday Review of Literature *(see Letter 157). In his article (9) Brown quoted Shaw as saying, 'There would be no wars if only men read my books. And took them to heart ... That's silly of me, really silly. I ought to know better. I have only to remember Patch ... Patch has typed all my stuff for me these many years. And what I have written has never had any effect upon her at all. She is bored with me and my work and abhors my ideas. You can tell she does not understand them by the mistakes she makes in transcribing them.' When Brown included this article as part of his book* Many a Watchful Night *(1944), the references to Blanche were omitted because she had written to the publishers, McGraw-Hill, 'in September 1944 threatening suit if the passage appeared in the book' (Stevens, 169).*

Dear Lady Astor

I did not send you any news from here because really there was nothing to say. GBS seems much as usual & sails along in his usual serene fashion quite oblivious of the many domestic trials & troubles that assail most of us nowadays. I sometimes wish that he'd had one or two daughters. They would probably have brought him to earth occasionally.

I shall probably retreat to London again; but he will be all right with our new housekeeper & on the whole happier having his meals by himself. Did I tell you that he told the American, John Mason Brown, who reported it in a New York paper that *I* was bored with his work & him & abhorred his ideas? He denies having said it & I've an inkling that he meant *he* was bored with me.

I hope Plymouth was not as cold today as it is here, but I read in an old Guide Book that Herts is a notoriously cold county & only the most robust constitutions can stand it.

Yours sincerely

Blanche Patch

178 / To Nancy Astor   Ayot St Lawrence, Welwyn, Herts.

19th November 1944

[TLS: Reading, Sykes (e)]

For a considerable time members of Nancy Astor's family had been urging her to retire from Parliament (see the Introduction, xxiii–xxiv, and, for example, the discreet account in Astor, 217–19). Nancy was more than reluctant, as her 28 December 1944 letter to Thomas Jones (NLW, Class Q, vol. 2, f. 78) reveals: 'I am not at all certain that I should leave Parliament at this moment. It was Waldorf's decision not mine. He was tired but as Bill [Astor] remarked why should Mother retire & not you? Well you know that tired minds are poor guides. L.G. [Lloyd George] is over 80. I am 65 & very spry & very strong with a good knowledge of politics.' The announcement on 1 December 1944 of Nancy's retirement ('Lady Astor to Retire,' The Times, 2 December) was surrounded by a flurry of celebrations of her twenty-five years in Parliament. The British Federation of Business and Professional Women gave one such celebratory dinner at Grosvenor House on 30 November. Waldorf, the only man present, spoke eloquently (if perhaps cynically in light of the impending retirement announcement): 'When I married Nancy, I hitched my wagon to a star. And then when I got into the House of Commons in 1910, I found that I had hitched my wagon to a shooting star. In 1919 when she got into the House, I found I had hitched my wagon to a sort of V2 rocket. But the star which is represented by Nancy Astor will, I am sure, remain a beacon light for all with high ideals' (The Times, 1 December 1944). The next day twenty-eight past or present women MPs honoured Nancy with a luncheon at the House of Commons and she took the opportunity to express her bitterness about the retirement announcement: 'Today I have done a thing that has been terrible for me

– one of the hardest things I have ever done in my life, but a thing that every man in the world will approve of. I have said that I will not fight the next election because my husband does not want me to. I have had twenty-five years in the House of Commons, and I am bound to obey. Isn't that a triumph for the men? But whether in or out of the House, I shall always stand for what women stand for' (Sykes, 474). Waldorf's insistence on her retirement led to a significant rift (maintained stubbornly on Nancy's side) in their relationship during the remaining eight or so years of Waldorf's life.

My dear Nancy

I really dont know what to say, because I dont know why you are being pressed to retire.

Sometimes people who are first rate for starting a movement upset it if they dont withdraw at the right moment and start something else.

Sometimes MPs stick to their seats too long, having worn out their authority, novelty, and patience with the futility of the House under the Party system.

Sometimes a project like the Plymouth Improvement, having been set going under dual control, reaches a phase in which single control is indispensable.

How am I to know what is in the mind of W[aldorf] and your serpent brood if they really want to hound you out of public life? They may have a dozen other reasons that I know nothing about. Obviously you have 20 years work left in you yet, and are getting deeper instead of being merely quick witted and inconsecutive.

Both you and your mate are in a false position as members of the Conservative Party, or indeed of any Party. You ought to be Independents, like Margery Fry with her University seat. When Hitler and Mussolini are finally steamrollered there will be only three parties: the Diehards, the Fascists, and the Communists. The regime will be Fascist, as Fascism, which is Capitalism established and endowed by the State, is too firmly established here, and too acceptable to the Trade Unions, to be shaken. The Opposition will be Communists trying continually to substitute State ownership for Capitalist ownership, and State enterprise for Capitalist enterprise. National banking and transport, municipalization of urban land, and collective farming, will be the Opposition programs in the rest of the century. Waldorf will be an Urban Land municipalizer or he will be nothing. That is to say, he will be a Communist, whether his party calls itself so or not. You in the Commons cannot go on voting with the Diehards against him. You will both be against the Fascists and for the Communists on every important division. You will both find yourselves in embittered conflict with your Cliveden guests, just as old Lady Carlisle (Britomart Undershaft), who by the way, was a bigoted teetotaller and an ungovernable live wire like yourself, found her social circle broken up when the Liberal party split over Home Rule. This monstrous caravanserai in which you and Waldorf live will be deserted by its rabble of Tory subalterns and public schoolboys and their relatives as the Carlisle mansion in Kensington Palace Gardens was deserted by the Chamberlain Whigs when I lunched there in the days of Gilbert Murray's courtship. It may end in your living sensibly in a twelve roomed villa as Charlotte and I did.

Now that Ireland is disposed of there is going to be a new split in the Liberal party over my case against legislation by Adult Suffrage (Anybody elected by Everybody) and against my insistence on a Constitutional Amendment making half the seats on all public authorities reserved for women only, no matter how they are to be elected or nominated or co-opted or how not.

Where would you stand on these two questions? Are you for the municipal system or the Party System? for Votes for Women or for human instead of masculine government? These are the things that will come up in your time. Look them intelligently in the face before you act on any shorter views in your domestic arrangements.

Now to change the subject.

Is that honest army surgeon who told Charlotte the truth about her illness (none of the private practitioners did: they couldnt afford to, poor fellows) still with you at the hospital? If so, will you ask him whether there is any practitioner in London, Russian or English, who knows about A.C.S., and can treat by it clinically. I know somebody who is going to die of arthritis just as Charlotte died of osteitis. A.C.S. is a serumpathy brought into practice by a Russian named Bogomolets. The papers are full of the miracles it does in the Red Army, mending up wounded soldiers in a week and stimulating patients to unprecedented bone repairs. Our private doctors know nothing about it; but the army surgeons must be keen on it, as they have nothing to lose and much kudos to gain by curing their patients.

Enough for today.

G.B.S.

Shaw is mistaken in thinking **Margery Fry** (1874–1958) held one of the university seats in Parliament. She was principal of Somerville College, Oxford (1926–31), and served on the University Grants Committee (1919–48). Until they were abolished by the 1949 Representation of the People Act, there were twelve seats in Parliament representing **university** constituencies, with Oxford and Cambridge Universities each returning two MPs. Only graduates of the relevant university were eligible to vote; however, they were also eligible to vote in their domiciliary constituency, and thereby could cast two votes in a general election. Lady **Carlisle**, Hon. Rosalind Frances Stanley (1845–1921) was a suffragist and the model for Lady Britomart in *Major Barbara*. She was the mother-in-law of the Greek scholar **Gilbert Murray** (1866–1957), the model for Adolphus Cusins in *Major Barbara*. The **honest army surgeon** may have been 'Colonel C.A. Watson of Victoria, British Columbia, the [hospital's] medical officer' (Thornton, 16). **A.C.S.** (antireticular cytotoxic serum) was made from animal (usually horse) bone marrow and was supposed to protect against disease and to prolong life. It was developed by the Russian pathophysiologist Alexandr Alexandrovich **Bogomolets** (1881–1946).

179 / To G. Bernard Shaw [9 Babmaes St, Jermyn St, SW1]
[December 1944]

[ALS: BL 50528, f. 104v]

Nancy Astor's letter (which is more disjointed and illegible than most of her autograph letters) is written on the reverse of a letter to her from Stewart Perowne (1901–89), orientalist, colonial administrator, and Shaw enthusiast. His letter of 23 November 1944 described his admiration of Shaw's work, humour, and quality of mind, and his desire to meet Shaw again in the future. Two similarly laudatory letters from Perowne to Astor (dated 6 January 1942 and 21 April 1942) are at Reading.

Dearest G.B.S.

Do read this [from] Stewart Perowne. A young friend of mine. I loved seeing you & you as always comfort me [dear G.B.S. mine?]! This blindness thing you & Philip [Kerr] understand me!! [*sic*]. I sound like an actress – you have never heard anything like this great [Debali?]. The [government?] is wholly Republican. The stupid king doesn't want to retire–. He wants to [live?] in [*illegible*] [Hotel?] with a certain Mrs Jones. He never wanted to retire so thats just eye wash.

Anthony Eden made a *6* hour [clear?] speech. But enough of politics. I love my [treats?] & I may have to take up residence with you! Admiral Stark purred all the way back. Much love. I keep fed. I go Cliveden until Wed. Here & Plymouth Thurs night.

Nancy

D.D. Lyttelton much older than you. Poor D.D.

Admiral Harold R. **Stark** (1880–1972) had supervised the U.S. Navy during its part in the Normandy Invasion in June 1944. He retired from active duty in 1946. Edith **Lyttelton** was, in fact, nine years younger than Shaw.

180 / To G. Bernard Shaw   Eydon Hall, Eydon, Rugby
                                          4th or 5th January [*sic*; 1945]

[ALS: BL 50528, f. 105]

At the heart of Nancy Astor's meandering letter of family news lies her festering resentment at being urged by Waldorf to retire from Parliament.

Dearest *GBS*

I hoped to come to you this week but my plans as usual have changed. Family again. My sister's boy Jim Brand aged 19 Coldstream Guards – was given this week's leave & rejoins his Regiment in France or Holland on [Monday?]. So I being his nearest relation am doing all I can to make his few days pass with as much pleasure as possible. So many of his friends have 'gone' lately that it's not easy. We are here until [Wednesday?] when we return Cliveden. London Sunday & I go to Plymouth Mon. for 10 days. – The more I think about the *push* on Waldorf's part to get me away from Plymouth the less inclined am I to go on in this new role of a docile obedient wife – How I wish I could get you to Cliveden for a week. I read your [counsel?] & [suffered?]. It's so cold here I don't want you to move even to rescue me. I wonder if you read the Economist? If not I will send you the bit about US & Gt B[ritain] which is causing nearly as much talk as one of *your* articles. I will come to you as soon as I can. Wissie [Phyllis Astor] & her children are at Cliveden. David [is] back. Michael has a bronze medal from US Army and a letter from 'Monty' saying he had seen him & should have known he was my son *as* he was charming & a good officer. I will send you what Michael wrote about M[onty] and M[onty] about Michael. You should get petrol & come to London, or send Miss Patch. Travel by rail hopeless – what 1945 Resolutions not Re*vo* Re*so* have you made?

Much love
Nancy

'Noble Negatives,' in *The Economist*, 147 (30 December 1944), 857–8 drew attention to an 'outburst of criticism and abuse' in America of virtually every aspect of current British policy. Britain was being denounced as 'imperialist, reactionary, selfish, exclusive, restrictive ... The only novelty in the present epidemic is the evidence that the American Government itself ... is more anxious to provide ammunition for the malcontents than to correct their wild misstatements.' **David** is David Astor. **Michael** Astor's citation, for his work at the American Corps headquarters in the Ardennes, noted that he had 'demonstrated a most successful combination of energy, intelligence and diplomacy in carrying out a difficult assignment' (BL 50528, f. 106). Nancy adopts Field Marshal **'Monty'** Montgomery's commendation of Michael as 'charming and a good officer' (BL 50528, f. 107).

181 / To Nancy Astor   Ayot St Lawrence, Welwyn, Herts.

14th January 1945

[TLS: Reading, Sykes (e)]

Although Nancy Astor's retirement from Parliament had been announced on 1 December 1944, she was thinking of rescinding her decision. Indeed, she never accepted the decision foisted on her. At a luncheon given by the National Council of Women on 14 December she said: 'I think ... it is a bad time for women to get out of the House of Commons and a bad time for any woman who knows how to fight shams and prick bubbles to get out of public life. We are going to have the same kind of shams after this war as after the last if we are not careful. The Left will have its wild people, and the Right will have its "dead-who-won't-lie-down" kind of people. Those two kinds would ruin Paradise if they ever got there' (The Times, 15 December). Shaw had those remarks and her speech on 1 December 1944 (see Letter 178) in mind as he advised her to weigh her position carefully.

My dear Nancy

Just a hasty line: I have nothing conclusive to say.

I take in The Economist: last week's article was a worse stinger than the one about America.

Your speech at the club lunch was virtually an appeal to the public against Waldorf.

Heaven forbid that I should interfere between man and wife! Both of you must, however, bear in mind that the question of your contesting Plymouth again is not a domestic one. It goes far beyond that. No man has a right to make his wife give up a public career to look after his grown-up and married family. No woman has a right to throw over her public work merely to make things comfortable for herself at home. So you twain must fight it out on other lines.

If your retirement would secure the parliamentary seat for a woman younger and abler than yourself then I should say that the 25th anniversary would be a good opportunity for retirement. But if it would reduce the number of women in the House by one, and substitute some ordinary male duffer, I should say hold on like grim death.

What the devil is Waldorf to do with you if you have no parliament to go to, and no children to bring up? You would be a grandmother, and would spoil your grandchildren; but you certainly wouldnt spoil Waldorf. He ought to thank God for Westminster.

G.B.S.

Last week's article in *The Economist*, 148 (6 January 1945), 1–2, entitled 'Deadlock in Europe,' discussed 'how the Allies have come upon military and political policies which are so painfully frustrating their victory ... This diversion of massive forces to the Far East may well have made the difference this autumn between complete victory and the long-drawn-out fighting which seems to threaten now.' In the 1945 general election on 5 July a **younger** woman did win Nancy's Plymouth seat: Lucy Middleton (née Cox, 1894–1983) became the first Labour MP to represent the division (1945–51).

182 / To Nancy Astor   Ayot St Lawrence, Welwyn, Herts.
                                                    20th January 1945

[ALCS: Reading, Letters, Sykes (e)]

While Shaw was content to relegate his relationship with Nancy Astor to the epistolary, she continued to send him invitations to stay with her or proposed visiting him at Ayot. Shaw was successful in fending off the former but not always the latter.

These excursions are wildly impossible for me at my age, even if I were not loaded with business that I cannot deal with apart from my papers.

Miss P[atch], losing her sanity by living in a shopless theatreless village with one very old man of whom she must be very tired, has braved the bombs and returned to London, which makes my presence here still more compulsory. The postal arrangements are worse than ever, my letters arriving half an hour *after* the one daily collection; so that I cannot answer by return.

You must get a younger understudy for Phil [Kerr]. My next journey will probably be to Golders Green; and you should in common prudence replace me betimes, however inferior the substitute.

G.B.S.

183 / To Nancy Astor   Ayot St Lawrence, Welwyn, Herts.

24th January 1945

[ALCS: Reading]

There is something in your letter which I cannot decipher; but it seems to threaten your arrival here on Monday the 29th with a carfull of Shaw sightseers.

DONT, for Heaven's sake.

When you bring a lot of people down you might as well stay at home, as I have to talk to them all the time; and neither of us can say a word to one another about our private affairs. And they immediately sell reports of what we *do* say.

I cannot write to W[aldorf]. I could not broach the subject with him unless he opened it. It is beyond all question that the decision rests with you.

G.B.S.

The **subject** was whether Nancy should rescind her decision to retire from Parliament and, instead, stand for re-election.

184 / To Nancy Astor   Ayot St Lawrence, Welwyn, Herts.

13th February 1945

[TLT: Reading, Sykes]

Even though the war was not yet concluded nor a general election announced, Shaw's letter makes clear the political jockeying for positions that was taking place already. His analysis of Nancy's vacillation over her Plymouth (Sutton) seat pinpoints accurately the factors involved.

My dear Nancy

With regard to Sutton I am really quite in the dark as to what you are going to do: for though your wish is to contest the seat your intention seems to be to succumb to family pressure, the real grounds of which I cannot make out, as all their interests point to your being settled in Westminster.

I must not interfere: all I can say is that your right to the seat if you want it is beyond all question, and the family opposition therefore inexplicable.

But as the constituencies are announcing their candidates in all directions the question is pressing. If a Conservative candidate is chosen in Sutton, or a Labor candidate with Waldorf's support, you will be checkmated; for the situation created would be intolerable if you then resolved, too late, to split the vote against Waldorf and your own party.

If you are going to contest the seat you must announce your change of mind at once, and thus make a split practically impossible. It all depends on who gets in first. Your claim must be jumped, and jumped quickly, or it will be equally impossible.

Keep this to yourself, or the other side will take the hint and jump first. It is now or never.

I cannot advise you: I can only warn you of the situation.

G.B.S.

185 / To Nancy Astor   Ayot St Lawrence, Welwyn, Herts.
6th April 1945

[TLT: Reading, Holroyd (e), Sykes (e)]

In the early months of 1945 a quartet of would-be caretakers of Shaw and his affairs jostled for position. Nancy's part has emerged already, and she was aided and abetted by Blanche Patch, who thought that Nancy was the best person for such a supervisory role and that she might retain more of her own influence with Shaw thereby. Her alliance with Nancy was fostered by their mutual anti-Semitism, which focussed on Dr Fritz Erwin Loewenstein (1901–69), a German Jew and founder of the Shaw Society, who had insinuated himself into Shaw's life, declaring himself Shaw's bibliographer. Later in 1945 Shaw appointed him as his literary executor, which frustrated the aspirations of a young Scottish journalist, John Wardrop (b. 1919), whose path into Shaw's life is described in his own words in Laurence, Letters, *636–7, and of whom Shaw said: 'He assumed not only the position of my literary agent but of my son and heir' (ibid., 739). Nancy must have voiced her concerns to Shaw about Wardrop possessing some of his manuscripts. Nancy's information may have derived from Blanche Patch, with whom Shaw discussed the situation: 'Wardrop has just burst in on me, with a suit case, frantic about Loewenstein and announcing that he had come to sleep here and live with me to protect his property (ME) against the Jew. He assured me that you entirely agreed with him. Of course I have packed him back to London after bullying him into comparative deflatedness if not into sanity. / With these lunatics to deal with we two must have a look at the whole situation' (ibid., 738). Shaw resolved that situation quickly. Wardrop 'proved impossible. He was too young, too excitable. The slightest encouragement turned his head ... Meanwhile another candidate has arisen in the person of F.E.L. I began with a violent prejudice against him because he arrived as the founder of The Shaw Society which threatened to become a nuisance to me ... But he made good in spite of me' (ibid., 739).*

My dear Nancy

You were so very crazy about Wardrop that I must tell you that he arrived here after your visit with three trunks and innumerable bales filled with my papers, of which he retains not a scrap.

I do not know why you have let the parliamentary seat go; but gone it is now.

Winston's mother was an American. England grossly insulted the United States by actually dethroning her king for marrying an American. To soften the smart of that, Winston should make you a peeress in your own right. Ask him flatly to do it. Keep at him until he does. Then join Lady Rhondda in an agitation beginning with the opening of the House of Lords to peeresses in their own right (consort peeresses are impossible) and carry the movement on for a constitutional amendment making all elected authorities consist of men and women in equal numbers, each voter having two votes, one for a man and the other for a woman.

This is program enough for the rest of your life. Consider it seriously; and do not let your Conservative riffraff persuade you that I am a society clown and write letters to amuse you. I am deadly serious. What alternative program have you if you are not game for it?

G.B.S.

PS   I am completely in the dark as to why the Cliveden family wanted to get you out of parliament, and how they have succeeded when you had the decision in your own hands.

Winston Churchill's **mother** Jennie Jerome (1854–1921) was born in Brooklyn, New York, and married Lord Randolph Churchill (1849–95) in 1874. Her second husband was George Cornwallis-West who, after their divorce in 1913, married Mrs Patrick Campbell in 1914. Churchill had supported **King** Edward VIII during the 1936 abdication crisis. Shaw appears unaware that on 11 December 1936 Nancy had broadcast to America and had stressed that the abdication was caused because Mrs Wallis Simpson was a divorcée and not because the King was **marrying an American** (see Sykes, 176). On 23 April 1945 Nancy did ask **Winston** Churchill to create her a peeress because 'she would wake up the House of Lords as she had woken up the House of Commons' (Nicolson, 451).

186 / To G. Bernard Shaw   [*no address*]
[7th April 1945]

[Holograph draft for TEL: Reading]
The draft of this telegram is written on the envelope containing the previous letter. Ironically, although Nancy Astor was relieved about John Wardrop being side-lined from Shaw's affairs, she despised his replacement, F.E. Lowenstein.

So relieved about W[ardrop]. Please don't educate him for job. Guarantee to get someone with wisdom & character. Will be back next week. Nan.

187 / To Nancy Astor   Ayot St Lawrence, Welwyn, Herts.
13th April 1945

[ALCS: Reading, Holroyd (e), Letters]

I see. Having neither wisdom nor character I am to be placed in the care of someone gifted with both, selected by you, and willing to act as my keeper and office boy. Splendid.

However, there is no hurry: I am getting along fairly well as I am. I have in me the makings of a first rate hermit. Even a bit of an oracle.

Only, as you wont consult me I can hardly be of any use to you, except to amuse you occasionally.

Mrs P.C. [Patrick Campbell] with her last breath called me Joey, and in her last letter Dear *dear* Joey. I am glad she got that much out of me. And now you also–!!

G.B.S.

188 / To Nancy Astor

4 Whitehall Court SW1
15th April 1945

[ALS: Reading]

This letter and Letter 190 are revealing both for Blanche Patch's account of events as she interpreted them and for her resentment of her declining position in Shaw's affairs.

Dear Lady Astor

No doubt you will have heard that I could no longer bear the lonely life at Ayot & came away some 3 months ago. And really there was nothing to keep me there as GBS & I have always worked together quite easily through the medium of the post, &, as regards his material comfort the servants look after him quite well. Also, he likes being alone, & I was beginning to feel that my constant presence at meals (the only time I saw him) was distinctly boring for him.

However, I must admit that what finally decided me was the presence of the non-stop smoking German Jew [Lowenstein] who now works there daily & has full permission to poke & pry wherever he pleases in the capacity of GBS's official bibliographer. It is no doubt unreasonable of me, as he is apparently highly approved of by GBS, but I just can't get over my antipathy to Jews – & this one is a German. The unfortunate man (though he thinks himself fortunate in having secured such a strong footing in the house) is by no means liked by the servants & I, being far too sensitive to atmosphere, just couldn't tolerate the uneasy one prevailing in that house in addition to spending my leisure hours in a very cold bed-sitting room.

I tell you this so that you should not think that I abandoned GBS thoughtlessly & I hope you will understand.

Yours sincerely
Blanche Patch

189 / To Nancy Astor   Ayot St Lawrence, Welwyn, Herts.

17th April 1945

[ALCS: Reading, Holroyd (e)]

Friday is Maggie's [Caskie] day off: Thursdays are better for us here; but we can manage.

I shall expect you on Friday unless I hear from you putting it off.

Sandwich is as far out of bounds as Cornwall: I shall never see these places again. The garden and plantation here are my world now.

G.B.S.

190 / To Nancy Astor   4 Whitehall Court SW1

19th April 1945

[TLS: Reading]

Blanche Patch's sideline commentary here focuses on the jostling between F.E. Lowenstein and John Wardrop to be Shaw's literary executor. Blanche's account of Wardrop occurs on a separate sheet of yellow paper included with her letter.

Dear Lady Astor

In case you should be seeing GBS again I thought I would try and let you know the position of the Wardrop-Loewenstein affair. I think both candidates quite unsuitable to represent GBS when he is no longer with us, but, at the moment, am rather in sympathy with Wardrop as GBS certainly did encourage him – much to my annoyance, I must admit. One of the amusing things is that Loew is a non-stop smoker, but GBS doesnt seem to notice the smell of his perpetual cigarettes. When I was there I forbade him to bring them into the study!

Perhaps you had better destroy the yellow sheet when you have digested it as I dont want there to be any record of my underhanded way of opposing GBS.

Yours sincerely

Blanche Patch

Mrs Wardrop told me the real reasons for leaving her husband [had] nothing to do with religion.

John Wardrop appeared on our horizon just before the war when he was about 19 and he arrived as a Scotch free lance journalist hoping to get work with London papers, and a passion for GBS's work in particular. He dropped in here from time to time and apparently amused GBS with his eagerness. He had to join up when the war came, but was out of the Army in 3 months – for reasons of health, I presume, but I never heard what was wrong. From that time and while we were at Ayot he paid us occasional visits (much to Charlotte's annoyance), wrote long letters to GBS and eventually got him to make some sort of suggestion that John should be his Literary Executor. But it is only a suggestion and I have been told by one or two business men that the Public Trustee will very likely take no notice of it. Then we all came to London and Charlotte died. GBS called in Wardrop to make lists of books etc (always when I was not here) and gave him a latch key so that he could have the run of the flat. He also told him he could remove the contents of 10 files to his, or rather his wife's, house so that he could straighten them out at his leisure. Then Loewenstein, the founder of the Shaw Society, appeared in the arena and the Wardrops joined his S.S. Immediately they were in disagreement and Mrs. W. told GBS that Loew's ideas were entirely contrary to GBS's teachings and that he ought not to allow a German Jew to be the head of a Shaw Society. The Wardrops left the Society and eventually Loew managed to persuade GBS to let him come to Ayot to write a bibliography of Shaw writings and since last July he has been there almost daily with permission to read all letters and anything he finds in boxes or cupboards – or wastepaper baskets. In addition he told GBS that he must have all the stuff removed by Wardrop (with GBS's permission) and has made the unfortunate Wardrop convey it all to Ayot. The latter is now spoken of as if he was an offender, but I can't help thinking that GBS certainly led him up the garden path before he shook him off in favor of Loew. He is now paying for his tuition fees so that he can qualify as a *barrister*, but as he has first to pass his London Matric[ulation] (which should have happened in his school days) he will be some years before he knows much about the law. As far as I can see Loew has every intention of being the future Curator of the house at Ayot, but, of course, the National Trust may put a spoke in that wheel.

Mrs Wardrop was Eleanor O'Connell, who was not actually married to John Wardrop, although Shaw treated them as a married couple.

191 / To Nancy Astor   Ayot St Lawrence, Welwyn, Herts.

30th May 1945

[ALCS: Reading]

In July Shaw went to London for appointments with his accountant (Stanley Clench), the Public Trustee, and others. He also encountered Nancy Astor there on his 89th birthday, as Judy Musters recalled in her 28 July 1953 letter to Nancy (Reading): 'I thought of you & of [Shaw's] birthday in 1945 when you lunched with G.B.S. & me at Whitehall Court as the results of the General Election were coming out, & the entire Press kept telephoning for Shaw's comments on being 89 AND on the election. He made none.'

Cliveden is impossible for me. I transfer to Whitehall on the 7th July, and remain there for most of the rest of the month – if the change does not kill me.

Maggie [Caskie] says you are coming tomorrow; so until then –

G.B.S.

192 / To Nancy Astor   4 Whitehall Court SW1

13th June 1945

[TLS: Reading]

At some point before Charlotte's death, Nancy Astor had written an 'amusing card,' which reads 'I G.B. Shaw will my wife Charlotte to my friends Nancy & Waldorf Astor' (Reading). In returning the card to Nancy, Blanche Patch also took the opportunity to indulge her prejudice against F.E. Lowenstein.

Dear Lady Astor

I feel that this amusing card, which I found when turning out some old boxes and drawers, should belong to you. Rather ironical that you made GBS dispose of Charlotte, and, as things turned out, she should have willed him to someone, but I think she always took it for granted that she would outlive him. One of my uncles, who lived to the age of 95, told his doctor that he wished the Dr to take charge of his wife at his death, but the Dr told him that although he could do as he liked with his wife in his lifetime he would have no power over her when he (the uncle) had left this world.

However, to return to the card. If I send it to GBS I know he will leave it lying about and it would most likely be purloined by that intruder [Loewenstein] down at Ayot. I am very allergic to him.

Yours sincerely

Blanche Patch

193 / To Blanche Patch   3 Elliott Terrace, The Hoe, Plymouth
                                                        25th June 1945

[TLS: Cornell, Holroyd (e)]

Nancy Astor's response apparently refers to an intervening, unlocated letter from Blanche Patch in which she mentioned film director Gabriel Pascal as well as Clare Winsten's paintings.

Dear Miss Patch

I was so glad to get your letter and also to know about Pascal. I can't bear that way of life and certainly won't go to see him!! Not I!

To tell you the truth, I don't like either of the Winsten pictures, nor do I want them, but how I am going to break it to G.B.S. I don't know.

I think I will have to look after you when I come back and I don't like the company you are keeping. As you say, it is certainly strange.!!! On Sunday too.

I must stay here to help these people over the Election. They've a hard job. I met a great friend of yours the other day. I've forgotten his name but not his face I liked him so much. I must try to remember – with love

Nancy Astor

I am fighting for my successor!

Nancy's **successor** was the Conservative candidate Laurence Douglas Grand (1898–1975), then a brigadier, who polled 10,738 votes; his opponent, Lucy Middleton, polled 15,417 votes (Craig, 216, and see Letter 181).

194 / To Nancy Astor   Ayot St Lawrence, Welwyn, Herts.
                                                        14th August 1945

[ALCS: Reading]

The substance of the first sentence of this letter may be connected with a later plan to induce Shaw to assist Yousuf Karsh with a forthcoming book (see Letter 198).

Dont dream of lugging down all that Karsh stuff: I know it only too well.
It is frontispieced to my last book, which you havnt opened. H.G. Wells
calls it my wicked old face.

I am not rested: I have begun a new play; and the struggle to keep up
with overwhelming business on top of it is impossible. Either I or it must
go smash.

On the 3rd I signed away all my Irish property and am no longer a
country gentleman. I am even renouncing my life interest in Charlotte's
estate.

G.B.S.

The photograph by Yousuf **Karsh** provided the frontispiece to *Everybody's Political What's
What?* (see Letter 141). Shaw's **new play**, eventually entitled *Buoyant Billions*, was not
performed until 21 October 1948 in Zurich. Shaw conveyed his **Irish property** to Carlow
Urban Council on 13 August 1945, but did not renounce his **life interest** in Charlotte's
estate because of the legal complications that would entail.

195 / To Nancy Astor   Ayot St Lawrence, Welwyn, Herts.
28th September 1945

[ALS: Reading, Masters (e), Sykes (e)]

*While Shaw told Nancy Astor he was 'old and dying,' he told Sidney Webb on 26
October 1945: 'This bachelor life with nobody to consult but myself... suits me very
well; it actually develops me at 90!' (Laurence, Letters, 757). Nancy did not heed
Shaw's injunction 'to forget and drop me': 'I took Michael and Jakie to see
Bernard Shaw last week. They were perfectly delighted to see him and he them' (17
November 1945 letter to Sir Edward Cunard (1891–1962) [Reading]).*

My dear Nancy

I havnt time to write, nor anything to write about. And I want you to
forget and drop me because I am an old and dying man (actually I am
dead and considerably decomposed) and you must find a Sunday husband young enough to last your time.

You are very puzzling about W[aldorf]. Have you separated? You write
as if you now have no latchkey of Cliveden, nor he of Rest Harrow. I
hope not. You will neither of you do better. But of course you should
both have Sunday spouses to keep you young.

Stalin must be worn out. Five years like the last would kill a giant.

G.B.S.

Epifania, the heroine of *The Millionairess*, defines a **Sunday husband** as 'a gentleman with whom I discuss subjects that are beyond my husband's mental grasp, which is extremely limited' (Act 1). As Shaw noted in Letter 58, Epifania was modelled after Nancy.

196 / To Nancy Astor Ayot St Lawrence, Welwyn, Herts.
14th December 1945

[ALS: Reading, Sykes (e)]

The Evening News *(11 December 1945) carried a report of Nancy Astor's 'speech at a dance given for Australian sailors in the Plymouth Corn Exchange last night ... Lady Astor informed the audience that when she retired from Parliament ... Mr Shaw wrote to her to say how sorry he was. A correspondence followed and Lady Astor read extracts from it. As thus:* Lady Astor: It is all my husband's fault. Mr Shaw: Well get rid of the fellow. Lady Astor: I will, if you will marry me. Mr Shaw: I don't want to, but I will. *When I asked Mr Shaw to-day for his comments he replied cautiously that he did not go to the dance at Plymouth.'*

My dear Nancy

The cheese arrived safe and very nearly sound. Do not bother about further supplies. Bolles Rogers has sent for some to America and wants to bring it with him on a second visit, which, as he is a likeable fellow I have consented to.

After your outrageous indiscretion in Plymouth the telephone was ringing all day. I enclose a sample of the reports.

Why dont you and Waldorf, now that you have done your job of repeopling the world, get married seriously and settle down to the real thing? 'The best is yet to come.'

G.B.S.

Bolles Rogers is unidentified.

197 / To Nancy Astor Ayot St Lawrence, Welwyn, Herts.
28th June 1946

[ALCS: Reading]

On 7 January 1946 the Astors sailed to the United States, visiting numerous eastern cities (Sykes, 482–8). They then 'joined the [Clarence] Dillons on their yacht, Nevada, *cruising about for several weeks, calling at Palm Beach, Hobe*

Sound, Boca Grande and other places' (Perez, 126). Waldorf left New York for England on 14 May, while Nancy returned on the Queen Mary, *leaving New York on 20 June.*

Pascal has just blown in with the news that you were in the ship with him. He proposes to drive you here on Sunday or Monday. Dont let him. We could not talk. Try to find some less ebullient car owner to transport you. Any day that suits you and does not suit him will suit me.

I may have to go up to Whitehall on the 21st July to give my domestic staff a holiday and have the house spring cleaned and chimney swept.

If this does not quite kill me the birthday fuss will finish the job. So come before the 21st.

G.B.S.

Gabriel **Pascal** had travelled to America to sort out his perennial financial problems and to drum up interest in his Shaw film projects (see Dukore, 189–91).

198 / To Nancy Astor Ayot St Lawrence, Welwyn, Herts.
27th July 1946

[TLT: Reading]

Shaw's aversion to celebrations of his ninetieth birthday on 26 July 1946 led him to try to subvert such preparations as had been made. Judy Musters wrote from Whitehall Court to Nancy Astor on 25 July (Reading) that at the last moment Shaw had informed her he would not travel to London as planned: 'A bombshell from Ayot: he is not coming to stay in town at all! Everything was arranged here & at 1 o'clock came the bomb from the blast of which I still suffer: blasted hopes are so much worse than blasted houses (no swearing intended).' However, Shaw did make a surprise afternoon visit on 26 July to the National Book League exhibition honouring his birthday, returning very tired to Ayot at 5 pm. Mrs Laden recalled Nancy's attempt to see him: 'I remember she phoned on his ninetieth birthday to say that she would be coming to see him. "Tell her I would rather she didn't come." A little later that morning a telegram arrived from her saying "My present to you is my absence"' (Minney, Recollections, 152). In May 1946, during her trip to the United States, Nancy was photographed by Yousuf Karsh: 'Long shall I remember the thoroughly stimulating time I had photographing you. It was a delightful pleasure, and I am so glad we were finally able to arrange an appointment'

(18 June 1946 letter, Thornton, 411). Karsh also enlisted Nancy's aid in trying to secure an introduction from Shaw to his forthcoming book, Faces of Destiny *(1946): 'Also, I am sending a collection of my original prints in the hope that you will show them to the Great Man. I am sure that the mutual affection you hold for Mr Shaw coupled with my earnest desire will yield a favourable outcome for the introduction to my book' (ibid). A photograph of Shaw appears in Karsh's book, which Leonard W. Brockington instigated: 'It was another friend, Leonard W. Brockington, who persuasively suggested to the Department of External Affairs and the Canadian Wartime Information Board that I go to London to photograph Britain's wartime great for the Canadian archives'* (Faces of Destiny, *8). Brockington apologized to Nancy after Shaw's refusal to contribute to Karsh's book: 'I am so sorry to have caused both you and Mr Shaw so much trouble about Karsh. I would not have thought of worrying either of you on my own behalf. I was concerned only with the needs and wishes of my friend who apparently had some hopes of success. Will you please present to Mr Shaw my apologies for what I agree was an indefensible invasion of his time and thought' (3 August 1946 letter to Nancy, Thornton, 413).*

My dear Nancy

Send the enclosed card the white one to Brock[ington], and make him understand that he is not behaving correctly. If K[arsh] cannot sell his wares on their own merits he shall not sell them on mine. And I am not a jobbing journalist.

All my arrangements are changed, to my inexpressible relief. Yesterday instead of going up to London for three weeks I went up for six hours and am now safe back here for good. I found 140 telegrams and over 200 letters waiting for me. I have spent the morning not opening them but writing to THE TIMES about the National Health Service Act and the doctors.

No more birthdays for me: another such would kill me.

G.B.S.

Shaw's letter to *The Times* (30 July 1946) was 'The Doctors' Powers,' in which he asserted characteristically that the **National Health Service Act** (approved in November 1946) would permit doctors to 'poison us or mutilate us professionally with virtually complete immunity and considerable pecuniary gain.'

199 / To G. Bernard Shaw   [*no address*]
                                                          29th July 1946

[TLU (c): Reading]

Irritated by her exclusion from Shaw's birthday, Nancy Astor here counters with gibes at Shaw's neighbours (presumably the Winstens) and Mrs Wardrop, wife of a rival would-be Shavian caretaker.

My dear G.B.S.

If you would only have let me arrange your birthday instead of your neighbours it would have been a peaceful and happy one.

I have heard from Judy [Musters] at least you are safe and well.

I am sorry about your not going to London. I hope to get down to you on Thursday as I couldn't for the Birthday.

I am lunching with Judy in London on Wednesday.

I notice you don't even have the politeness to sign your name to Brockington and yet no doubt Mrs W[ardrop] will be receiving love letters from you. You can't think what sorrow your middle-age is causing.

   your devoted

                                                          [Nancy Astor]

Mrs W might also be Clare Winsten whom Nancy disliked. However, Shaw was fond of Mrs Wardrop: he visited her house after Charlotte's death, and she visited Shaw in hospital during his final illness (Holroyd, 461, 511).

200 / To G. Bernard Shaw   9 Babmaes St, Jermyn St, SW1
                                                          19th August 1946

[TLS: BL 50528, f. 108]

This letter reveals Nancy Astor's persistence on every front, including sniping at Clare Winsten's portrait of Shaw (see Letter 162). Two doubtful words in the letter are the result of Nancy's holograph additions.

Dearest G.B.S.

Did you get the letter from Sargent? – you remember the Naval Officer I used to bring down? He has sent you an article he has written about you & asks me to find out if you will pass it.

One more last appeal about a word for Karsh, the photographer. I have just received some more of his photographs. They are magnificent, world famous, and two lines would not hurt you and would do an awful lot for good photography. I think he is the best in the world & his picture of you better than *some* Portraits!!

Ward Price and the Turk came away full of your youthful charms. I came away a little sorry that I had brought them as there were many things I wanted to talk to you about.

I will try to get down early next week or probably this Friday afternoon, in case you have that free. I wish I could [persuade ?] you to Sandwich! Your Wells article was one of your best. Frank but not too truthful – Much love & really [*illegible*] – as you look too young for safety!

Nancy

Sargent and **the Turk** are unidentified. George **Ward Price** (1886–1961) was a correspondent with the *Daily Mail* and author of several books, including *I Know These Dictators* (1937) on Hitler and Mussolini. Shaw's H.G. **Wells article** on the late author (who died on 13 August) was 'The Man I Knew,' *New Statesman and Nation*, 32 (17 August 1946), 115 (the typescript is BL 50699, ff. 149–52); reprinted in J.P. Smith, ed., *Bernard Shaw and H.G. Wells* (Toronto: University of Toronto Press, 1995), 210–13.

201 / To Nancy Astor　　　　　Ayot St Lawrence, Welwyn, Herts.
31st August 1946

[ALS: Reading, Holroyd (e)]

Nancy Astor's morale-boosting gesture of sending Mrs Laden ballet tickets reflects both her innate generosity and her desire to ensure Shaw's well-being by keeping his housekeeper happy. Mrs Laden wrote to Nancy on 2 September (Reading) to thank her and to express her enjoyment of the ballet. She also told Nancy not to look for the temporary cook Shaw mentions in this letter, since she was not going to take a holiday immediately.

My dear Nancy

The ballet at Covent Garden (your gift to Mrs Laden thereat) was an enormous success. She turned up this morning herself again, rejuvenated, smiling, and utterly repudiating the possibility of leaving me on any terms. But I must force her to take a holiday, and still would like a temporary vegetarian cook to save me from Whitehall.

After you left I went over and had you described by the great sculptress [Clare Winsten] as an American chorus girl, married to a rich Polish Jew, and grossly ignorant of how to speak to an English lady and a distinguished artist.

Blanche Patch is here for the week end. She tells me that you have let fly at Judy [Musters] and are driving everybody mad by your effervescent activity now that the House of Commons no longer absorbs it. Why not make Attlee open the House of Lords to women and the King make you a peeress in your own right?

G.B.S.

202 / To G. Bernard Shaw

Rest Harrow, Sandwich, Kent
3rd September [1946]

[ALS: BL 50528, ff. 109–10; Sykes (e)]

In responding directly to the previous letter, Nancy Astor here reveals her often prickly relations with other people. Although David Astor's Swiss wife, Melanie (née Hauser), receives only passing mention (and apparent approval), David, knowing of his mother's fierce opposition to her other sons' wives, 'had kept his relationship with his wartime fiancée a secret from his mother until shortly before he set off to marry her in Paris in 1945' (Fox, 455). They were divorced in 1951.

Dearest GBS

I am relieved to hear about Mrs Laden. She seemed to enjoy the [dress ?] up. She really loves & cares & [appreciates ?] you *so* I am not jealous of her–! If [Blanche] Patch can't find a cook you really must face Whitehall for Mrs L's sake. Judy [Musters] says she is ready. I've *never* had a scene with Judy. You know, I like you can make a scene when necessary. Your distinguished artist [Clare Winsten] made the scenes. I swiftly told that young lady what some of your friends felt. You know that I loved the way you took it – But I am sorry it took you to the 'Crows nest' – your distinguished artist has a great insight. She should concentrate on my Polish Jew. If she can make you spend hundreds, she could make Waldorf spend thousands! Its not that I grudge her the money but I grudge her the way she extracts it – uses you in other ways – common ways. Now if you really want someone to coach, why not get someone who is worthy of *your* distinguished gifts! Make another Ellen [Terry?]. I will find you 6 to pick from.

No I won't go to the H[ouse] of L[ords]. I am very much occupied – I started out to make myself a Christian. So far I have utterly failed. Now at long last I will start fresh. It's a big job – & a very narrow way. Yet it seems to me it's the only way left to poor mortals. You can't make Christians of others – but we know some have succeeded with themselves. If I succeed I might even help your neighbours–! I said *help*. I dare not show Waldorf your letter. I believe he feels he made a mistake. Yet he never says so – that card you wrote advising me not to listen to him was not a success. – Had he taken your advice – well – at least I could have gone on my wicked way. Now I am forced to face up to my [own?] short (oh so short) comings–, so another way you could have given him [*illegible*] & company (of a sort) in solitude should you retreat & come here – It's very bracing & we do get sun occasionally. I wish you could see David's wife. She's very lovely–! You might 'open the seal' – I can't. Please don't let my past life on the stage put you off. Tell Mrs W[insten] I am thinking of [becoming?] a *great* actress & to do so may mean I must share Ayot – for there's only one master for me.

Bless you & thank God for Mrs Laden & your faithful girl friend I who may become good – after all.

Nancy

203 / To Nancy Astor   Ayot St Lawrence, Welwyn, Herts.
1st October 1946

[ALCS: Reading]

Shaw had served on the St Pancras Borough Council (1897–1903) and was to receive the freedom of the Borough on 9 October 1946. In the event, all did not go quite as planned (see Letter 204).

The cistern here is worn out and leaking; and the house will be waterless and uninhabitable next week while the builders and plumbers are at work on it.

Also on Wednesday the 9th, at 2.30, the St Pancras Borough Council is to make a grand parade of making me its first Honorary Freeman.

So I am moving to Whitehall on Monday next, the 7th, returning on the 12th or 14th or whenever the cistern work is completed.

Mrs Laden takes the week off; and Maggie [Caskie] sleeps in the village.

That is absolutely all my news.

G.B.S.

204 / To Nancy Astor   4 Whitehall Court SW1
9th October 1946

[ALS: Reading]

On the day before he was to become the first honorary freeman of the Borough of St Pancras, Shaw, while rising from his swivel chair to greet his Polish translator, Florian Sobieniowski (1881–1964), fell and injured his leg. When Shaw still experienced discomfort the next morning, a doctor was called in to treat him. Shaw was obliged to record his acceptance speech, which was broadcast later that day by the BBC ('Accident to Mr. Shaw: Freedom Conferred in His Absence,' The Times, 10 October 1946. See also Henderson, 263).

Dear Lady Astor

I see that this will now not reach you until Friday morning; but I've not had a moment until this evening to sit down & write.

A great relief to us all when the X Ray photos shewed no sign of any cracks or displacements; but the morning was simply hectic. Dr Cooper, the osteopath here before GBS had finished his breakfast, & it was he fixed the X Ray affair. Then there was getting in touch with the St Pancras people, which led to the Mayor & Town Clerk arriving here, & they immediately got on to the B.B.C. to send their recording van so that GBS could make his speech from his bed. At one time we had the 2 X Ray men with apparatus, & the 3 very nice young BBC fellows, & the Mayor & T[own] Clerk popping in & out of the bedroom as opportunity occurred. In addition there were yards of rubber tubes being thrown from the windows to the apparatus in the street. Then later when the news got about that GBS was not at the function the newspapers got very busy on the telephone.

However, on the whole, I think GBS has had rather an amusing day, finishing with a visit from [Gabriel] Pascal just back from U.S.A. & who says he was met at the airport by newspaper men who said that GBS had had a stroke & was calling for him!! I must finish the bulletin by saying that GBS tottered from his bed at 6.15. to hear the wireless recording of his speech – and thought it very good. I may add that he made an extremely good lunch & dinner. The enclosures are photos of the Winsten family the single figures being Mr & Mrs W. The bust was done by Mrs & is the one shewn at the Nat. Book League, & of which Lady Scott said 'Shaw after he was hung.' I think I told you this morning that Ruth, the daughter, has written saying that she had been admitted to the Roy. Academy of Dram. Art. I wonder if she has any future as an actress.

Yours sincerely
Blanche Patch

Dr Cooper may be '[William] Cooper the osteopath' identified in Laurence, *Letters*, 396. The **Mayor** and **Town Clerk** were Councillor F.C. Combes and R.C.A. Austin respectively. Sculptor Kathleen **Scott** (née Bruce, 1878–1947) was accorded the rank of a K.C.B.'s widow after the death of her first husband, Robert Falcon Scott, 'Scott of the Antarctic' (1868–1912). She became Lady Kennet when her second husband, Sir Edward Hilton Young (1879–1960) was created 1st Baron Kennet in 1935. Her daughter, **Ruth**, does not appear to have had a significant career as an actress.

205 / To Nancy Astor 4 Whitehall Court SW1
2nd January 1947

[TLS: Reading]
Blanche Patch grew increasingly annoyed that F.E. Loewenstein was appropriating her position. There are extensive examples of Loewenstein handling Shaw's correspondence during this period in BL 50565, tasks that would have fallen previously to Blanche Patch.

Dear Lady Astor

Alas, I fear that nothing can be done about these cryptic messages. At one time GBS used to send all these letters to me, scribbling on top of each one the gist of what he wanted said or written, and I used to polish it up politely, but for some months he has allowed Loewenstein to do it all although GBS has envelopes addressed to me, and into which he can easily slip the letters. Now I only get his articles and long letters which he writes in shorthand for me to transcribe, and I am really so tired of all these queer helpers that he likes around him that at times I feel he is meditating retiring me altogether.

Mrs Laden was here two days ago and reported GBS as being very well; but he has, as I know to my cost, these silent days and probably one was on him when you were down there.

I shall be very pleased to have a talk when you happen to be in London, but am not very hopeful as to our being able to move the Mountain.

Yours sincerely
Blanche Patch

206 / To Blanche Patch   [*no address*]
4th January 1947

[TLT: Reading]

Dear Miss Patch

Miss Dowie is going to post this to you when she gets back to London today, so please forgive my not being there to sign it!

Yesterday I motored to see Jakie's [Astor] new country house and on the way I stopped by and saw G.B.S. for a second. I told him about Loewenstein incident and he assured me that he told Loewenstein to write the card. He looked extraordinarily well and seemed very cheerful.

Mrs Laden told me that the Irish woman was going down to see him Sunday (you know the one whose husband he has helped).

I may be coming up to London next week and will try my best to see you. I am writing this in haste just to let you know what happened.

Best wishes for 1947.

Yours
NANCY ASTOR

The **Irish woman** is unidentified.

207 / To Nancy Astor   4 Whitehall Court SW1
3rd February 1947

[TLS: Reading]
This brief note shows Blanche Patch providing Nancy Astor with ammunition

against F.E. Loewenstein with which she could taunt Shaw. As Letter 208 reveals, Nancy lost no time in using the information.

Dear Lady Astor

In case you do not see the Evening Standard I thought this enclosure might amuse you. Rather funny, I think, that Dulanty, the Irish High Commissioner, calls the Shaw Society 'a tuppenny ha'penny affair.'

Yours sincerely
Blanche Patch

An examination of the *Evening Standard* for this period has not revealed exactly what Blanche Patch's **enclosure** might have been. John W. **Dulanty** (1883–1955) became Eire's ambassador to Britain in July 1946.

208 / To G. Bernard Shaw   Cliveden, Taplow, Bucks.
                                    [*c.* 5th February 1947]

[ALCS: Cornell, Holroyd (e)]

Dearest G.B.S.

I see that Dr FEL[oewenstein] the founder of the Shaw Society which Dulanty called a tuppenny ha'penny affair has got the [place of power?] – Charlotte would rise in her grave. Mercifully I am not in my grave nor you in yours – So I feel as your *guardian* (self appointed) I must take active steps. Perhaps you could advise me–as to what they should be! Who wrote the [*illegible*], you or the Dr! What a Doctor! He will have to take an *overdose* if he goes on pursuing you. –

Yours in Earnest Love & Positive Authority!
Nancy A

209 / To Nancy Astor   Ayot St Lawrence, Welwyn, Herts.
                                4th April 1947

[ALCS: Reading, Sykes]

Nothing to write about.
    Under such circumstances it is my point of honor not to write.
    Duty letters and duty visits are intolerable curses.

I care for nobody, no not I; and nobody need care for me.

Waste no care on the old: make young friends–young enough to outlast you. I only waste your time. Activities are what you need, not the society of dotards. Be warned: I am a dotard; and I *know*.

G.B.S.

Shaw has modified the lines from Act 1, Scene 2 of the comic opera *Love in a Village* (1728) by Isaac Bickerstaffe (1735–c. 1812): 'And this the burden of his song / Forever used to be,– / **I care for nobody, no, not I**, / If no one cares for me.'

210 / To Nancy Astor   Ayot St Lawrence, Welwyn, Herts.
11th April 1947

[ALS: Reading]

Under Nancy Astor's influence, Waldorf had been a Christian Scientist since the mid-1920s. He was in relatively poor health, but despite their estrangement Nancy sought out Shaw's advice on places that might provide appropriate treatments for Waldorf.

Dont come on Monday. I have business with [Gabriel] Pascal then.

Free the rest of the week so far.

If Waldorf is not recovering there is something wrong with him or with his way of life. Make him go for a month to some clinic like Battle Creek, or Scripps's Metabolic Clinic in La Jolla, California, or the place at Tring. Have him overhauled by an osteopath or chiropractor. He need not follow the medical treatment further than to get a diagnosis. If they can find anything wrong he can depend on Christian Science to cure it. It may be some mechanical lesion, or something in his diet that is wrong *for him* and has nothing to do with C.S.

Anyhow he must make some change if he is not getting better.

G.B.S.

The **Battle Creek** Sanitarium in Michigan was founded by John Harvey Kellogg (1852–1943), a physician and health-food pioneer of cornflakes fame. Shaw had received an account of Kellogg's work from Charles Helin (23 November 1944 letter from Helin, BL 50524, ff. 228–30). Gabriel Pascal had entered the Scripps **Metabolic Clinic** in February 1947 for a check-up (see Dukore, 212–13). The **place at Tring** was probably Champneys Nature and Health Care Clinic in Wigginton, near Tring, which had been established by Stanley Lief (d. 1963), the founder of the British College of Osteopathic Medicine.

211 / To Nancy Astor   Ayot St Lawrence, Welwyn, Herts.
                                              17th April 1947

[ALS: Reading]

The changes in the day of Gabriel Pascal's visit mentioned in Letter 210 and here are probably attributable to telephone calls between Shaw and Nancy Astor. In them Nancy may also have raised the possibility of a visit to Shaw by presidential hopeful Henry A. Wallace.

My dear Nancy

Pascal is coming on Saturday, not on Friday.

If by any chance Wallace should be curious to see me, and you manage it for him, make sure that he brings his wife.

One never can estimate a man's chances of the Presidency without taking into account his wife's fitness and desire (or the contrary) for the White House.

But let the initiative come from him.

G.B.S.

Henry A. **Wallace** (1888–1965), whom Shaw supported, was the former Vice-President of the United States (1941–5) who was about to run as leader of his left-wing Progressive Party in his failed attempt to become President. There is no record of the two men meeting.

212 / To Nancy Astor   Ayot St Lawrence, Welwyn, Herts.
                                              29th April 1947

[ALCS: Reading]

On the advice of Nancy Astor, Shaw used to have his hair and beard washed and trimmed by the hair stylist Bertha Hammond, who maintained a shop at 16 Old Bond Street, London. During the war he ceased the practice despite Bertha sending him a postcard imploring him to return to her because she missed him very much. In addition, she asked Shaw to give her an autographed copy of one his political works because, jealously, she was sure Nancy also possessed one (5 July 1944, BL 50524, f. 71). Nancy visited the United States during May and June 1947 and spent most of her time at Mirador, Virginia, visiting her very ill nephew-in-law John Polk (d. 1948), who was married to Virginia Brand (1918–95). However, in a letter to Nancy (16 June 1947 [Reading]), Waldorf Astor implies that an additional motive for her visit was because Nancy could not get her own way in various matters including the direction of the Observer. *David Astor was currently the paper's foreign editor and was to become editor in 1948.*

Bertha Hammond writes that she is in hospital at Rochester U.S.A. with a broken hip and no money. All gone on doctors.

I cannot get permission to send pounds to America, as it depletes our stock of dollars.

Can we do anything for her?

Are you really going nursing to the States? If you have not yet sailed, I could send a contribution to your bank for her; and you could disburse. £10 would be my limit.

G.B.S.

213 / To G. Bernard Shaw

[*no address*]
8th May 1947

[TLU (c): Reading]

Nancy Astor had heard from Sir Sydney Cockerell (1867–1962), director of the Fitzwilliam Museum in Cambridge, at the beginning of May. Cockerell, who had known Shaw since 1891 and who was instrumental in introducing T.E. Lawrence to Shaw in March 1922, apparently wanted Nancy to arrange a meeting with Shaw. In a letter to Cockerell (2 May 1947, BL 52703, f. 216) Nancy wrote that she 'telephoned at once ... to ask permission of the Great Man for a visit. He says he will be delighted if I will bring you down to see him ... I can't tell you yet which day it will be ... as I am leaving for America on the 18th and am trying to live in three places in the meantime ... P.S. You will be glad to know that the Winstens are things of the past!' Nancy and Cockerell visited Shaw on 14 May; her glee over the Winstens was unfounded (see the distinctly favourable account of Shaw and the Winstens in Brockway, Towards, *170–6).*

Dearest G.B.S.

£10 won't be much use to her [Bertha Hammond] if she is in such a bad way, and anyhow you can't get it to her in America. If you give me her address, when I get there I will try to see if there are any people out there who would be willing to help her. I do hope we can do something for her.

Yes, I am going as nurse to Virginia and must see you before I go for I may be away for months.

I propose bringing Sir Sydney Cockerell (who wants to see you) down on Wednesday. I wonder if you would rather have us for luncheon or afternoon? Please get Mrs Laden to telephone to me at Cliveden tomorrow and tell me. I will then let Sir Sydney Cockerell know.

I have just seen two remarkable American women – one a decorator and the other a weaver. I wish your Russian friends could see what is being produced in that capitalist country of mine. They are the loveliest things you ever saw and open up another world altogether – so bright and gay.

I wish I could take you with me.

[Nancy Astor]

The **remarkable American women** are unidentified.

214 / To Nancy Astor   [Ayot St Lawrence, Welwyn, Herts.]
                                                    [10th May 1947]

[ALCS: Reading]

All right: come on Wednesday with S.C. [Sydney Cockerell] but not until 4. That is the village post hour; and if I have visitors earlier it upsets my whole day.

Bertha [Hammond] gave no address except the hospital in Rochester.

G.B.S.

215 / To Nancy Astor   Onslow Court Hotel, Queen's Gate SW7
                                                    2nd June 1947

[ALS: Reading]

Nancy Astor was staying at Mirador in Virginia, where Blanche Patch's letter is addressed.

Dear Lady Astor

... I spent last week-end with GBS, & in my opinion he seemed better able to bear this heat wave than most of us. Anyhow he was pretty well, & told me, with much laughter, of the fixing of the St Joan statue & how Mrs Winsten had wanted it moved 'a ¼ inch'! & how he eventually wrote her a note in which he said 'in the utmost friendliness I hereby consign you to hell' – or words to that effect. Also you may like to know that in speaking of Loewenstein he referred to him as 'that ruffian.' All the same the man is firmly established there, & as GBS really makes use of him, as he'd make use of his hairbrush – that is he doesn't look on him as having feelings to be hurt, there is no more to be said, as I can do his shorthand transcribing in town – Mrs Laden looks after his physical welfare – & he doesn't want company in the house. He & Charlotte never seemed to speak to each other much – he preferred the racket of the wireless!

Yours sincerely
Blanche Patch

Shaw had commissioned a statue of **St Joan** from Clare Winsten the previous October. A copy of the statute now stands in the garden of 'Shaw's Corner' at Ayot; the original was damaged beyond repair by vandals.

216 / To Nancy Astor   Onslow Court Hotel, Queen's Gate SW7
4th July 1947

[ALS: Reading]

Dear Lady Astor

Your letter has just arrived &, also from U.S.A, the enclosed cutting, which I don't think necessary to send on to GBS. I'm sorry to say that the sentiments expressed in it are held by a good many Americans. Not that he'd care tuppence. Still it just shews how the wind blows sometimes. He is perfectly well (I spoke to Mrs Laden today) & is reeling out 'sheets' of shorthand which he sends to me to transcribe. But he'll have to hold off for the next 3 weeks because I'm just off to Sidmouth for that period (back on the 25th). Judy [Musters] is not coming to town this year – & its really not necessary. Last year he gave her practically nothing to do, & wouldn't now even if she were at Ayot where Mrs Laden looks after his physical needs, & doesnt allow any interference with her department. Quite rightly, of course.

As long as rationing goes on its impossible to pay more than occasional visits to Ayot. The maids have only just enough for their own requirements, & I can take nothing with me to supplement.

I don't think you realize what a deadly little village Ayot is. No means of getting out of it, no shops, & absolutely no one with whom one can be friends in the real sense. GBS *prefers* to eat his meals in silence – or with the radio blaring – & mealtime is the only time one sees him. It's a mystery to me how I existed there during the war when Charlotte was alive because, to be perfectly frank, she was a very bad tempered old lady in the family circle. She did keep intruders like Wardrop, Loewenstein & the Winstens at bay, & my own opinion is that the relaxation of her control has excited him to do as he pleases. I'm sure she'd have left him had he insisted on having them in the house – & he knows perfectly well why I can't stay there for more than a week-end.

However, he is perfectly satisfied with the way his affairs are managed &, for his age, is remarkably well. Considering he is all but 91 there is nothing to worry about.

Yours sincerely
Blanche Patch

Pascal is in Rome planning to film Androcles & the Lion. I don't know if he'll try to hire the Coliseum for the lion scene!

Nancy's **letter** and the **enclosed cutting** have not been located. Shaw signed a contract for the filming of **Androcles and the Lion** on 8 September 1947 (see Dukore, 223–6, and passim). *Androcles*, produced by Gabriel **Pascal** after Shaw's death, premiered in America on 14 January 1953 and in England on 16 October 1953 (Dukore, 267).

217 / To Nancy Astor   Ayot St Lawrence, Welwyn, Herts.
                                                        17th October 1947

[ALCS: Reading, Holroyd (e)]

From the next two letters it would appear that Blanche Patch had complained to Nancy Astor about her financial condition, hoping to enlist Nancy's influence with Shaw. Two years earlier Blanche had complained directly to Shaw about being underpaid (Laurence, Letters, 758–60). After Shaw's death Blanche was upset that Shaw's will failed to specify that his bequest of £500 a year to her should be tax-free: 'The Estate now deducts 9/6 in the £ which means that I get only £262-10-0 a year, and if I had not a very little of my own I should be in Queer Street. In addition to the £500 he used to pay my P.A.Y.E. tax and other incidental expenses like holidays and dentists. Day, the chauffeur, is in the same position and feels bitter about it' (26 July 1952 letter to Nancy Astor [Reading]).

Dowdy!

Blow your £58! I paid £98 for a fur coat to keep her [Blanche Patch] warm last winter. Dont worry about her: she is jolly well provided for.

Antony & Cleopatra is not by me but by a man named Will Shakespear.

Anyhow it is my iron rule NEVER to autograph a book for sale. Else I should spend my life doing it.

So there!

G.B.S.

In a non-extant letter to Shaw, Nancy, either innocently or deliberately, must have confused Shaw's *Caesar and Cleopatra* with Shakespeare's **Antony and Cleopatra.**

218 / To Nancy Astor   Ayot St Lawrence, Welwyn, Herts.

21st October 1947

[ALCS: Reading, Holroyd (e), Letters]

B.P. [Blanche Patch] spent the week end here. She was at the top of her form. I could detect no trace of the half starved, raggedly dressed, cruelly exploited, moribund victim I had been led to expect from recent conversations.

So be easy.

G.B.S.

219 / To Blanche Patch   2049 East Elm St, Tucson, Arizona

18th March 1948

[TLS: Cornell]

The Astors, together with son Michael and his wife, visited the United States from late January to May 1948. As Nancy indicates in her final paragraph, Shaw had not been writing to her, which accounts for the gap in their correspondence (which from mid-1947 had in any case slowed to a mere trickle). Nancy's holograph additions are responsible for some illegible words.

Dear Miss Patch

I can't thank you enough for your letter with the enclosures. It really is amusing that [the] Winstens still [hang?] on. Also it is good to hear that G.B.S. is so spry and it is amazing [and] I am delighted to have the shorthand and the translation. How on earth he can do without you I do not know, and as a matter of fact he was not doing very well!

Sybil Thorndike went down to speak for the Socialist candidate [at Croydon?]. I was horrified. I had no idea she was Red.

I would so like to get you out here next year. Tucson has a really marvellous climate and it has done Lord Astor so much good. Dry & lovely sun-[but dusty?]

I am going to give your name to one of my friends and I hope you get a package as I know how desperate things are. We of course can't send them as we have so little money over here. – What do you most need. Please write me c/o Astor Estate 535 Fifth Avenue New York.

I have endless letters & GBS would be horrified if he heard me on England & [Ireland?] too. I get a sec[retary] in occasionally but she doesn't seem to understand. I think I am too [quick?]. So forgive this letter. We sail 29 – Queen Elizabeth – of April – had [*illegible*] has had Patrick Day Parades – The Palestinian question I hope is settled. I had a nice letter from Sir Sydney Cockerell. Please give the Great Man my love – He never writes me, so I just don't write him. – I hope Mrs Laden has not frozen or been starved. [So sent with many thanks?] & keep going!

Nancy Astor

The **socialist candidate** for the hotly contested by-election at North Croydon held on 11 March 1948 was Harold Nicolson, who failed by 11,664 votes to win the staunchly loyal Conservative seat. His opponent, F.W. Harris (1915–79), was a local businessman supported by Winston Churchill, who castigated Nicolson as an 'imported' careerist (*The Times*, 25 February 1948). On Nicolson's 'North Croydon crucifixion,' see Lees-Milne, 215–20. Extensive Jewish immigration to Palestine in the twentieth century led to conflict between Arabs and Jews. In 1947 the United Nations recommended that Palestine should be partitioned between the opposing factions, a suggestion the Arabs rejected. An independent state of Israel was declared in May 1948. The **Palestinian question** was still unresolved in 2004. Nancy voiced her anti-Jewish sentiments with regard to Palestine during her 1947 visit to America (Sykes, 494).

220 / **To Nancy Astor**   4 Whitehall Court SW1
                                                 1st April 1948

[TLS: Reading]

Dear Lady Astor

I was very pleased to hear from you and delighted to know that the air of
Tucson has done good to Lord Astor. I will pass on the news to GBS. He
seems much as usual, and in this I include the fact that one or two have
found him in one of his contrary moods – that is, refusing to comply with
their modest requests.

Very kind of you to have given my name to your friend for a Gift
Parcel, and as you tell me to mention what is useful I can say that a tin
of biscuits (cookies, I think, in America) is always acceptable. I can't
buy them here because my little hotel takes all my points, and they
don't go in for buying biscuits. Or a tin of apricot or strawberry jam is
pleasant – also milk chocolate is unobtainable here – but that you
probably know.

We had a fearful gale yesterday with torrents of rain. The latter was
much wanted, but the gale did much damage – one thing it did was to
hurl a flower pot from a window sill at our house, and it hit a passer-by on
the head. She rushed to the front door and threatens to sue the manage-
ment for damages. A search was made as to which room was responsible,
but naturally no one will own up as to the possession of the pot. Has
anyone told you of Joad's misdemeanour in travelling from London to
Exeter without paying a sufficient fare? Apparently he'd done it several
times, and the dining car waiter seems to have spotted him. The case is
not yet finished, but I should think he'll get a pretty heavy fine. I wonder
if the B.B.C. will allow him on the Brains Trust, the new session of which
starts next week. As you know Donald McCullough is on a world tour,
and I had a letter from him yesterday posted in Melbourne.

I was with GBS about 2 weeks ago and for the Saturday evening he
refrained from having the wireless on all the time, but whether that was
out of kindness to me, or because there was nothing he wanted to hear, I
can't say.

We had a glorious afternoon for the Varsity Boat Race, which I saw
from a house in Hammersmith. Four doors further on I saw Attlee and

A.P. Herbert at a window of the latter's house. A veritable posse of policemen of course in the narrow street at the front.

Sincerely yours

Blanche Patch

Just received a truly marvellous certificate from America admitting me to the Order of Seraphic Secretaries, and many virtues attached. Mine is No. 379, so I suppose many other secretaries have received the same trophy. Darius Benham appears to be the sender. Could he be a descendant of the King of Persia in the Book of Ezra! ·

C.E.M. **Joad**, Nancy's co-panelist on the 'Brains Trust' in 1942 (Letters 110–11), was convicted on 12 April 1948 of travelling on the railway without paying his fare. As a result, he was removed from the 'Brains Trust' panel. **Donald McCullough** (1901–78), writer and broadcaster, was chairman of the 'Brains Trust' program. The annual **varsity boat race** between Oxford and Cambridge Universities is rowed on the River Thames. Sir Alan Patrick **Herbert** (1890–1971) was a writer, dramatist, barrister, and Independent M.P. **Darius Benham** is unidentified.

221 / To Nancy Astor   4 Whitehall Court SW1
3rd May 1949

[TLS: Reading]

Although there is a year-long gap in the correspondence, Nancy Astor continued to see Shaw from time to time. One such occasion occurred on 20 January 1949: 'G.B.S. was very well; very bored at seeing me; busy all day long, and well looked after by Mrs. Laden' (20 January 1949 letter to Sydney Cockerell, BL 52703, f. 219). More welcome was Nehru, who had written to Shaw on 4 September 1948 (Elliot, 300–1) and recollected hearing Shaw address a meeting in Cambridge, England, where Nehru was an undergraduate. He also expressed the hope that he might visit Shaw during 1948; however, there was insufficient time to arrange a meeting at that time, and Nehru did not visit Shaw until 1949. There is perhaps some significance in the fact that Shaw did not invite Nancy Astor to participate in the occasion. Blanche Patch's schadenfreude over Shaw's difficulties with Clare Winsten over Buoyant Billions was justified: 'The printer William Maxwell noted in his personal copy [of the play] "It would have been a typographical masterpiece but for [Shaw's] surrendering to the ignorant blandishments of Clare Winsten, her daughter Theodora and her husband. ... just look at the horrible title page by Clare and the silly inept caricatures by Theodora on front and back covers"' (Laurence, Shaw, I, 254).

Dear Lady Astor

I thought it might interest you to know that the Pundit's visit to Ayot
went off very successfully. He stayed much longer than we expected
which shewed that he felt at his ease, and he and GBS skimmed lightly
over every subject – politics, religion, Russia etc etc. Our car had been
sent to town to escort his car and was supposed to lead him back, but the
Pundit said this was quite unnecessary, and as I had intended to return in
ours he said that I must, of course, come with him. So I returned in great
style with detective sitting in front and Indian flag flying from the
bonnet.

I was vastly entertained to find that GBS is having quite a scrap with
Mrs Winsten over the illustrations for this very expensive Limited Edition of the new play, Buoyant Billions. Its refreshing to know that he has
difficulties with his more than peculiar friends – though perhaps I ought
not to say so.

Yours sincerely
Blanche Patch

Jawaharlal **Pundit** Nehru (1889–1964) was the first prime minister (1947–64) of independent India. His visit to Shaw at Ayot on 29 April 1949 is recounted in more detail in Patch,
106–8. The **very expensive** limited edition of 1025 copies of *Buoyant Billions A Comedy of No
Manners in Prose by Bernard Shaw and in Pictures by Clare Winsten* was eventually published on
15 May 1950. The play received its British premiere at the Malvern Festival on 13 August
1949.

222 / **To Nancy Astor**   Ayot St Lawrence, Welwyn, Herts.
5th May 1949

[ALS: Reading, Rose (e)]

*Although Nancy Astor's concern for him irritated Shaw, it was genuine since she
also enlisted other people to visit Shaw, as Shaw's letter (5 June 1949) to Sydney
Cockerell implies: 'Take no notice of Nancy's nonsense. She tells everybody to come
down here and see that I am properly taken care of while she is away. / If they came
I should have to buy a ferocious dog' (Meynell, 190).*

My dear Nancy

The 13th is quite impossible. There is work to be done in the house which has obliged me to promise Mrs Laden not to have any more visitors for the next three weeks.

And I am at the end of my tether as to entertaining your car lenders or even yourself. I am working from early rising to late bed going; and recent visitors, including Nehru, Danny Kaye, and my publisher, have taken so much of my time that I dont want to receive anyone on earth until two books that I have in the press are finally published. I have to read all through my meals and cut out my post-lunch nap.

Keep off, keep off, keep off, keep off.

Do you want to kill me?

G.B.S.

Danny Kaye (né David Daniel Kaminsky, 1913–87), the American entertainer, comedian, and singer, appeared in variety at the Palladium Theatre, London, beginning 25 April 1949 (*The Times*, 26 April 1949). His visit with Shaw on 3 May is recounted anecdotally in Gottfried, 156–8. Shaw's **publisher** was either his long-standing publisher at Constable, Otto Kyllmann (1860–1959), or possibly Max Reinhardt (1915–2002), who began publishing in 1947. Shaw was among Reinhardt's first authors.

223 / To Blanche Patch   3 Elliott Terrace, The Hoe, Plymouth
                                                        6th May 1949

[TLS: Cornell]

Dear Miss Patch

Thank you so much for writing me about the visit. I longed to hear, and it was kind of you. I have been here for a fortnight so I am out of touch.

I wrote and told G.B.S. that I wanted to come on the 13th and got a most extraordinary letter back, that he had to work during lunch-time and close the house for three weeks! & he hoped I would not come. I don't know that I shall pay any attention to it, and may pass by on my way to Hatfield.

Delighted to hear about Winstens but I heard that Mr Winsten had got Danny Kaye to see G.B.S.

Is he really tired? Or shall I pay no attention and go down on the 13th? Please let me know what you think. I shall be at Cliveden on Monday and London Tuesday.

Have you had any American parcels? Please let me know.

Hope you will go away this summer – If not you must come to Cliveden for a good rest. I know you need it.

[Sincerely?]
Nancy Astor

224 / To Nancy Astor　　　　　Ayot St Lawrence, Welwyn, Herts.
8th May 1949

[TLT: Reading, Holroyd (e), Letters, Masters (e), Rose (e), Sykes, Wilson (e)]

My dear Nancy

You must positively not come on the 13th. If you will not let me manage my work and my household in my own way you must not come at all. I have arranged with Mrs Laden that there are to be no visits for the next three weeks; and no visits there shall be.

All this nonsense about my having to be looked after, and the job bequeathed to you by Charlotte, is a worn-out joke which you are beginning to believe in yourself. Let me hear no more of it. You need looking after far more than I do; and nobody knew this better than Charlotte, except perhaps your unfortunate secretaries. You must upset your own household, not mine.

I write in great haste, and am rather angry with you for forcing me to put my old foot down and make you understand that in this house what I say, goes.

As the keeper of a mental patient you are DISCHARGED.

Quite unchanged nevertheless
G.B.S.

225 / To Nancy Astor　　　　　Ayot St Lawrence, Welwyn, Herts.
27th June 1949

[TLS: Reading, Holroyd (e), Sykes (e)]

As Shaw's final holographic paragraph in this letter explains, he was in the process of moving from Flat 130 to a smaller, two-roomed, furnished flat, number 116, at Whitehall Court.

My dear Nancy

I gave a general instruction to Sothebys to clear everything out of Flat 130 and sell every stick and stone. They wanted to pick and choose; but I said it must be all or nothing. They consented, but handed over the commonest stuff (in their judgment) to two other auctioneers. Auctioneer B sold a small lot for £25, including £18 for the best bed: Charlotte's: a beauty. I did not bother to study the catalogues, as I would have paid anybody handsomely to rid me of my superfluous belongings.

But when Auctioneer A announced tomorrow's sale, I looked through his catalogue and found in it 'a Terra Cotta bust of Mrs Sidney Webb,' without any sculptor's name. As I possessed no such object I realized at the last moment what it was, and hastily warned Sothebys and Auctioneer A that as a bust of Beatrice, and fictitious at that, it would fetch a few shillings; but as a bust of you by Strobl it might fetch billions.

Auctioneer A instantly wrote to you for a bid. You (or your secretary) telephoned Loewenstein, my domestic German Jew, Doctor of Philosophy. He came to me and asked me what he should say – what I was going to do about it. I, being busy, shouted 'Oh, let them go ahead and sell it; I want money, money, money.' Dr L., deeply shocked, said I could not possibly do such a thing. I reminded him that I am practically on the point of death; and what, I asked, will become of the bust then. But he stuck to his point, and at last wakened my sense of decency. I have written Auctioneer A to withdraw the bust from the sale, and keep it until I have ascertained your wishes.

There are three courses open to me. I can present the bust to the House of Commons as a memorial of its first woman member. I can present it to the Plymouth Municipality. Or you can have it back and be damned. I do not advise this last, because the bust ought to be in some Pantheon as a memorial of you: and as you cannot well present it yourself it would stick in Cliveden as a museum piece for ever after the place had passed into the hands of the National Trust and its purely accidental association with you forgotten. Still, you might sell it.

Make up your mind promptly about this while the subject is topical.

My domestics are having their holidays in July. Mrs Laden begs me to have no visitors until August.

The hero of the bust episode is decidedly Loewenstein.

I am not leaving Whitehall Court, as I must keep an office there for Miss Patch and a bed for myself in case this house should by fire or fever become uninhabitable. So the address and telephone are unchanged, except that Flat 130 is now Flat 116, cheaper, and furnished by the Court.

GBS

226 / To G. Bernard Shaw   [*no address*]
                                                                [27th June 1949]

[TEL: Patch]

DO I GET MY BUST OR DO I BUY IT?

[Nancy Astor]

227 / To Nancy Astor   Ayot St Lawrence, Welwyn, Herts.
                                                              28th June 1949

[ALCS: Reading]

If after receiving my long letter you decide to sell by auction, all you have to do is to write to Sothebys, 34 New Bond St W.1 instructing them to put it up for sale at the forthcoming auction of my effects.

G.B.S.

It is a pity that this statuette only 17 inches high is not life size in bronze. Strobl intends coming back to London presently.

228 / To Nancy Astor   Ayot St Lawrence, Welwyn, Herts.
                                                              20th July 1949

[ALCS: Reading]

The bust question is settled. The Clerk and the Speaker [of the House of Commons] accept it. It will be kept in the Speaker's house until it is quite certain that you cannot discredit it. Then it will be transferred to public view.

The first elected woman member was Constance Markievich; but you are the first to take the seat.

G.B.S.

Constance Countess **Markievich** (née Gore-Booth, 1868–1927) was a Sinn Féin leader who was elected to the House of Commons while she was imprisoned in 1918. She refused to take her seat.

229 / **To Nancy Astor**   Ayot St Lawrence, Welwyn, Herts.
10th February 1950

[ALCS: Reading, Holroyd (e)]

It is perhaps appropriate that the last significant letter from Shaw to Nancy Astor should concern politics. He did write one more, on 1 March 1950 (Reading); however, it is only an enigmatic note: 'I have written to Thérèse; so you need not bother about her.' A general election was held on 23 February 1950, when Labour's majority over all other parties was reduced to five seats. Three of Nancy's Astor sons were Conservative candidates: Michael stood for Surrey (East), Bill for Buckinghamshire (Wycombe), and Jakie for his mother's old Plymouth (Sutton) seat. Michael was the only one to win. Nancy continued to visit Shaw; for example, she and Judy Musters saw him on 25 October 1950, when they discussed his recently written but incomplete playlet Why She Would Not *(Henderson, 665). In her 2 April 1955 letter to Nancy (Reading), Judy Musters pointed out that she had typed* Why She Would Not, *and not Blanche Patch. Nancy was also greatly in evidence during Shaw's final illness, death, and funeral.*

I do not understand. You have not a son standing in Slough and Eton, have you?

Fenner is an old Conchy and I.L.P. stalwart. I could not refuse him my coupon. Why should I?

Churchill will lose the election for you, as he did in 45. In home affairs he is a century out of date. Your game is to fight to *the Left* of the Labor Party: Tory Democracy, not Stick-in-the Mud Conservatism.

You cannot shut Winston up; but try to keep him on foreign policy and Glory.

G.B.S.

Shaw had known **Fenner** Brockway (1888–1988), journalist, author, activist, and Labour MP for East Leyton (1929–31) and for Eton and Slough (1950–64) since 1910. During the First World War Brockway was jailed for a total of three years as a conscientious objector (**conchy**). The **I.L.P.**, the Independent Labour Party, was founded in 1891 and split from the Labour Party in 1932. Shaw told Brockway in a 26 July 1922 letter: 'The truth is I have never been able to understand what *raison d'être* the I.L.P. has had since the Labor Party was established in Parliament' (Brockway, *Outside*, 201). Shaw's **coupon**, or endorsement, for Brockway was: 'Slough and Eton ... are inhabited largely by political nitwits who read nothing but betting pools, and simple-souled stick-in-the-muds who dread reformers more than serpents and dragons. The wiser few must do their utmost to outnumber them on the forthcoming Day of Destiny.' Brockway's opponent tried to take full advantage of Shaw's insults, but Brockway won the seat – for which Shaw claimed credit: 'My coupon and my advice has secured you the one Independent triumph of the election in an impossible constituency' (Brockway, *Towards*, 170). The term coupon in this sense derived from the 14 December 1918 general election; letters of endorsement that candidates supporting the coalition government received from their party leaders were derided by opponents as 'coupons.'

Table of Correspondents

Unless noted otherwise below, the letters were written by Bernard Shaw and Nancy Astor.

References

Astor, Michael. *Tribal Feeling*. London: John Murray, 1963.

Bentley, Eric. *Bernard Shaw 1856–1950*. Amended edition. New York: New Directions, 1957.

Brockway, Fenner. *Outside the Right: A Sequel to 'Inside the Left.'* London: Allen and Unwin, 1963.

– *Towards Tomorrow: The Autobiography of Fenner Brockway*. London: Hart-Davis MacGibbon, 1977.

Brookes, Pamela. *Women at Westminster: An Account of Women in the British Parliament 1918–1966*. London: Peter Davies, 1967.

Channon, Sir Henry. *Chips: The Diaries of Sir Henry Channon*. Ed. Robert Rhodes James. London: Weidenfeld and Nicolson, 1967.

Chaplin, Charles. *My Autobiography*. New York: Simon and Schuster, 1964.

Chappelow, Allan. *Shaw the Villager and Human Being: A Biographical Symposium*. London: Charles Skilton, 1961.

Collis, Maurice. *Nancy Astor: An Informal Biography*. New York: E.P. Dutton, 1960.

Conolly, L.W., ed. *Bernard Shaw and Barry Jackson*. Toronto: University of Toronto Press, 2002.

Coward, Noel. *Autobiography*. London: Methuen, 1986.

Craig, F.W.S. *British Parliamentary Election Results 1918–1949*. Glasgow: Political Reference Publications, 1969.

Dent, Alan, ed. *Bernard Shaw and Mrs. Patrick Campbell: Their Correspondence*. New York: Knopf, 1952.

Dukore, Bernard F., ed. *Bernard Shaw and Gabriel Pascal*. Toronto: University of Toronto Press, 1996.

Dunbar, Janet. *Mrs G.B.S.: A Portrait*. New York: Harper and Row, 1963.

Elliot, Vivian. *Dear Mr Shaw: Selections from Bernard Shaw's Postbag.* London: Bloomsbury, 1987.

Ellis, E.L. *T.J.: A Life of Dr Thomas Jones, C.H.* Cardiff: University of Wales Press, 1992.

Ervine, St John. *Bernard Shaw: His Life, Work and Friends.* London: Constable, 1956.

Evans, T.F. 'Myopia or Utopia? Shaw in Russia.' *SHAW: The Annual of Shaw Studies* 5 (1985): 125–45.

Fox, James. *Five Sisters: The Langhornes of Virginia.* New York: Simon and Schuster, 2000.

Geduld, Harry M., ed. *The Rationalization of Russia by Bernard Shaw.* Bloomington: Indiana University Press, 1964.

Gibbs, A.M. *A Bernard Shaw Chronology.* New York: St Martin's, 2000.

Gottfried, Martin. *Nobody's Fool: The Lives of Danny Kaye.* New York: Simon and Schuster, 1994.

Grenfell, Joyce. *Darling Ma: Letters to Her Mother, 1932–1944.* Ed. James Roose-Evans. London: Hodder and Stoughton, 1988.

– *Joyce Grenfell Requests the Pleasure.* New York: St Martin's, 1977.

Grigg, John. *Nancy Astor: A Lady Unashamed.* Boston: Little, Brown, 1980.

Halperin, John. *Eminent Georgians: The Lives of King George V, Elizabeth Bowen, St. John Philby, & Nancy Astor.* New York: St Martin's 1995.

Harris, Kenneth. *Attlee.* London: Weidenfeld and Nicolson, 1982.

Henderson, Archibald. *George Bernard Shaw: Man of the Century.* New York: Appleton, Century, Crofts, 1956.

Holroyd, Michael. *Bernard Shaw: Volume 3, 1918–1950, The Lure of Fantasy.* New York: Random House, 1991.

Irving, Clive, et al. *Scandal '63: A Study of the Profumo Affair.* London: Heinemann, 1963.

Johnson, A.E. 'Encounters with G.B.S.' *Dalhousie Review* 31 (Spring 1951): 19–22.

Jones, Thomas. *A Diary with Letters 1931–1950.* London: Oxford University Press, 1954.

– *Whitehall Diary: Vol. II 1926–1930.* Ed. Keith Middlemas. New York: Oxford University Press, 1969.

Kavaler, Lucy. *The Astors: A Family Chronicle of Pomp and Power.* New York: Dodd, Mead, 1966.

Krause, David, ed. *The Letters of Sean O'Casey 1942–54.* New York: Macmillan, 1980.

Lash, Joseph P. *Eleanor and Franklin: The Story of Their Relationship, Based on Eleanor Roosevelt's Private Papers.* New York: Norton, 1971.

Laurence, Dan H. *Bernard Shaw: A Bibliography.* 2 vols. Oxford: Clarendon Press, 1983.

Laurence, Dan H., ed. *Bernard Shaw: Collected Letters 1926–1950.* London: Max Reinhardt, 1988.

– *Platform and Pulpit: Bernard Shaw.* New York: Hill and Wang, 1961.

Laurence, Dan H. and James Rambeau, eds. *Agitations: Letters to the Press 1875–1950.* New York: Ungar, 1985.

Lees-Milne, James. *Harold Nicolson: A Biography: Vol. 2 1930–1968.* London: Chatto and Windus, 1981.

Mackenzie, Norman, ed. *The Letters of Sidney and Beatrice Webb, Volume 3, Pilgrimage 1912–47.* Cambridge: Cambridge University Press, 1978.

Mackenzie, Norman and Jeanne, eds. *The Diary of Beatrice Webb, Volume 4, 1924–1943: The Wheel of Life.* Cambridge, MA: Belknap Press, 1985.

Masters, Anthony. *Nancy Astor: A Biography.* New York: McGraw-Hill, 1981.

Meynell, Violet, ed. *The Best of Friends.* London: Rupert Hart-Davis, 1956.

Michalos, Alex C., and Deborah C. Poff, eds. *Bernard Shaw and the Webbs.* Toronto: University of Toronto Press, 2002.

Minney, R.J. *The Private Papers of Hore-Belisha.* London: Collins, 1960.

– *Recollections of George Bernard Shaw.* Englewood Cliffs, NJ: Prentice-Hall, 1969.

Nicolson, Harold. *The War Years 1939–1945: Volume II of Diaries and Letters.* Ed. Nigel Nicolson. New York: Atheneum, 1967.

NLW National Library of Wales, Thomas Jones Collection.

O'Casey, Eileen. *Sean.* London: Macmillan, 1971.

Parliamentary Debates: Official Report: 5th Series (House of Commons) [title varies], 1909–80.

Patch, Blanche. *Thirty Years with G.B.S.* London: Victor Gollancz, 1951.

Pearson, Hesketh. *G.B.S.: A Full Length Portrait.* New York: Harper and Brothers, 1942.

Perez, Robert C., and Edward F. Willett. *Clarence Dillon: A Wall Street Enigma.* Lanham, MD: Madison Books, 1995.

Pugliese, Stanislao G. *Carlo Rosselli: Socialist Heretic and Antifascist Exile.* Cambridge, MA: Harvard University Press, 1999.

Rattray, R.F. *Bernard Shaw: A Chronicle.* New York: Roy, 1951.

Rose, Norman. *The Cliveden Set: Portrait of an Exclusive Fraternity.* London: Jonathan Cape, 2000.

Smith, J. Percy. ed. *Bernard Shaw and H.G. Wells.* Toronto: University of Toronto Press, 1995.

Stevens, George. *Speak for Yourself, John: The Life of John Mason Brown, with Some of His Letters and Many of His Opinions.* New York: Viking Press, 1974.

Sykes, Christopher. *Nancy: The Life of Lady Astor.* New York: Harper and Row, 1972.

Thornton, Martin, ed. *Nancy Astor's Canadian Correspondence 1912–1962.* Lewiston, NY: Edward Mellon Press, 1997.

Tompkins, Peter, ed. *To a Young Actress: The Letters of Bernard Shaw to Molly Tompkins.* New York: Potter, 1960.

Weiss, Samuel A., ed. *Bernard Shaw's Letters to Siegfried Trebitsch.* Stanford, CA: Stanford University Press, 1986.

Wilson, Derek. *The Astors 1763–1992: Landscape with Millionaires.* New York: St Martin's, 1993.

Index

Since the names of Shaw and Nancy Astor appear on most pages of this volume, they are not included in the index except where Shaw's works or specific aspects of Nancy Astor's career are mentioned. The location of theatres is London unless otherwise indicated.

Ely, Gertrude, 29
Eydon Hall, 150

Fabians, 8–9, 45, 57, 127, 139
fascism, xx–xxi, 57, 133–4, 142, 171–2
Fitzroy, E.A., 14
France, 79, 108, 112, 169
Franco, General Francisco, 73
Fry, Margery, 171–2

Gallacher, William, xv
Gandhi, Mohandas Karamchand
   'Mahatma,' 40–1, 45, 129
Garvin, James Louis, 75–6
general election: May 1929, 13–15;
   October 1931, 38; November 1935,
   69; July 1945, 168–9, 176, 184–5;
   February 1950, 213–14
George V, 55
George VI, 71, 93, 129, 192
Germany, xx–xxi, 55–6, 73–4, 78–9,
   91–2, 108, 113, 128, 144
Gibson, Charles Dana, 6
Gibson, Irene, 6, 53, 71, 106
Gilbert, Fred, 39
Goebbels, Joseph, 113–14
Golders Green, xxv, 110, 133, 139, 177
gold standard, 39, 45
Gosford Park, 144
Gould, Bruce, 117
Greenwood, Arthur, 27–8
Grenfell, Joyce, 93, 95, 111, 114, 139
Grigg, Sir Edward, 8–9
Guild Theatre, New York, 68
Guinness, Bridget, 89–91
Gusev, Feodor Tarasovich, 137–8

Hadfield, Sir Robert, 63–4
Halifax, Edward Frederick Lindley
   Wood, Earl of, 84, 124–5

Hamilton, Lady Emma, 156–7
Hamilton, Mary Agnes, 17
Hammond, Bertha, 199–201
Hardwicke, Cedric, 25
Harris, F.W., 205
Harrison, Rex, 102
Harrison, Rosina, xv
Hatfield House, 92
Haw Haw, Lord. See Joyce, William
Hearst, William Randolph, 34–5, 51
Henderson, Arthur, 36–7, 57–8
Herbert, A.P., 207
Higgs, Clara, 24, 104, 121, 127, 132,
   135–6, 138–9, 143, 148, 154, 162,
   164–7
Higgs, Harry, 121–2, 154, 164–7
Hiller, Wendy, 70, 102
Hitler, Adolf, xx–xxi, 58, 66, 74, 79–82,
   102, 108, 115, 129, 142, 171, 191;
   Mein Kampf, 115
Home, William Douglas, xxiv–xxv
homosexuality, 32–3, 45–8
Hore-Belisha, Leslie, 85

Imperial Chemical Industries, 147
Independent Labour Party, 26, 35,
   213–14
India, 40–1, 45, 129
Inge, Mary Catherine, 41–2
Inge, William Ralph, 41–2; Vale, 63
Ireland, 70, 80, 83, 113, 115, 139, 147,
   159, 186
Israel, 205
Italy, 108, 128

Jackson, Sir Barry, 8–9, 41, 68
Japan, 45, 51, 62, 67, 103, 128
Joad, C.E.M., 117, 206–7
John, Augustus, 146–8
Johnson, A.E., 7

Selected Correspondence of Bernard Shaw

Bernard Shaw Theatrics, edited by Dan H. Laurence

Bernard Shaw and H.G. Wells, edited by J. Percy Smith

Bernard Shaw and Gabriel Pascal, edited by Bernard F. Dukore

Bernard Shaw and Barry Jackson, edited by L.W. Conolly

Bernard Shaw and the Webbs, edited by Alex C. Michalos and Deborah C. Poff

Bernard Shaw and Nancy Astor, edited by J.P. Wearing